Hiring Fairs and Market Places

May Blair

Appletree Press

This book is dedicated to my farming forefathers
- the Warnocks and Flemings

First published in 2007 by
Appletree Press Ltd
The Old Potato Station
14 Howard Street South
Belfast, BT7 1AP

Tel: +44 (0) 28 9024 3074
Fax: +44 (0) 28 9024 6756
E-mail: reception@appletree.ie
Website: www.appletree.ie

Title page image: Market Day, Pomeroy courtesy of Ian McCullough.

A catalogue record for this book is available from the British Library.

Hiring Fairs and Market Places

Paperback ISBN: 978 1 84758 010 8
Hardback ISBN: 978 1 84758 038 2

Desk and Marketing Editor: Jean Brown
Copy-editing: Jim Black
Editorial Assistant: Laura Armstrong
Designer: Stuart Wilkinson
Production Manager: Paul McAvoy

9 8 7 6 5 4 3 2

AP3541

CONTENTS

Courtesy of William Mehaffy

William Mehaffy gathers potatoes with his children, Will, John, Myrtle and hired man Willie Alcorn (far right).

FOREWORD

Life is very different in the early years of the 21ˢᵗ century from it was fifty or a hundred years ago. Technology has changed all our lives whether by the power and scope of computers, the convenience of credit cards, the development of the mobile phone or the genetic modificatoin of crops to mention but a few.

It is therefore pertinent that we pause from time to time to look back at the past in our own small country to remind us of the difficult times our farming forefathers came through to survive. This book, so thoroughly researched and so well-written by May Blair paints a comprehensive picture of what farm life was really like in the past. It brings out the hardships the farming community had to endure and how farmers rose to the challenge of marketing and selling their produce to eke out a living.

It is appropriate that the Royal Ulster Agricultural Society decided to launch this book at its Balmoral Show, the shop window for the Northern Ireland Agrifood sector. Having been involved with this event over many years, it gives me great pleasure to write the preface and to commend Hiring Fairs and Market Places as a must-read by both the rural and urban communities.

I have been privileged to scan the manuscript and its associated illustrations and know that everyone who reads this book will find it fascinating. It will make them aware of the hard times endured by our rural population in the past and will also allow them to reflect that, despite the problems which agriculture is currently facing, we are fortunate to be living in the relative comfort of the 21ˢᵗ century.

William H Yarr

Chief Executive, Royal Ulster Agricultural Society 1978-2003

William Mehaffy closing drills.

INTRODUCTION

This book aims to record a way of life which disappeared during the twentieth century. It is about farm life and how farmers marketed their produce in times past. It covers mainly the 1900s as remembered by farmers and their workers, but does not claim to be either comprehensive or definitive. It aims rather to capture the atmosphere of the fair and the hard times endured by people who lived by the land.

An important feature of the fair was the twice-yearly hiring, when farmers looked for workers and workers looked for employment. The traditional dates for hiring were the twelfth of May and the twelfth of November, though in reality hiring took place on the fair day nearest these dates. Mostly the farmer and his wife respected their workers and would not have asked them to do anything they were not prepared to do themselves e.g. Alex Erskine and his servant man Tom White, but sometimes they were looked down upon, even despised, and treated worse than dogs – like the unfortunate Robert Higgins (*Co. Antrim, Chapter 1*). The situation was made worse in that land-owners were in the main Protestant and servants Roman Catholic, and compounded in the west of the province by the fact that many of the young people for hire came from Donegal, having little education and speaking only Irish. For well over a century they sought 'a place' in hiring fairs which were held in almost every town and village throughout Ireland. In this book however the study is confined to the six counties of Northern Ireland.

Hiring goes back a long way. Possibly the earliest reference has its origins in the pre-Christian, Greek or Roman feast in honour of Cybele, the mother of the Gods. This was the fore-runner of Mothers' Day or Mothering Sunday, when daughters in service were allowed home to visit their mothers on a day during Lent. Then we read in *Matthew 20 v.6 & 7*:

> *And about the eleventh hour He went out, and found others standing idle, and saith unto them,*
> *'Why stand ye here all the day idle?'*
> *They say unto him, 'Because no man hath hired us.'*

The custom must have continued uninterrupted throughout the centuries for according to popular legend, St Patrick was hired to tend swine on Slemish in the fifth century.

There is little doubt that hiring once took place in Belfast. A map of 1660 shows it to be a compact town of 150 dwellings at that time, cattle and cattle-related products being the mainstay of the people. The main market area was High Street, the central feature of which was the River Farset, now culverted but at that time open to the sky and spanned by several bridges, the most important of which was the Stone Bridge situated near the Market House. It was here that unemployed men assembled in the hope that someone would come along and offer them work, and employers got into the habit of sending 'to the bridge' for a man. No doubt there were similar systems operating in older towns like Carrickfergus and Downpatrick, but there are few records to confirm this.

As for hiring fairs, these were common in England and Scotland for many years before they came to Ireland. They can be traced back to the fourteenth century when an Act of the English Parliament was passed, fixing the wages of farm labourers and declaring that they be made known to all concerned. This Act was called the Statute of Labourers and new wages were declared at Statute Sessions. Since both employers and labourers had an interest in what was said at these sessions, they were common ground on which to meet, and naturally enough some made their agreements there and then.

The earliest written reference to hiring here comes from an inventory made at Legecory in County Armagh in 1717, where a debt entry states: *Due to Danaill McClellen for one quarter's wages…6s 6d and Due to Elinor Stevenson for halfe a year's wages…16s 6d.* Whether Danaill and Elinor were hired in a fair is not stated.

Music and poetry played a big part in the lives of farm workers. Every district had its poet who would record for posterity his view of important, amusing or even traumatic events. As these were designed to be recited or sung at local firesides they were seldom written down and many were subsequently lost. Songs tell us a great deal, not only about the times in which they were written but also about the attitudes of those that wrote them. They are in fact unique social and historical documents. Most of those included in this book were written by people who had experience of both the drudgery and freedom of farm life. They vary from John Clifford's rollicking *The Hirin' Fair* to Sara Savage's poignant poem about the parting of a mother and daughter to hire in different parts of the country. Their contribution to history is obvious.

Commercial fairs really began in the twelfth and thirteenth centuries with the arrival of the Normans. These fairs were of such importance that the legal right to hold one could only be granted by Royal Charter. Such a right was granted to John de Courcy by Henry II, with the instruction that he was 'to subdue Ulster, obtain land, set up feudal fiefs and establish fairs'. There is little doubt that he also claimed lordship over some of the old native fairs (oenachs). It was common during the Norman era for a symbol of the fair to be paraded through the town and then hoisted above the roof-tops for the duration of the fair. In Greencastle in County Down the symbol was a ram, which was lifted above the castle walls and given the title 'King of The Benns'.

As it turned out, Ulster was to be a thorn in the flesh of England for the next few centuries culminating in the nine years war between Elizabeth I and the powerful Gaelic lords led by Hugh O'Neill. Shortly after the war ended a number of Irish chiefs (including O'Neill, O'Donnell and Maguire) took ship and fled the country to the continent together with their entire families. The year was 1607 and the event was to become known as the Flight of the Earls. By this time Elizabeth had been replaced on the throne by James I. To remove the threat of Ulster once and for all, James decided on a policy of Plantation, encouraging English and Scottish settlers to make a new life for themselves in a difficult and often hostile environment. Two counties (Antrim and Down) were not included as they had already been settled by some influential Scots and Englishmen towards the end of the previous century. These introduced settlers to the Ards Peninsula, Lagan Valley and the shores of Belfast Lough (at that time known as the Bay of Carrickfergus). Monaghan was also excluded as eight of its chiefs had in 1591 surrendered their territories to the queen and received them back to hold according to English law. Nor was Londonderry included as it was soon to become the responsibility of the Irish Society and the wealthy London Companies who have left their mark so indelibly across that county today. Armagh, Fermanagh, Tyrone, Cavan and Donegal were the counties selected for Plantation. These were to hold their grants directly from the king.

The charter usually included a patent to hold fairs and markets. In those days the main commodities sold revolved around cattle and the linen industry, and the customers were in the main farmers and bleachers. As time went on fairs and markets began to supply the needs of most rural households, and provided an outlet for surplus items such as poultry, eggs, butter, linen and yarn. They were also frequented by such people as coopers, tinsmiths, shoemakers, creelmakers and livestock castraters. Most importantly they provided a place where farmers could buy and sell farm animals. Selling at fairs was always fraught with risk. Besides the vagaries of the actual dealing, there were other disadvantages. Animals might have been driven for anything up to twenty miles along dusty roads, and would already have lost some of their value by the time they arrived. The prospect of a return trip therefore made selling imperative. On top of this there was a time when local landlords or city corporations claimed a toll on each item sold, thus adding to the farmer's costs.

In the beginning fairs fell at the turning points in the pastoral year: spring horse fairs in February and March; cattle fairs in May when the grass started to grow; Lammas fairs for sheep and wool in July and August; cattle fairs again in October and November when rents fell due. By the middle of the nineteenth century, when farmers began to depend more on the land than the loom, the number of fairs increased to the extent that in many places they were held monthly. In the last quarter of the century farmers were paying fairer rents, and they began to take more interest in making the soil productive. This was largely due to land reform by Liberal Prime Minister William Ewart Gladstone, and the Land Purchase Acts which enabled farmers to become owners of their farms.

The horse was however still the mainstay of the farmer and was to remain so until the 1930s. It was during the '20s and '30s that mechanic Harry Ferguson spent much of his time experimenting with machinery, determined to produce an alternative to the heavy dangerous tractors then in use. His work in the roof-space of a garage in Belfast's Donegall Square East was to produce an agricultural revolution. He produced his first prototype tractor in 1933 and within a few years the first 'wee Grey Fergie' came off the production line. It was to become famous worldwide, and Ferguson's principles are embodied in 85% of tractors in use today.

Harry Ferguson's ideas have survived into the twenty-first century but the local fair is no more. It has been replaced by the highly efficient cattle mart, usually situated on the outskirts of a town, with ample space for lorries to load and unload. A few survive as pleasure fairs, giving us a glimpse of the life lived by a past generation, the most famous being the Lammas Fair at Ballycastle.

This book will leave a record, however incomplete, of what farm life was like in the recent past, what fairs were and what they meant to the people concerned. Much of the drudgery of farm life is also no more, thanks to the genius of Harry Ferguson, the quiet farmer's son from County Down.

Courtesy of George McKibbin

Harry Ferguson with one of the tractors which revolutionised agriculture.

COUNTY ANTRIM

Our big horse Billy, a good brown bay,
He draws the straw and draws the hay,
And butter, and buttermilk, far away
To Durham Street in the morning.

–William Fee McKinney (1832-1917) Personal Notebooks, Sentry Hill, Carmoney

Farmers in south Antrim (like those in north Down) marketed much of their produce in Belfast, the only difference being that growers in north Down by and large specialised in growing potatoes and vegetables, while those in south Antrim concentrated mainly on dairy produce.

Belfast as a market place goes back to the advent of Sir Arthur Chichester, Lord Deputy of Ireland in 1604, who for services to the Crown received a grant of the town, manor and castle of Belfast and adjoining territory forfeited by the O'Neills. The grant included provision for fairs and markets. Sir Arthur is said to have fostered the 'little hamlet', encouraged immigration and advanced the prosperity of the place so far that in 1613 the town received its charter of incorporation and the right to return two members to Parliament. It was still, however, only a

Photograph © Ulster Museum

High Street, Belfast as depicted by John Nixon. The building with the tower was the market house.

8

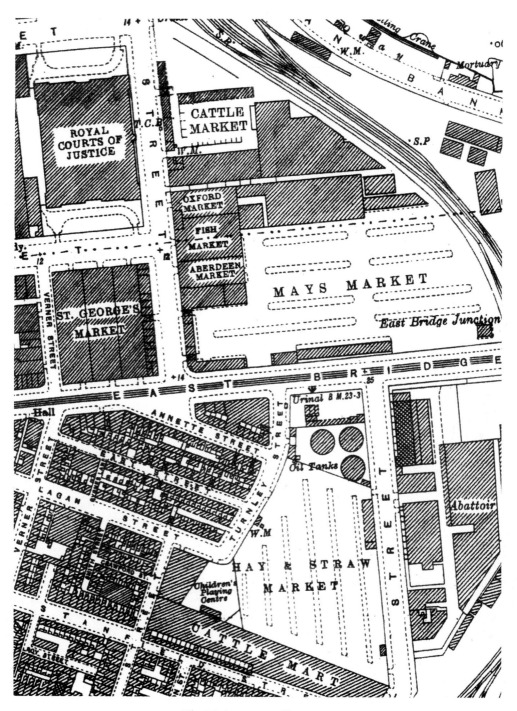

The Markets area, Belfast, 1939.

(Reproduced from the 1939 Ordnance Survey of Northern Ireland Map)

cluster of straw-thatched mud hovels dotted about the site of the present Castle Junction and High Street (then called Front Road).

The first Belfast Fair was held on 1 August 1604. Regular markets were established soon after and by and by a market house was built nearby. It stood at the junction of Cornmarket and High Street for the best part of 200 years until it was demolished in 1811. By 1660 Belfast was a compact town of 150 dwellings set in a rural area. The heart of the town was the River Farset (later culverted below High Street) which even then was lined on either side with shops. Traders, at their own expense, erected bridges across the Farset, the most prominent of which was the Stone Bridge. The commercial life of the town was within a stone's throw of this bridge (slaughterhouses, tanneries, etc.) and markets and fairs were held in its vicinity until the nineteenth century. On market days there were stalls in front of the houses on both sides of the river. The Stone Bridge became a meeting place for unemployed men, and employers got into the habit of sending 'to the bridge' for a man. Here in fact was Belfast's first place of hiring.

By 1760 a new market had been established on the outskirts of the town at Smithfield. It was convenient to Hercules Lane (now Royal Avenue) known at that time as the street of the butchers, and was also close to the slaughterhouses situated in the corner enclosed by Hercules Lane and Castle Lane. Smithfield became a thriving market place over the next century, with an open market for miscellaneous goods, hides, wool, delph, farm produce, cattle, horses, mules, asses and much, much more. It had all the attractions of a country fair – amusement booths, Punch and Judy shows, ballad singers, storytellers. Fruit and vegetables were sold nearby in Castle Lane. The streets were busy, thriving places too; full of the traffic of carts and long-shafted drays piled high with unbleached yarn and linen. These would eventually find their way to the Brown Linen Hall, then situated on the site of the present St Anne's Cathedral in Donegall Street.

In those days farmers from south Antrim brought their produce to market via the Malone Road, passing the turnpike house as they approached Sandy Row. This led to the old Carrickfergus Road past the Pound, through Durham Street, Barrack Street, Millfield, Carrick Hill, North Queen Street and the Shore Road. Traffic heading to market could turn off to the right at the junction of Barrack Street and Mill Street (known as Watson's Corner) which led straight down to High Street, or it could turn left off Mill Street towards Smithfield. At Watson's Corner you would have seen a long line of carts piled high with hay and straw or fresh green vegetables, for here the weighbridge keeper had his hut and collected tolls from farmers as they passed by. These came from such places as Ballinderry, Glenavy, Hannahstown and Upper Falls to sell their produce wherever it fetched the best price.

By 1820 yet another market had opened on reclaimed land by the River Lagan. It was used mainly for the sale of butter, eggs, potatoes and vegetables. By 1845 the need was felt for bigger and better markets. The Corporation of Belfast applied for and obtained an Act of Parliament giving the Town Council powers to borrow up to £150,000 for improving the town. The Belfast Improvement Act 1845 enabled the Corporation to purchase all the existing markets. Ground for new markets was purchased from one of the town's chief magistrates (Stephen [later Sir Stephen] May) who owned meadows and fields (May's fields) stretching eastwards to the river's edge. From then on most of Belfast's markets were held in this vicinity, the main market area being known as May's Market. It was to this market that most of the flax, pork, butter, eggs, fish, potatoes, fresh vegetables, onions, straw, meadow hay, upland hay and unthreshed seed hay were brought from 1850 onwards. Seed hay was in great demand for feeding the carrier horses

ESTABLISHED 1842   TELEPHONE No. 190.

ROBSON'S
ROYAL VICTORIA HORSE BAZAAR,
General Posting & Funeral
Furnishing Establishment,
SALE
AND COMMISSION MART,
31 & 33 CHICHESTER ST., & 11 & 13 MONTGOMERY ST.,
BELFAST,
One of the Largest and Best Equipped Establishments in the
Kingdom.

Posting and Funeral Departments.
Carriages of every description turned out in first-class style
in a few minutes' notice.
Well trained matched Carriage Horses (with or without
Coachman) let on Job by the week, month or year.
Carriages of every description let on hire by the week, month
or year.
First-class Wedding Equipages.
Pic-Nic and Excursion Parties contracted for. Well
appointed Four-in-hand Drags for Race Meetings, &c.
Easy Carriages, Bath Chairs and House Chairs, suitable for
Invalids, on Hire with option of Purchase.
Funeral Requisites of all descriptions. Funerals fully Fur-
nished and Conducted to all parts in best style and with economy.

Sale and Commission Departments.
Accommodation for 200 Horses, and Standing Room for 350
Carriages.
Auction Sale of High-class Horses, Cows, &c., on the First
Wednesday in each Month (being the Fair Day).
Auction Sale of Horses, Cows, Carriages, Harness, Saddlery,
&c., on the Second Friday following each Fair Day.
Periodical Sale of Pedigree Shorthorns and other Cattle,
also Sheep, Poultry, Dogs, &c.
Horses and Stock Sales Conducted in all parts of the country.
Horses trained to Double and Single Harness.
Always on hands for Private Sale, a large stock of New and
Second-Hand Carriages, Harness, Saddlery, &c.
Carriages Warehoused for any period.
Terms Strictly Moderate.
JOHN ROBSON, Proprietor.

Telegraphic Address—"ROBSON," BELFAST.

Robson's advertisement from 'Bassett's County Antrim' 1888.

and (later) the horses that pulled the trams in the city's streets. In 1893 the Belfast Tramway Company had a stable of 800 horses. Across the street in the variety market (St George's) buyers could purchase butchers' meat, poultry, fresh butter, cheese and eggs; also such things as tongs, a crowbar, outerwear, underwear, furniture (both new and second-hand) – in fact anything the then town of Belfast might ever need.

The livestock markets and Fair Green were also situated in May's fields and sold horses, black cattle, sheep, pigs and goats. In the early days poultry, cage birds, pigeons and greyhounds were also available. The new market heralded the arrival of a new system of selling (by auction) though selling at fairs, at the farm, and direct selling to shops was to continue for a long time yet. The main auctioneering establishments in those days were Robson's Royal Victoria Bazaar, founded in 1842 and sandwiched between Victoria Street, Montgomery Street and Chichester

May's Market, Belfast in the late 1920s.

Street, and John Colgan & Sons which was first established in Glasgow in 1850 and came to Belfast in 1900. Robson's later moved to roomier premises just beyond East Bridge Street. In 1926 two of Robson's employees, R.J. Allam and W.N. Orage set up their own auctioneering business in Oxford Street and these three (Colgan's, Robson's and Allam's) dominated Belfast's trade in cattle and sheep for many years. By then many animals were being transported by train. They were loaded onto wagons at stations and sidings all over the country, some even coming from as far away as Cork. In those days animals were hand reared and were much tamer and more easily handled than they are today. Even so, animals arriving in Belfast, never having seen anything in their lives but hedges and green fields, must have felt both nervous and bewildered on arrival in the city.

One County Down farmer, who purchased three cows in Colgan's mart for £30, with three ten-shilling notes handed back for a luck-penny, got more than he bargained for. On the ten-mile walk home one of the cows lay down by the roadside, having decided that the time had come to produce her calf. This she proceeded to do and the new owner, William Scott, had to leave mother and newborn calf with a farmer at Carryduff overnight. They completed their journey to the Scott farm at Carricknaveigh the next day.

Jim Scott was one of three sons in that family who set up in business in Belfast. Two ran a grocery business at 164 Shankill Road. The third, Jim, served his apprenticeship with W.J. Gordon, a provision merchant in Church Lane, before setting up as a butcher at 3 Lisburn Road. In those days pigs were butchered on the farm and Jim purchased his pork through an agent who either collected it there or bought it in the markets throughout the country. Beef and mutton were purchased at the livestock sales, usually Colgan's or Allam's. Selling was by then an efficient undertaking run by business people rather than farmers, who were by now educated to know the value of their stock. It was a far cry from the days when a farmer could

Jim Scott (right) with his assistant and a customer at his shop on the Lisburn Road.

14

Belfast docks from where thousands of cattle were exported.

spend all day trying to sell a cow. Most of the animals arrived by train, unloading at sidings and going into pens at East Bridge Street and Oxford Street. Animals purchased by local butchers went across to the abattoir in Stewart Street to be slaughtered. Those bought by farmers were penned prior to being walked or lorried out to the farm. The remainder went into lairage pens situated between Stewart Street and the Lagan, where they were examined by vets before setting off on the mile-long walk (along Laganbank Road, Oxford Street, Ann Street, Victoria Street, Corporation Street and Garmoyle Street) to the docks. Here they were again penned before being loaded onto boats destined for Glasgow, Birkenhead or Heysham depending on who had purchased them earlier in the day.

This journey from May's fields (now called Maysfield) to the docks was a running sore with Belfast Corporation for many years, mainly because of the disruption to traffic but also because of perceived cruelty in that ash plants were used freely as sticks by the drovers who accompanied the animals. Police kept a lookout at the appropriate time each morning and evening in an effort to enforce a Corporation bylaw but it was impossible to watch all of them all of the time and lapses often occurred. A report in the *Belfast News-Letter* of 1 May 1931 stated that salesmen at Birkenhead were complaining of animals arriving with stick marks. This reduced their value.

Ministry of Agriculture figures for October 1931 state that 24,556 cattle, 19,796 sheep and 2,508 pigs passed through the Port of Belfast that month, most of these having travelled on the hoof along some of Belfast's busiest streets. The Corporation felt that the problem could be solved by moving the auctioneers, lock, stock and barrel to Duncrue Street beside the docks. They succeeded in moving the abattoir but the auctioneers refused to move from their traditional site. However, changes were already taking place. The Pigs Marketing Board (established 1934) now controlled most of the pig sales. Cattle and sheep were being sold by weight instead of by the head. Marts were springing up in towns all over the North to conform to new regulations. The days of Belfast's nightly 'Wild West show' were numbered and they came to an eventual end in 1968.

Many pubs in the area had accommodation in the back yard where horses and milk cows could be kept on the night before or after the sale. The best known was Alfie Lavery's on the corner of Verner Street. There was another in Eliza Street. Johnny McKeown, a blacksmith, also lived in Eliza Street. Johnny shod the horses which pulled the breadcarts used in delivering bread for the nearby Inglis's Bakery. Fodder for the horses was supplied by Ballycarry farmer Edward Sturdy who had a contract with Inglis's for the supply of hay to 100 of their horses. This kept seven of Sturdy's own horses and carts busy three days every week. Another dealer came from Aghalee. It was a common sight between the wars to see him with two loaded carts, one immediately behind the other, trundling down the Lisburn Road towards the hay market, the second horse's nose almost buried in the load in front. Some dealers fitted a frame to the cart to enable them to carry a larger load.

During the eighteenth and nineteenth centuries and into the twentieth a large quantity of butter (sold in 56lb weights called firkins) and buttermilk (sold in small barrels called runlets) was carted into Belfast and delivered directly to shops and bakeries. Much of it came from the Carnmoney area which at that time was very rural even to the point of having its own fairs for which a patent was granted in 1772. There were just two in the year and they were used mainly for

Courtesy of J.E. Blair

William James Blair and 'Kate' the mare at Balmoral on their way to market in 1925.

the sale of black cattle and pigs. They were also used by the farming community for the purchase of earthenware, pedlar's goods, huckstery; and hiring the occasional servant man or woman. Potatoes were either taken directly to shops or sold in the market. The roads in the Belfast area were excellent by the standards of the day and farmers thought nothing of setting off for the city in the early hours of the morning in the knowledge that they would get a good price for their crop when they got there. They converged on the town from all directions – Newtownards, Dromore, Antrim, Larne, and Islandmagee. Those coming from the northern shores of Belfast Lough approached by the Shore Road. Those from the Lisburn direction made their way down the Lisburn Road (completed in 1821) into Bedford Street, turning right at the back of the City Hall (formerly the White Linen Hall) when they reached the city centre. This led through May Street to Oxford Street where the markets were held until the Balmoral Market opened in 1975. At the height of the season growers queued along Oxford Street as the gateman struggled to cope with collecting the market dues. Sometimes the queue turned the corner into Laganbank Road, at that time known to farmers as the Sand Quay as that was where lighters coming from the interior unloaded their cargo of sand. This queue often formed in the autumn when farmers were in the market every day with potatoes.

Farmers seldom returned home with an empty cart. Some brought back coal but more often it was a load of horse manure – or onion boxes. Onions in those days came in wooden cases divided into three compartments. Turned on their side they made good nesting boxes for hens. Manure could be readily procured all over the city. A notice in the *Belfast Commercial Chronicle* dated 26 January 1818 advertised 'Several Parcels of Excellent Street Manure to be sold by auction at one o'clock precisely commencing at the rear of the fountain in Queen Street and proceeding by Great George's Street. Ready bank notes only accepted in payment.' This trade in manure continued well into the twentieth century.

South Antrim farmers usually returned home via Cromac Square and Donegall Pass. Tiredness and lack of sleep often caught up with them on the journey home. One farmer woke one morning to find he had fallen asleep in his cart. He had nodded off about Finaghy Crossroads and his mare had brought him safely to his own farmyard near the Halfpenny Gate – about six miles beyond Lisburn. The mare had probably stopped at several drinking troughs along the way without disturbing the sleeping occupant of the cart.

Taking the hay to market was the job of the hired man and one that he looked forward to immensely, though it held some risks. A ton or more of hay was loaded onto the cart the evening before. The man set off at two in the morning (in the case of Islandmagee) for the six-hour journey to the hay market. He sometimes sat on top of his load and sometimes walked with the horse. When he reached the outskirts of the city he allowed the cart wheels to slip from the cobble stones into the tram lines and it was full steam ahead then, providing he wasn't caught, for the practice was illegal. During the Troubles of 1921 he had to bury himself in the hay or risk being hit in the crossfire of opposing factions. The farmer set off a few hours later travelling by train for he liked to do the actual selling himself. When the deal was completed the hired man was given the address to which the hay had to be delivered, and more often than not he had to fork it onto a loft when he arrived. The horse was treated to some hay and the hired man had a bap and a mug of tea before the pair set off for home.

The homeward journey also held risks. There was always the possibility that thieves would be lying in wait to relieve farmer or servant of the day's takings. The thieves worked in pairs, one grabbing the horse by the reins to stop him in his tracks and the other jumping into the cart to attack the driver. The farmer's line of defence was to lift a side board off the cart and hit his attacker with it. Archie Brown of Islandmagee was just a small boy when these things were taking place but he often heard his father speak of them in later years.

A horseman, a stockman and a servant girl were hired full time on the Brown farm with extra hands being brought in for the harvest. These were either hired in Larne or engaged locally. On a couple of occasions Archie's father negotiated privately for a lad from the Nazareth Home in Belfast but often these were unsuitable as they had neither the background nor interest in farming. Three horses were kept at Brown's, two for working the land and one for odd jobs like pulling the trap. In addition to this, blood [throughbred] horses were specially bred and broken in for selling as officers' horses during the 1914-18 war.

One of the jobs that fell to the young Archie was taking the horses to be shod. The best-known blacksmiths in Islandmagee were the Mitchell brothers who could shoe a horse, mend machinery parts or hang a scythe to perfection. The scythe parts (the snead [handle] and the blade) were bought in Larne and taken to the blacksmith who twisted the metal part at the neck of the blade and hung it so that the blade lay at the correct angle according to the customer's height and the length of his arm. Archie looked forward to going to the smithy as, apart from meeting and talking with neighbouring farmers, he enjoyed listening to the fine voices of the Mitchells who often sang as they worked.

By the outbreak of the Second World War Archie was farming 600 acres, keeping cows, pigs and poultry – but never sheep. Later he was to hire someone from whom he would learn the rudiments of sheep farming. At the time the man (Nat Sloan) was hired with a well-known hill farmer outside Larne. Nat knew he was well off where he was but he was restless for a change. Archie heard about this and asked him if he was interested in coming to Islandmagee. He was; and within a short time Archie found himself buying sheep to accommodate the interests and skills of his hired man. It was the beginning of a partnership that was to last several decades.

But not all hirelings were as fortunate as Nat Sloan. Robert Higgins' experience was just the opposite, for every place he hired was to prove worse than the one before. When Robert ran away from home at the age of eleven and took a job with a farmer at Cairncastle he little realised what he was letting himself in for. On his first morning he, another hired man and the servant girl were called at four o'clock. Robert's first job was to milk the cows and take the milk to the road to be collected by the creamery cart. After that he cleaned out the byre. By then that morning's milk had been lifted and the previous day's empty cans were waiting to be brought to the yard and washed.

By eight o'clock it was time for breakfast, which consisted of buttermilk and half a soda farl spread with margarine and jam. For dinner he got a salt herring and two potatoes. At supper time a plate of porridge was set down with two spoons, one for Robert and one for the other hired man. They supped from the same plate. Each had his own mug of buttermilk.

Robert left that place after six months and fared better at his next place, though worse was to come. It is possible Robert's account is exaggerated but it is just as likely to be true:

I left there and I went to a man called Thomas Wilson of Ballyalbana. Well, it was a good house. There was no two tables in Tom's house. He was a gentleman tae work till and everybody sat at the same table, but I still had only five shillin's a week an' my meat an' bed. But the house was too wee and I had to sleep in an outhouse. It was their old dwelling house and they kept the meal down below and I slept up the stairs. But it was comfortable.

After the six months Tom was going to stop labourin' [growing crops] so I went to Larne Hiring Fair. I went down to the bottom end of the Town Hall and all us boys that was for hirin' stayed down at that door and talked about farm life and what sort of man he had worked till and what his last six months was like. I hired that day with a man who was the sexton of Glenwherry church. Tom Wilson stepped forward and told him that I was a good worker and he would guarantee me to work if I was left alone.

'But,' he says, 'he's a bit hasty-tempered but if you work him the right way you'll have no fault and he'll stay the six months.'

Nobody could tell me anything about *him*; whether I was going to a good place or not. Well, there wasn't much meat about it but there was plenty of bloomin' hard work. When I went to him in the month of May he had no crop in, so I helped him to put all the crop in and when it came the month of November all the crop was out – the turnips an' all snedded. Most of the time I stayed away from him and he stayed away from me. I never seen the inside of Glenwherry church while I was there even though he was the sexton. I was never invited to go to that church and even when they were saying prayers at night I was dumped up the stairs to bed. He had two daughters and a son. Well, the son got hardened to the father and couldn't do with him at all and he went out to Australia. Then he found out where the son was, and he sent him the money to come back home because he was an old man and couldn't run the farm without him.

The last I remember about the old man: I asked one of the daughters could I have a piece of bread and a cup of milk at night for supper.

The old man said, 'Did you challenge [ask] Lizzie to get you a cup of milk and a piece of bread at night? Why, what's wrong with your porridge that you can't take it?'

I said my heart didn't lie to porridge.

'Och well,' he says, 'You'll just sleep better without it,' and I had tae go to bed without any supper. I got nothing at all!

When my six months was up I went to see the doctor in Larne and he said I was badly nourished and badly run down and didn't he advise me to go to the Cottage Hospital in Ballymena. When I came out of hospital Tom Wilson was there waitin' to take me back to his place but I had made up my mind to go to the next hiring fair in Larne.

We were all standing in a group and this man said to me, 'Boy, have you got a place?'

'Naw, I haven't got a place yit.'

'If you don't get a place here, what are you goin' to do?' he said.

And I said, 'If I don't get a place here I'll go to Ballyclare Fair.' (Ballyclare's fair was held later in the month.)

'Well,' this man said, 'Robert, I have a man here but he takes a lot of drink and he's hard tae work with. Any man that has ever been with him has never finished the six months.'

I says, 'That's a bloomin' recommendation you're givin' me!' But I hadn't got a place and I said I'd go. He was a wee man that lived at Hall's Crossroads outside the town.

He says, 'What's the wages?'

Main Street Larne and Henry McNeill's Hotel.

'I'll take what I was gettin' from the rest of them – £6 for the six months,' I says. But by God I didn't know what I was in for. He daled [bought and sold] a lot in horses – and was maybe away for a week at a time.

He would come home late in the afternoon and he would say, 'Go over to Sam's and get him to run you to the Border [dividing line between Northern and Southern Ireland] in the lorry and you can bring home a few horses.' At the Border I met the man that had the horses and he told me what field they were in, and at night I had tae go into that field, put the ropes on them and bring them out. Usually there were six, sometimes four. I roped them two abreast, got on one in the middle and away I went. Between gettin' a ride and walkin' it was a long journey. It took three or four days.

When I got them home we fed them, got them up nicely and as long as I could work with them he guaranteed that they were quiet in harness in all farm work. So when it come the horse fair in Belfast – I think it was the first Wednesday in every month in the market at Allam's – I had to have the horses in that fair before eleven o'clock because that's the time they got them numbered and put through the ring. And what he didn't sell I had tae turn roun' and walk back home and when you got home you were hungry and all you got was tea and bread.

Then the boss would have come in and said, 'Robert you're not that tired, boy. Yoke [harness up] that oul mare there stannin' in the stable and cart out manure 'til it's bedtime.' I seen me that when I went down to say my prayers at night I was that tired I wakened up that same way in the mornin'.

20

If it was rainin' he would say, 'Go to Larne and redd out that man's midden and when you get home put the manure in that field.' (You see lots of people in Larne kept animals at that time.) And off you set in the early hours of the mornin' for a load of manure. And if there was no dung to be got, you went down to the sea for a load of wrack instead, and spread that over the land. But you couldn't use too much of that because of the salt in it. It would have poverised [impoverished] the ground.

I mind one time he had a field that was full of cutworm. So I said to him, 'I'm goin' to plough that oul bog down there.' The boss's father come over to me when I had it half ploughed and he says, 'Robert, what are you doin?'

Says I, 'I'm goin to put corn in this.'

'You might as well go home an' lie in bed,' he says, 'because my brother-in-law ploughed that fiel' for years an' they never could grow anything in it because it was full of cutworm.'

'Well,' says I, 'To hell, I'll try it. I'm goin to Larne for two load of manure in the mornin'. I want a lend of your cart and horse. I'm goin' to scatter dung over it and plough it in.'

'Ye need'nae bother.'

But instead of goin' to Larne for two load of manure, I went to Carrick for two load of gravel salt and I spread the gravel salt and killed the cutworm, because nae cutworm would live where it was. Well, I went down to Mounthill and I got five cwt of seed corn. And the boss comes home and he says, 'What did you plough that oul bog for?'

'Well,' says I, 'I put corn in it. I don't know if it'll grow or not.'

Says he, 'You've a brave braird [first shoots] in it anyway.' The dickens, it grew as high as the house!

Some people went home between fairs. I never went home because I had a stepfather and he wasn't good to us. But on the eleventh night (the night before the fair) we all gathered at the crossroads and we had a jolly night then. Somebody would have had a melodeon, somebody else a fiddle and maybe somebody an oul fife or something. You had your six poun' in your pocket and a bottle of beer was only sixpence. When you got a few bottles of thon heavy Guinness in you, you enjoyed yourself. Then there was one time we used to grow a terrible lot of flax in this country. When it was ready it was put up on the laft where you slept and then the rats and mice come in. I remember one night I was that tired after workin' hard about the farm, when I riz in the mornin' my face was all scratched and bleedin' so I had to go to the doctor to get an injection. I always thought that it was rats or somethin' that ate the side of the face nearly off me.

About that time I got married. It was the 'hungry thirties' and you couldn't get a job anywhere, so I bought the *Belfast Telegraph* one night and I read where a man wanted an all-round farm-hand, with a free house and 29s 0d a week. But when we got to the house half the slates were off it, and I had to put bits of tin under the slates to keep the water out. There was no free food or nothin' there. If you got a stone of potatoes or half a pint of milk it was taken out of your wages. By this time we had a child but the child wasn't allowed inside that man's house. My wife had to work the same as I had for the 29s 0d and I had to get up at three in the mornin' to have the milk at the end of the loanin [lane] for six. The horses were ready for me when I came out from my breakfast and I had to wait for daylight so that I could see the first fur [furrow] before I could start. He used to give me a hurricane lamp so that I could find the cows in the field in the mornin' to bring them home for milking.

I used to listen to them sayin', 'Rule Britannia. Britons never shall be slaves,' but Larne was one of the biggest slave markets ever I come across in my life. Once you hired you were down for six months slavery and you needn't expect from any farmer an easy time because you did not get it.'

In actual fact Larne hiring fair was no worse than any other, but Robert's perception of it was coloured by bad experiences in the places where he had hired. Hiring day was a day of freedom – a day when servants could say 'yea' or 'nay' to their masters; a day which could herald the beginning of a new life in a new home in a new place for the next six months. It was a day when the country people took over the town in a big way. It was a big day for the farmer too. He perhaps sold a few cattle or a cart load of pigs. He met and chatted with his neighbour or treated him to a drink.

To the townsfolk it was a novelty. The stalls were always more alluring than the shops with their profusion of gingerbread, apples, hard nuts, dulse and yellowman. Larne Fairs are remembered with affection by many people and admirably described by John Clifford in his poem 'The Hirin' Fair'.

1
The corn is stacked, the prittas dug,
The cattle housed a' neat and snug
November's breath is in the air
And brings yince mair Lairne Hirin' Fair.
Frae ivery fairm for miles aroon
The lads an' lasses mak' the toon,
Wi' shiney boots an' shiney faces,
They seek mair wages an' fresh places.

2
The past six months they've worked like mad,
For maisters, middlin, guid or bad;
Some weel-fed, happy an' respected,
But ither craiters, starved, neglected.
Yet on this happy day o' cheer
They soon forget the past half-year,
An' flock in droves for guid or ill,
Tae Cross Street, near the Lairne Fair Hill.

3
An' hopeful there they take their stan',
Each servant lass an' servant man,
Tae seek a job an' better pay,
For six lang months, frae noo till May.
There's servant men frae Killyglen,
That hasnae shaved since Lord knows when;
Lang, lanky raw-baned Mounthill toughs,
An' gangs o' big Kilwaughter roughs.

4
They come frae Ballynure an' Straid,
Frae doon the shore, aye an' the Braid,
Gleno, Raloo an' Islandmagee,
Frae Feystown, Magheraban, Rashee.
A' dressed up in their Sunday suits,
They've creeshed their hair an' blacked their boots,
Intent for yince tae cut a dash,
An' buy some fun wi' hard-earned cash.

5
There's watches goin' for three an' six,
There's cork-screw knives an' walkin' sticks;
Drinks, apples, nuts an' yellowman
An' spae-wives there tae read yer han'.
That's where you'll find the servant girls
Before they go in search o' erls,
For maybe printed on their han'—
Is some 'rich, handsome, dark young man.'

6
This is their day, their faces show it;
They're brave weel-like, an' man they know it,
An' mony a match that's made this day
Is clinched in kirk afore next May.
These sonsy dacent weel-wrought lasses,
Though a wee bit blate, are no' sich asses,
But show ambition, pride and zeal,
An' dae their best tae marry weel.

7   *Wi' some mysterious seventh sense*
The fairmer knows wi' half a glance,
That this young lass, dress't up tae kill,
Has niver wrought in toon or mill.
But knows the way tae milk a coo,
Tae feed a calf or stroke a soo;
At threshin' time cud gie' a han',
Fork hay or corn wi' ony man.

8   *He sidles up – ' I s'pose,' says he–*
'Ye'r hirin'.' – 'Aye, A am,' says she;
They bargain, argue, chap, divide,
Till lang at last the erls is paid.
Guid ploughmen are in big demand
Tae coup Carncastle's heavy lan',
They'll get their keep an' ten poun' clear,
An' that's no' bad for yin half-year.

9   *An' then there's useful handy chaps,*
Sae guid at diggin' dykes an' sheughs;
Can milk a coo, or feed a pig,
Can swing a scythe, or set a rig.
They'll clean the horses, plait their manes,
An' gie a han' at mindin' weans.
Sich chaps as these at this Lairne Fair
Can get six guineas – less or mair.

10   *Av coorse, there's ither thaveless bein's*
Saft, hairmless, feckless doits – the lea'ins;
They're happy hokin' in a sheugh,
Or dungin' byres, or somethin' rough.
They get a bed, a bite tae eat,
A dud o' claes, clogs tae their feet;
An odd half-croon frae time tae time,
An' this arrangement works oot fine.

11   *You'd nearly think some unwrit law*
Provided places for them a',
The way they fitted in sae weel,
Like cogs in some great nick-ed wheel.
An' as the efternoon descends,
The fun begins, the hirin' en's.
They're a' fixed up for six months mair,
But still hae time an' cash tae spare.

12   *Their youthful healthy appetites*
Go oot in search o' toon delights,
For tay an' buns, an' pig's feet broth,
Or pints o' porter topped wi' froth.
The fairmers slowly trickle hame
And lea' the boys an' girls alane
Tae spend an hour or twa thegither,
Makin' trysts wi' yin anither.

13   *These golden hours – how soon they flee,*
Yet what great happiness they gie,
Convoyin' some young lass, an then–
A cuddle at some loanin en'.
How better end a perfect day?
I've only yin thing mair tae say –
It's this – ' I'm no ashamed tae tell
I've sipped these simple joys mysel'.

In the early days much of the produce brought to Larne was exported to Scotland but as roads improved and demand increased at home, farmers began to market their produce in Belfast. Larne had a hinterland of good farming land and the usual industries associated with farming, i.e. spinning, weaving, tanning, milling and threshing. There were in addition three rope manufactories and salt pans which by the 1830s had fallen into disuse.

East Antrim was one of the earliest areas to be settled by the English and Scots (chiefly the latter). They landed at Carrickfergus and proceeded to the districts allotted to their leaders where they occupied themselves with farming and weaving. They were a Presbyterian family called

Edmonstone to whom a patent was granted to hold a monthly market in Ballycarry. The market was used for the sale of yarn and cloth. To encourage excellence the Edmonstones offered first, second and third premiums to the families which produced the most and best quality of yarn. This worked well for many years but when the premiums stopped the markets quickly followed suit. Fairs (never more than four in the year) were originally held at the Black Hill about a mile outside the town but later moved to the village itself.

Neighbouring Mounthill had never more than two fairs which were also established early in the 1600s. They were held on the first days of July and October. The Fair Green was at one time let out by the landlord to one or other of his more prosperous tenants at a yearly rent of between five and ten pounds. Anyone who wanted to hire a tent on the day of the fair could do so for a half-crown. Ballycarry and Mounthill fairs had much in common. Both witnessed scenes of drinking and fighting which caused their fortunes to rise and fall over the years. The following poem entitled 'Mounthill Fair' by John Clifford captures the atmosphere:

1   *Them was the days lang lang ago,*
When Mounthill Fair was like a show;
And folk frae a' the district pairts
Come trottin' in the low-wheeled cairts.

2   *Frae early morn, afore 'twas clear,*
There meres and foals they wud appear;
And kye and heifers tae as weel,
And cairts o' pigs wi' mony a squeal.

3   *The hale Fair Hill frae end tae end,*
Was covered thick wi' beasts and men;
Frae Tammy's corner richt alang
Tae Robert Howie's was a thrang.

4   *And jist inside the oul' Fair Hill,*
Ach, boys a dear, I see her still;
Was Jean, her stall sae spic and span,
Wi' apples, nuts and 'yellow man'.

5   *And then the lasses – man o dear,*
They'd mak' ye smile frae ear to ear;
And mony's a match for guid or ill
Was made inside the oul' Fair Hill.

6   *The gipsies wi' their piebald steeds,*
Their weemin wi' their scarves and beads;
Like folk frae some far foreign shore,
You'd see them there, full mony's a score.

7   *The foals, them days, was something great,*
They bred them roun' and strong and straight;
The Mullaghsandal boys for years,
Held pride o' place for sheltie meres.

8   *Ructions wud start in Robert's bar,*
There's arguments, there's threats, there's war;
The lads come runnin' frae the hill,
Like warriors flockin' tae the kill.

9   *There's scattered teeth, there's bla'kened e'en,*
The wildest mess you've ever seen;
Ivery man's your friend or foe,
Speak oot o' turn and doon ye go.

A cockfight was held at Mounthill on the evening before the fair. The drinking started then and continued until the day after – generally called the Old Fair Day. The first day of July 1840 turned out to be very wet. Around 200 horses were sold that day (about half the usual number), some 250 each of black cattle and beef cattle, 150 pigs on the string, 20 cart loads of young pigs and about 100 sheep. At the same fair there were forty tents selling whiskey alone! There were also stands for the sale of gingerbread, sweetmeats, tinware, soft goods, wooden vessels, hardware and baskets.

The formation of Farming Societies in the 1830s (two such were the Templecorran and the Kilroot Farming Societies) did much to promote improvements in both farming methods and the quality of farm implements. All three blacksmiths in Ballycarry began making iron ploughs and an 'excellent description' of farm cart was introduced. There were numerous horse-operated threshing machines and at least one driven by water. The water was conveyed about a quarter of a mile in a pipe under the ground and thirty-three yards by a wooden trough supported by five stone pillars. It could work all seasons of the year in spite of sharing the stream with a corn mill and a flax mill. A lean-to for storing straw was attached to the main building.

The Six Mile Water and its tributaries once provided the power for a score or more mills, not to mention its fertile valley and a number of towns and villages once associated with fairs and farming. These included Antrim, Ballyclare, Templepatrick, Roughfort, Parkgate, Oldstone, Ballynure and Straid (once known as Thomas Town). The original patent for fairs in the parish of Ballynure, which included Straid, was granted by James I on 8 July 1608, when John Dalway was given liberty 'to hold a Friday's market and a fair in each year at Thomas

People for hire used to gather around the Cunningham Memorial in Ballyclare.

© Green Collection, Ulster Folk and Transport Museum

Hiring Fairs and Market Places

Town, within the cynament of Ballynure.' These transferred to Ballynure village around 1790 when they were held on the Fair Hill which was on the site of the old castle built by Dalway in 1609. There was a second piece of common ground just off the main street in Ballynure where locals were in the habit of grazing their goats and geese. It was known as the Shilling Hill. The name had nothing whatever to do with money but rather indicated a draughty place where farmers could separate the shellings (or husks) from grain. The farmer or housewife shook the oats in a riddle and the wind took away the waste. Ballynure was in those days notorious for its horse dealers but famous for the quality and quantity of its butter which was generally marketed in Belfast.

The fairs at Parkgate – which was situated on the ancient road from Antrim to Carrickfergus – date back to 1787 when William Ferguson of 'Thrushfield' near the village was granted the patent for holding monthly markets and quarterly fairs. Markets were never held there but the fairs flourished. Two fairs started in Roughfort around the same time and continued throughout that century and the next. Livestock and farm produce were sold in both places: hiring also took place. The February fair, in Parkgate in particular, brought in hundreds of horses, mostly of the kind used for farmwork. There could have been any number up to 700 animals. The May fair had fewer horses, but a greater number of cattle as the grazing season got underway. The August fair was mainly for the sale of beef cattle and sheep, though there was always a certain number of every kind of animal at all the fairs. The November fair was said to be poor compared with the other three, though a few cattle would have been sold to pay land rents or make up servants' wages. Pedlar's goods, old clothes, fruit and huckstery were sold at all of them.

> Here cantin' varlets, thrawn [awkward] an' cross,
> Wi' ballad singers skirl:
> There blackguard boys at pitch-an'-toss,
> Gar baw-bees crimbly birl;
> There's ginge bread wives and tinkler jades,
> In garbs o' monie a texture,
> With folk o' a' kinds, callins, trades,
> Mak' up the motley mixture.

From *The Summer Fair* by Samuel Thompson, *New Poems* (Belfast 1799)

On one occasion a prankster put up posters advertising that a representative of the Persian Government was coming to Parkgate to buy cats. Another version of the story states that the purchaser was coming from Peru. In any case his country of origin is irrelevant as no one turned up at all. Numerous people, however, arrived at the fair with cats for sale. When it became evident that it was all a hoax they released hundreds of cats on the unsuspecting villagers of Parkgate.

A copy of *Old Moore's Almanac* records horse fairs at Oldstone until the outbreak of World War II but local people cannot recall any being held in the 1930s. They took place at what was known as O'Neill's Bullock House at the junction of the Ballyarnott Road and the Oldstone Hill. Today there is no evidence at all of the former twice yearly event.

Centuries ago, the nearby town of Antrim was said to consist solely of wooden houses; the floors, walls and doors being made of oak and the roofs of shingles. The town was destroyed in the rebellions of 1641 and 1798 but its position on the main route from places like Carrickfergus and Downpatrick, to Londonderry and the North West, ensured that it recovered quickly in the years that followed. Around the latter date, stage coaches (The Champion, Commerce, Reformer and Lark) passed through regularly. It also had a phaeton and gig and a good supply of four-wheeled caravans and jaunting cars. All these were said to be well horsed and appointed, and travelled on average at the rate of five Irish miles per hour.

In those days Antrim had just one street with three lanes branching off it, namely Bow Lane, Paty's Lane and Mill Row. The town had three fairs held on New Year's Day and the twelfth days of May and November. The first was held basically for the sale of cows, pigs and farm horses. The others were for the hiring of farm labourers. Those for hire could be found standing on the Massereene Bridge or near the hotel on the High Street. The *O.S. Memoir* of 1833 comments on male servants in Antrim carrying a rod to indicate that they were available for hire. The usual assortment of pedlar's goods, old clothes, cakes, apples, shoes, tinware, ironmongery and crockery was displayed for sale along the street. Cows and pigs were sold on the hiring days but never horses.

The town's two inns did a good trade, particularly in summer when parties called on their way to the Giant's Causeway and Shane's Castle. The downside was the influx of undesirables along with the visitors. This quote taken from *O. S. Memoirs, Parishes of County Antrim* Vol.29, P.24 states, 'From the circumstances of Antrim being such a thoroughfare and pass, their intercourse with strangers, though it may in some respects have tended towards their civilisation, still it also had its injurious effects in bringing many strolling and improper characters.' Not much had changed a century later when Alexander Irvine wrote:

> *The annual fair day in Antrim was a great occasion for the poor. The main street was lined with stalls which were crowded with gingerbread and candy.*
>
> *Petty merchants came from far and near to display their wares. [...] The whiskey places did a roaring business – so did the peelers [police].*
>
> *Farmers brought cattle, pigs, fowl, grain and hay. It was a great day for beggars, wanderers, thimble-riggers, acrobats, conjurers and queer people who live by their wits. I remember a time when my greatest ambition was to be old enough for a farmer to lay his hand on my shoulder and ask me to serve him for the following year. [...] I think I was more enamoured with the prospect of three meals a day than I was with agriculture.*

From *The Chimney Corner Revisited* by Alexander Irvine

There was always a good supply of meat at these fairs, though vegetables and fruit were often in short supply. Flax and grain were sold when in season. Lough Neagh trout, pollan and salmon were plentiful, as were Myroe oysters, Strangford cockles and Carrickfergus cod-fish. Poultry of all descriptions was usually available.

Although close to Antrim, Shane's Castle and Milltown once had their own fairs. Both died out during the eighteenth century. Templepatrick had two which were often used by the McKinneys of Sentry Hill for the sale of their farm produce and livestock. They also used other local fairs and of course, the bustling fairs and markets of Belfast. Fairs increased in many places during the nineteenth century and Antrim was no exception. They increased from two to

Hiring Fair in Antrim, May 1924. The main building (with the tower) is the market house.

fourteen at that time and to seventeen early in the twentieth century. In 1938 for instance they were held monthly, with an extra one in January, April, May, June and November. This included the two hiring days.

Hiring also took place in Ballyclare, though never at any time over the centuries were there more than four fairs in the year, two of which included hiring. The preferred site for hiring was the Market Square which in the early days was the old Fair Green. A wooden market house was built on it sometime during the eighteenth century. This was replaced by a stone one in 1866 and improved and enlarged several times afterwards. A monument was erected nearby in memory of a Doctor James Cunningham and from then on this was the focus for both selling produce and hiring labourers. When the monument was removed in the interests of traffic flow in 1951 the focus moved back to the market house, by now a fine building known and used as the Town Hall.

By tradition the fair was never held earlier than the third Thursday in the month, making it one of the latest fairs in the district. Ballyclare's fairs date back to 1756. George II saw fit to grant Arthur, Earl of Donegall 'two fairs yearly, also a weekly market to be held at the town aforesaid on every Wednesday forever; also a Piepowder Court to be held in the said town during the said fairs and markets.' However it is certain that these go back further, for *Watson's Almanac* records four fairs in Ballyclare in 1745. Ballyclare has always been famed for its livestock markets – especially horses. It was regarded as an excellent fair in which to purchase horses for cavalry regiments or draught horses for gun carriages or other military vehicles during World War I.

During 1818 a farming society was formed in the nearby village of Doagh under the patronage of the Marquis of Donegall. The society held a ploughing match in spring and a cattle show in the autumn. Prizes were awarded to the best ploughman, the best brood mare, foal, bull, cow, butter, etc. The marquis's patronage was short-lived however, as within a few years he became so embarrassed financially that he was obliged to grant leases to farmers in perpetuity in return for immediate cash, after which farmers held large farms at almost nominal rent.

For centuries Carrickfergus enjoyed prestige both as a stronghold and as a flourishing seaport. It was the Assizes Town for the county until the nineteenth century, when that position was usurped by the up and coming town of Belfast. It was also an important market town. Fairs and markets were established there by the Normans as far back as the thirteenth century, when John de Courcy received a charter from Henry II. The charter included a patent to hold fairs and markets. Other charters were granted over the years, one being that granted by James I in 1613. This stated that two annual fairs were to be held and two weekly markets, one on Saturday but no day was specified for the other; also a Piepowder Court. The number of fairs increased to four in the nineteenth century.

Horse racing was held at various venues in the town over the years – at the Commons, for instance and at two other places, named by the Ordnance Surveyor as Kirkshall (or Kirk's Fall) and the Reagh Hill; and at a time by the seashore on the Gallows Green. 'Human' racing also took place. For this the tail of a medium-sized pig was shaved and soaped, after which its head and neck were decorated with ribbons. It was then turned loose in a large area where it was pursued by hundreds of people all intent on securing the prize (the pig), which could only be won by catching it and holding on to its soaped tail.

The town grew around its market place which lay within the triangle formed by the castle, the friary and St Nicholas' Church. In its centre in medieval times was a fine market cross. In 1881 a monument in the form of a large gas lamp with a drinking fountain was erected near the site where the old cross had been. This was known as the Big Lamp and was a prominent feature of the town until it was removed in the late1950s.

But the big changes took place in the eighteenth century. These included repairs to the castle and harbour and the erection of a number of new buildings, including a customs house, a courthouse and gaol, a horse barracks and, most importantly, a fine new market house. The next century was to bring even greater changes, particularly to the economy of the town, in the form of growth in the textile industry, the opening of a shipyard and the establishment of salt mining as a major enterprise.

In 1835 a market yard was built in North Street beside the newly built Presbyterian Church which had replaced an earlier thatched one on the same site. The markets then moved to that area. The most prominent feature in the street was the North Gate, the only one to survive out of four built when the town was walled in the seventeenth century. Farmers agitated to have it removed around 1880 so that they could more easily transport their hay to market. They did not succeed and it was restored in 1911 to mark the coronation of George V. The general market day was Saturday. Pork and butter were sold on Monday. No tolls were collected but a charge was levied for a stall or other accommodation in the new market. The main commodities sold were farm produce and fish. Oysters, turbot, haddock, plaice, sole, cod and herring were all sold when in season. Large quantities of fish also went to Belfast Market or were peddled from door to door in the town. An assortment of potato baskets, brooms, riddles, delph, crocks, tinware, whips, canes, turf and a hundred and one other commodities were also sold. Fairs were by then held on the first days of May and November and the first Saturday in February and August. Pigs and cattle were the main animals bought and sold.

A rather unusual trial took place at Carrickfergus Courthouse in 1808. It concerned a sorceress and a cow. The people of the county were superstitious in the old days. The existence of fairies was confidently and generally believed in; omens, charms and witches too. Witches, it was said, could take away the luck or spoil the milk of a cow. An example of this came to light at the trial of fortune-teller Mary Butters. The story began in 1807 at the home of an Alexander Montgomery who lived close by Carnmoney Meeting House. Alexander's cow, the sole provider of milk and butter for the family, was still doing her duty as regards the milk but the milk simply would not churn into butter. A number of cures were tried including a blessing of the cow by twelve witches but to no avail. Alexander's wife was convinced that the cow had been 'blinked' – had the 'evil eye' of a witch cast toward it – and that they would have no butter until the cow was charmed back to full health. To this end Alexander consulted the aforementioned Mary Butters as to what, if anything, could be done.

Mary arrived at the Montgomery home at ten o'clock one August night and took charge. Alexander and a young man called Carnaghan, she said, should stay in the byre. They were to turn their waistcoats inside out, position themselves at the ailing cow's head and stay there until she sent them a message to come into the house. This they did until night began to change into day, by which time they were becoming alarmed at the delay in being summoned. They decided to investigate and to their horror found four people lying on the floor of the house as if dead. Two (Alexander's wife and son) were indeed dead and an old lodger, Margaret Lee, died shortly afterwards. The pair dragged the fortune-teller outside and threw her on the nearby manure heap, where a few kicks brought her speedily back to life. The cottage was filled with the smell of sulphur, which came from a brew of the contents of the charm, which also included milk, needles, pins and crooked nails. At the inquest in Carnmoney, the jury found Mary Butters guilty of causing the deaths of the three victims through the use of noxious ingredients in an attempt to cure a sick cow. However she was discharged by proclamation when tried at the Spring Assizes in Carrickfergus in 1808. Alexander is said to have married again within a few weeks.

Very few towns south of the Six Mile Water corridor had successful fairs and markets, no doubt because of their proximity to the excellent markets in Belfast. Exceptions were Lisburn and Crumlin, both of which had good fairs. Attempts were made to establish markets in several other places. Nicholas Grimshaw tried to start one in Whitehouse for the convenience of the workers in his cotton mill. It did not last long but the town did have a busy wharf, with lighters landing large quantities of coal. On the far side of the county Largy's Lane Ends had a patent for holding fairs but party feuds prevented them from rising to any importance. Four fairs once held in Ballinderry also petered out. Upper Ballinderry had, however, an excellent corn mill (Walkington's) built in 1822, improved in 1837 and manufacturing 5,400 x 4 cwt sacks of meal annually.

Glenavy did not fare much better. Under a patent granted by Charles I, markets and fairs were once held there on the first Wednesday of every month, but these were discontinued around 1805 on account of the number of outrages which took place at them. Attempts were made to revive them by offering incentives such as premiums of up to one pound for both the buyer and seller of the highest priced horse, beef animal, sheep or pig; also to the seller of the largest quantity of yarn spun at the residence of the seller. Still they did not succeed. It was, however, a good farming area and there were numerous associated mills round about. One was a bleach mill (situated in the townland of Ballyvorally) which exported all its linen to New York. Its green extended to twenty-six acres.

The natural resources of south west Antrim led to some occupations peculiar to that area alone – basket making for instance. These were made from osiers [willow twigs] which grew by the shores of Lough Neagh. The lighter, finer osiers were used for the baskets (potato baskets were a speciality), and the stronger, thicker ones were made into firkin hoops. Potato baskets were sold through hardware merchants or directly to farmers at local markets. Some were exported. Women gathered rushes for making seats for rush-bottomed chairs. Other occupations included fishing and the inevitable farming, spinning and weaving.

Crumlin in 1750 consisted of a public house, a smith's forge and two houses. It must have improved soon after, for an advertisement in the *Belfast News Letter* of 5 July 1765 stated:

> *Wanted: an honest careful man who can be well recommended to work in a flax mill in Crumlin. He can be furnished with a house and a piece of land if he wants it and constant work the whole year. For further particulars, enquiries to Samuel Campbell in Crumlin or Robert McMurry in Magheragall who will treat with him for the same. There is also selling at the same mill some choice good flax by wholesale.*

In that same year the MacCaulay family arrived in Crumlin and built extensive flour and corn mills. The town probably owes its success to that family, for seventy years later it was described in *The Ordnance Survey Memoir* as 'a neat, regular built and improving little town.' By then post cars were calling at the inn on the main street. A market was being held regularly on the first Monday of every month, when the usual assortment of cows, sheep, pedlar goods, yarn and crockery was exposed for sale. No tolls or customs were levied by either of the landlords – the Marquis of Hertford or Lord Pakenham of Langford Lodge. Attempts at starting a horse fair in Crumlin failed, possibly because of the already well-established horse fairs at Antrim, Parkgate and Oldstone. Many farmers took their produce to Belfast, a distance of fourteen miles, and brought back lime from Shankill.

Lisburn's position on the main canal, road and rail route into the interior of the country, not to mention its being on the main road from Belfast to Dublin, ensured its continuing success since its foundation early in the seventeenth century. It was destroyed by fire in the rebellion of 1641 and again (by accident) in 1707 but recovered rapidly afterwards in each instance. By the end of the eighteenth century there were twelve public coaches passing through the town daily besides other conveyances. The town was by then well supplied with hostelries including the Hertford Arms and the King's Arms, the latter having been established nearly a hundred years earlier. Add to this its fame as a market and linen town, its flour mills, grist mills, tanneries and brick fields and its success was assured. Its Tuesday markets have existed since 1627 when Charles I granted Edward, Viscount Conway the right to hold them. A new market house was built a few years later and parts of it can still be seen within the present Irish Linen Centre and Lisburn Museum. In those days the main goods sold were linen yarn, wool and their related products; also hides, butter, tallow and salt beef. These were mainly sold around the market house.

The meat shambles was in the vicinity of Smithfield but the meat, along with pork and herrings, was sold in Market Square. In 1796 the Marquis of Hertford saw to it that new

Making baskets occupied many people in the Gawley's Gate area near Lough Neagh. These were used for gathering potatoes.

Morgan Greer.

slaughterhouses were erected at Brown's Entry, which ran behind the Market Street shops from Smithfield to Bow Street, with a narrow exit onto the latter. This was known as the New Shambles and consisted of five slaughter houses and a piggery. The By-wash or Bow River took away the effluent. By the late 1920s these slaughter houses had gone and meat was prepared privately behind butchers' shops. There were several of these in Bow Street, including Green's, Cumins's, Drake's and Pat Laverty's, all of which conveniently backed onto Smithfield where cattle were sold. It was to Smithfield that the young **Morgan Greer** made his way in 1929 to sell his first bullock:

You took your cattle out and you sold direct to the butcher. The butcher came out to the market to buy it. Sometimes they came to the farm. The very first animal I had was a black cross-bred bullock. I reared him and fattened him on turnips and yellow meal. I brought him to Smithfield to sell him. Jacob Green bought him. The bullock had to be weighed first. There was a big lump of manure hanging to his tail. Jacob came forward and cut the lump off. He didn't want to be paying for the manure you see! Jacob was what was called a master butcher. He had a shop in Bow Street [still known as Green's]. Every butcher had his own abattoir in those days at the back of the shop. The shop backed onto Smithfield. I had to walk the bullock over to the abattoir myself. That was my first venture on my own.

Wee pigs were sold in Smithfield too. I think pigs were sold every Tuesday. Cattle would have been only once a month; horses every two months. They brought the pigs in with the horse and cart. They lined up in the open market. First they took the horse out and let the shafts down. Then they stabled the horse, lifted the pigs out and dropped them into a big box or crate. They were well fed and well washed. The buyers could look in and see what sort of pigs they were. They would reach away in and get one by the tail to see that there weren't any small ones in them. You had maybe ten pigs. You sold them to a man and he finished them – fattened them into pork. Then the Pigs Marketing Board came in and pork pigs – sold for pork, rather than bacon – went away by train. They were weighed at the goods station just off Antrim Street and went off to curers in Portadown and other places. They were graded before they left. A man called Gilliland used to put his hand into the cart and give them a grade. Sometimes we killed pigs on the farm and sold them as pork. We used to sell pork to G. & H. Bell's in Hillsborough or sometimes we took it to Lisburn. You lined the cart with clean straw before you loaded them and put a white cloth on top. The cloth was usually made from a bleached flourbag. Pork was sold in Smithfield too.

Horses were sold at the Market Place end of the Dublin Road. They were lined up there from Fergie Dornan's to R. & D. Thompson's corner. They used to trot the horse so that the buyer could see his action. The man that was selling him, he ran alongside. Then some men would be feeling down the horse's leg for side-bones; a wee bone at the side

Jacob Green and his staff in front of his butcher's shop.

Courtesy of Rowan Black

of the shin. If a side-bone developed he wouldn't have been so mobile and he might have had a few years on him. Sometimes a professional man would have 'choked' him to see how he coughed, to test his wind.

The main provision market continued for centuries at the Market House in Market Square. Here you could buy hen eggs, duck eggs, onions, cheese, clothes (both new and second-hand), socks, stockings, china, tin-ware, earthenware, books, pig troughs, potato baskets, stable brooms, hatchets, shovels, spades, rakes, hemp ropes, bee skeps, cabbage plants, wash tubs, tables, chairs, churns, saddlery, old spinning wheels. Many items could be bought at a penny or less and hardly anything cost more than a few shillings. The market was always well supplied with poultry, milk, fish, pork and wool; also vegetables when in season. At one time meal, grain and potatoes were sold in the Square too. A new grain market was opened in Smithfield in 1828. Some time later a hay market was built with its own separate entrance and weighbridge in Smithfield Street.

Lisburn prospered in the seventeenth century with the rapid development of the linen industry. This began with the arrival of English settlers and was boosted in 1696 with the removal of a tax on Irish linens entering England. It was further boosted in 1698 with the arrival of Louis Crommelin, a French Huguenot settler with a special interest in the manufacture of high quality linen. In those days the main market for linen was Dublin.

Around 1750 a Linen Hall, described as 'a large square court surrounded by a piazza of brick' was just one of several buildings erected in Smithfield at the expense of the Marquis of Hertford. This was good news for the weavers as it was attended by 'the most eminent linen merchants of the day', many of whom lived in or near the town. It had an excellent brown linen market, the largest in Ulster in 1816, even exceeding such places as Dungannon and Armagh. Add to this the fact that Coulson's damask manufactory in the town (built in 1766) was said to be the finest in the world and we have an idea of the pride taken by the people of Lisburn in the quality of their linen. But none of this was to last. Around 1820 the cottage industry began to fail, and the town commissioners sought other uses for the Linen Hall premises. The meat and herring market moved in nearby, much to the relief of those living in Market Square, as it took with it the smell emanating from the meat and bones. The building was later adapted to suit the markets for fowl, butter and, at a later date, eggs too. It would seem a far cry from linen to fowl, butter and eggs but it was the same people who brought all of these things to market.

The new grain market proved to be a great asset to the town. It was situated on the far side of Smithfield beside the Dublin Road and encompassed the markets for hay, grain and flax. As well as the weigh-house it had a number of sheds for the sale of potatoes. It had two main gates, one for carts entering the market and the other for carts leaving it. A third, smaller gate accommodated anyone who wished to leave the grain market and enter the main Smithfield area where animals were sold. The centrepiece was a 'weighing' or market house which contained the weighbridge, weigh-master's office and stores. This had a steeple containing a bell which was rung to announce the commencement of the market. The steeple was surmounted by a fine weather vane. There were one or two other buildings – a house for a care-taker, for instance, and a shed for cutting up meat.

A small charge was levied for weighing. It ranged from a half-penny for a small sack of potatoes to two pence for a sack weighing three cwt or more, and sixpence for a cart load. A load of chaff cost sixpence too. There were strict rules governing the operation of the market. No grain could be disposed of without a weigh-master's ticket. Empty carts were to be arranged in an orderly fashion at the back of the Market House and there was a fine of five shillings for the owner of any horse found in the market after the load had been taken off the cart.

Men were appointed to see that these and other market rules were observed. A court leet held on Saturday 19 September 1835 resolved that, among other things, John Cannon should receive £1 for keeping the market house open for labourers and clear of carts and cars. Joseph Thornton was to get £1 for ringing the market house bell and a further £1 10s. for winding up the clock. At the same time William Gregg (seneschal) was to see to it that £10 was spent on repairs to the weighbridge and market. He was given an additional £14 to pay six men to attend Glenavy Fair and to enforce market regulations. Presumably this was during one of the attempts to get that fair going again. His many other duties included looking after the sewers, pumps and fire engine and providing coats for the town bailiffs, the night watchmen and the men who looked after the butter market. Denis Kennedy was to receive one guinea for attending to the weighbridge at the butter market, £4 for keeping pigs and beggars off the street and two guineas for acting as town crier (Denis was still doing these things at the age of seventy-nine). William Close was entrusted with taking care of the meat market. His yearly wages were increased from £4 to £6 in 1837. It was his job to inspect the meat and issue certificates to the vendors stating that it was good and fit for sale.

© Irish Linen Centre and Lisburn Museum Collection

Horse fair at Market Place, Lisburn.

Animals were sold over the years at various locations within the general area of Smithfield. For centuries they were sold between the Shambles and the grain market (now a car park). A map of 1903 shows the cattle market within the precincts of the grain market, and during World War II it moved across the road to the area between Smithfield Street and Christ Church on the Dublin Road. Horses were sold at the Market Place end of the Dublin Road (as previously indicated by Morgan Greer).

In the early days customs were charged on animals sold (but on nothing else) and there were just two fairs in the year, held in July and October to coincide with horse racing at the Maze. Dealers in small items often took their wares to the racecourse after the market. As in so many other places, Lisburn's fairs were being held monthly by the nineteenth century and into the twentieth. In the 1930s the Variety Market moved from Market Square to the former grain market area of Smithfield: recently it moved again across Smithfield Street when the new Smithfield Square shops were built. The grain market was used for other purposes too. In the near famine years of 1831, 1835 and 1837 the indigent poor could go there and avail themselves of free soup on Wednesdays and Saturdays. (Lisburn's workhouse did not open until 1841). And it was to the grain market that people flocked in their thousands to sign the Ulster Covenant in 1912.

Lisburn had other claims to fame. A few miles away, the round tower at Trummery was said to be a favourite haunt of highwayman Redmond O'Hanlon at the end of the eighteenth century. The longest working life ever recorded in the United Kingdom was that of Susan O'Hagan (1802 – 1909). She was in domestic service with three generations of the Hall family of Lisburn for ninety-seven years – from the age of ten to light duties at one hundred and seven.

The most important market town in mid-Antrim was Ballymena, with Randalstown and Portglenone holding their own for many years. All three started off with just two fairs, increasing to twelve in the nineteenth century. After that they almost faded out altogether in Randalstown and Portglenone but increased to twenty-one in Ballymena – more about Ballymena later.

Randalstown, formerly called Mainwater and then Ironworks, was granted a charter in 1683. In addition to its two fairs it was granted monthly markets which were known far and wide for the high quality of the linen sold at them. At that time it had an extensive bleach-green and was described by the Ordnance Surveyor of the 1830s as 'a neat little linen-bleaching town'. It was once a pot-walloping borough, i.e. anyone who boiled a pot (of yarn) and lived within the borough was entitled to vote. However, although it benefited from its situation on the main coach route to the North West, it was overshadowed by the excellent linen town of Ballymena. As a result all its markets declined – even its once renowned grain market. Farmers then decided to take their wheat to Belfast, where it fetched a higher price and there was the added advantage of being able to collect a load of lime at Carnmoney on the way home.

Nearby Toome also had monthly markets and a fair on Easter Monday but these were poor and said to be held more for entertainment than business. At one time stage coaches stopped daily at the inn on the main street to change horses. The village came to life from June to March for the eel fishing. The Donegall family held the fishing rights, renting them out annually to Lord O'Neill. The Donegalls also owned the right of ferry across the Bann. There were two boats, a large one for animals and a small one for foot passengers. The fare ranged from a penny for a foot passenger, sheep or pig to sixpence for a loaded car. Lord O'Neill also collected the tolls at the bridge, which wasn't unreasonable since he had built it at his own expense in 1792. He also

Former Market House, Randalstown, now a library.

38

rented out portions of bog, generally a rood in each piece for half a guinea, or two guineas per acre. These were in great demand and through time the bog became dotted with sod huts 'of the most wretched description'. The only other fair in this part of Antrim was held at Staffordstown 'by a large oak tree in a cluster of houses'. The patent was taken away, probably as early as the eighteenth century, because of the terrible fights which took place there.

Portglenone suffered a similar fate to Randalstown. Its sales of brown linen dropped from around 2000 webs to less than 100 in each market in the 1820s. Its fairs and markets for other goods, however, continued to flourish. There was a small market for meal, yarn, potatoes and flax every Tuesday and the first one in the month was Fair Day, when the usual animals (with the exception of horses) were exposed for sale. G.H. Bassett does not mention a fair in Portglenone in his list for 1888. This may be an omission, or it may have been revived soon after, for the town had twelve in 1895. Portglenone had the advantage of being close to water transport. Heavy goods such as timber, coal and slates could be brought all the way from Belfast by lighter.

Ahoghill, Broughshane, Kells and Connor also suffered from their nearness to Ballymena. Ahoghill was once famous for its fairs, its bleach greens and a good small market at which linen was sold but these fell away while those in Ballymena prospered. Broughshane was probably named after Shane O'Neill who had a residence nearby in the sixteenth century. Its market was held on Wednesday but again it was a small affair, people preferring to walk or ride the three miles to Ballymena. Two fairs were held annually in the village and a third across the river at the O'Neill residence at Tullymore.

Kells and Connor held four fairs each but they were never held in opposition to each other, those in Kells being held in January, March, June and September and those in Connor taking place in February, May, August and October. The cattle and pigs sold at these fairs were mostly bought by dealers. The villagers were mainly weavers, though most had a few acres of land on which they grew a little flax which they manufactured themselves. When mill-spun yarn was introduced they accepted yarn for weaving from the proprietors of the mills. As in other parts of the county, many derived support from cutting and drying turf during the summer and selling it from door to door or in the market place in winter. The people of Connor and Kells helped the poor whenever they could. A beggar at the door was usually given a gowpen (two handfuls) of meal or two gowpens of potatoes. In addition to this, a special sermon was preached and a collection made at Connor Meeting House at the beginning of winter for the purpose of buying blankets for those who needed them. A similar service took place in spring to provide the poor with some flax seed. The Presbyterians of Connor and Kells were almost to a man engaged in the rebellion of 1798, as were many other 'respectable' persons in the neighbourhood, encouraged no doubt by their church ministers.

The landscape around Ballymena is dominated by Slemish, the mountain over which Saint Patrick himself roamed day after day for six years as he herded swine for his master Miliuc in the fifth century. The same Slemish was to dominate the landscape where John Sherriff farmed at the turn of the twentieth century. His farm was situated in the townland of Drumcrow a few miles outside Glenarm. It consisted of two or three mountains and eighty-four acres of good arable land. John kept a few hundred black-face sheep which were usually purchased at Cushendall Fair in the month of August, costing from four to eight shillings apiece. Since Cushendall was twenty-eight miles away it took two days to bring them home. This entailed an overnight stay at a lodging house in Carnlough with accommodation for the lambs in an adjacent field. John also kept bullocks (usually Galloways), a few sows, a bull, fifteen cows, three horses, two goats and a pony for the trap – used mainly for going to town and taking the family to church.

John had very decided views about everything, including putting in crop. Although he had a fiddle for sowing corn he never used it, preferring instead the old-fashioned way of throwing grain from a sheet slung over his shoulder. He had honed this to a fine art, so many handfuls to so many paces, to ensure an even distribution of seed. He used the same method to sow flax. When the corn was being harvested he left a corner of the field uncut for the birds. The winnowings of the barn were also given to the birds. On New Year's Day he threw a sheaf of corn to the cattle. John was very particular about his midden. The manure had to be shovelled up, and the heap built neatly into a square. He expected the ground around it to be brushed and cleaned so that no muck lay underfoot. Nor would he tolerate any broken windows about the place. These had to be mended right away.

John was a Presbyterian of Scottish descent and like many of his ilk and generation he ruled with a rod of iron in his own house. He subscribed to Shakespeare's theory, 'Such duty as the subject owes the prince, even such a woman oweth to her husband.' He considered himself a Christian, although he did not attend church. He had fallen out of that habit after being thrown from his horse, thereafter walking and talking with the aid of a stick. (He waved the stick about as he laid down the law to his household.) However, he expected his wife and family to attend church whether they were thus inclined or not. They had to change into and out of their best clothes and go back and forth to services and prayer meetings several times every Sunday.

Nor did 'the oul fella', as his son Joe irreverently called him, allow anyone to read a newspaper or any other secular material on the Sabbath. On that day the open Bible was placed on the wide window sill in the big farm kitchen and anyone who wished could read a few verses of scripture. He himself spent hours on end reading sermons. The minister visited twice a year and made prayer. The family usually had an idea when he was coming, for the name of the townland was announced from the pulpit the previous Sunday. Father McKillop also visited – on account of the servants. After a few exchanges about the crop and the weather, John would take him 'up the house' and offer him a glass of whiskey, which he always accepted. He never did this with the minister.

John was friendly with Henry McNeill who owned the King's Arms Hotel in Larne and ran a business hiring horses and traps to tourists during the summer. The two had been reared in the same part of the country and counted themselves almost kinsmen on that account. John supplied the hotel with potatoes and fresh vegetables (mainly carrots and onions); also corn and hay for McNeill's sixty or seventy horses that toured the coast road with visitors at the height of the season. When the season ended about fifty of these wintered on the Sherriff farm. No money changed hands for this but if John wanted to, he could use a couple of them while they were in his care.

His attitude to wakes was, to say the least, unusual. No one in the family was allowed to attend a wake – in his opinion they were 'a lot of nonsense, only giving a family under stress more trouble. Sure people are only there for a day or two and then they are gone and they are on their own anyway,' he would say. Nor would he have any truck with Orangemen or Orangeism, and references to Orangemen were not complimentary. 'A man was better off looking after his house and family than running after such things,' he averred.

Huge quantities of tea were needed, especially in summer when extra workers were drafted in. This was bought in chests from S.D. Bell's of Ann Street in Belfast. Whole webs of cloth were

John and Josephine Sherriff.

also purchased and laid by until the travelling tailor arrived. He normally stayed for a week or two, depending on how many in the house needed a new suit. Leftover bits were utilised by Mrs Sherriff for short trousers for the boys. That lady also found time to spin and card wool. Black wool was mixed with white and knit into socks for the family – thick heavy socks suitable for hob-nailed boots. The hired girls were given wool to knit socks for themselves.

In short, Mrs Sherriff worked her fingers to the bone in an endless round of washing, ironing, baking, cooking, milking, churning, knitting, jam making and the thousand and one other jobs to be done on a busy farm. Her husband acknowledged this from time to time by announcing loudly to all and sundry 'Man works from dawn 'til setting sun, but a woman's work is never done.' Mrs. Sherriff knew that this was all the thanks she was likely to get.

John hired his men in Ballymena, setting off early in the day. The men travelled to and from the fair under their own steam, which was just as well as they often went out on the tear and didn't put in an appearance again for several days. Like most towns, Ballymena had a good supply of public houses. William Street had at least a dozen, holding the record for any one street. The town's fairs date back to the reign of Charles I, when a patent was granted to William Adair Esq. to hold two fairs annually. These prospered throughout the centuries, together with an extensive market held every Saturday for the sale of butter, hides, yarn and linen. By the nineteenth century around five thousand pieces of linen, each twenty-five yards in length, were being sold there every week. The webs were exposed for sale in the linen hall off Castle Street. The purchaser wrote his name on the web and arranged to meet the weaver afterwards in a rented room in one of the inns or hotels to pay for it. Some merchants bought houses in the town for this purpose, thus saving the rent. At one time Ballymena attracted buyers from Belfast, making it one of the most successful linen markets in Ulster. Its linen hall was the only one in the county still being used for its original purpose in 1888. By then weavers were using yarns given out by manufacturers. There were, in addition, spinning and hem-stitching factories, foundries and establishments for handling pork and beef. Much of the pork was presented for sale on carts in the open streets, as were yarn and flax. There was also a small grain market. Customs and tolls were payable to the above-mentioned William Adair (or his descendants) who claimed from both buyer and seller, in spite of which the town prospered and gradually absorbed the markets and fairs of the neighbouring towns and villages.

The meat market, fish market and shoe market were held in Bridge Street. The market house, weighbridge and public crane stood at the junction of Bridge Street and Shambles Street. Up to forty people sold meat there on Saturdays, the price ranging from one to five pence per lb. Mutton sold at from three to five pence, bacon and salt meat at from four to five. Fish cost from twopence per lb for pollan [a white freshwater fish] to a top price of sixpence for best salmon. Shoes were made of kipskin and sold at from three to five shillings per pair. Miss Courtney's hotel, where coaches used to stop daily for a change of horses, was also in Bridge Street.

Anyone wanting to buy potatoes, lime or bricks went to Wellington Street. Castle Street was reserved for stalls selling soft goods. Cattle, horses, pigs, sheep and goats were sold in the general area of the Fair Hill and Market Yard just beyond William Street. At one stage there was a separate Fair Hill for the sale of horses. Police sometimes used a nearby house as a temporary lock-up for drunks.

By the nineteenth century Ballymena's fairs were being held on a monthly basis. Many lasted two days and included the sale of horses, by now a big industry in the Ballymena and Randalstown area. Poor quality horses were bought in the South and West of Ireland, fed and nurtured until they were in show-yard condition and then sold on for the English and Scotch markets.

Hiring of course took place at the appropriate times. At the turn of the twentieth century you would still have found several hundred people presenting themselves for hire in the town. Adam Lynn catches the atmosphere in the poem 'A Country Lad's Observations on the Hiring Fair in Ballymena'.

1
The hale toon seemed tae be aware
That Sethurday was Hiring Fair,
And that ferm-servants wud be there
For a big day;
Who meant tae hae a treat sae rare
Wae six months' pay.

2
Here and there wus a wee ban'
The centre-piece a big ould man,
What mak's his leevin' off the lan'
Without a doot;
Bit see him view the horny han'
'Ere he spak' oot.

3
'Tell me, my man, noo can you sow,
And can you milk, and plough and mow,
And build a load of hay or stro'
For market day?
If you can do these things, say so
I'll fix your pay.'

4
Then some yins want a servant lass
That desnae use the luckin'-glass,
But can dress butter that will pass
And tak the badge.
And hae wrists strong enough to mass
A prata fadge.

The same characters and entertainers turned up at these as at Strabane, Limavady and a dozen other places – Pat McAllister, whose magic rub promised to make old people young; Seequaw, who claimed he could perform miracles but whose real talent was for pulling teeth; and Tie-the-Boy, who could escape no matter how many yards of rope were used to ensnare him.

One of the long-established and more notable fairs took place at Crebilly, where twelve townlands had been granted to the O'Hara family by Henry II in the twelfth century. Held in July and August, these were said to be very large, with hundreds of cattle, horses, sheep and pigs being sold at them. Again, tents selling whiskey were much in evidence, resulting in the usual party riots towards evening. These started with stone throwing and ended with beatings with weapons called colts. Made with plaited osiers of woodbine and loaded at each end with a lump of lead, these were pliable and not easily fended off with a stick. Tolls at these fairs were collected by the O'Haras, on whose land they were held. Two fairs were listed at Crebilly in *Old Moore's Almanac* in 1938, one on 27 June and the other on 22 August.

Of the cluster of villages that lay between Ballymena and Ballymoney in the distant past, the most noteworthy were those at Cloughmills, Clogh, and away to the north of these, at Loughguile. Each of these had two fairs in the early days, increasing to four in Clogh

Advert from 1888 describing McNeill's Tours.

and Loughguile in the nineteenth century. The patent for fairs in Cloughmills stated that they were to be held in the townland of Drumadoon about half a mile outside the town. They took place in June and November for the sale of black cattle, pigs, sheep and horses – mainly Highland ponies. The cattle and pigs were bought by dealers and exported. Around 1870 Cloughmills started a weekly market for pork, butter, eggs, flax and linen webs, and the fairs moved into the village. Twopence was charged in tolls for a horse or cow and a penny for a sheep or pig. The recipient was Sampson Moore Esq. The same rate of tolls applied in Loughguile. The Ordnance Surveyor of 1833 described the people from the mountain areas around Loughguile as a 'wild lawless uncivilised race' which frequently created disturbances at neighbouring fairs. One particular family called Murray were renowned cattle thieves. A member of that family who had been transported, returned to be gaoled almost immediately for the same offence.

Clogh also had an influx of Highland ponies on Fair Day and in addition a good market for milk cows in May and bullocks in November. Martinstown, Dunloy, Cargan, Braid, Newtowncrommelin and Rasharkin had fairs too. The last had just one, held annually in November. Again the proprietor of the area was Sampson Moore Esq., who received the money collected annually in tolls. But whether the proprietor collected tolls or offered premiums as an incentive (as in Dunloy) most of these fairs succumbed eventually to the success of those in Ballymena and Ballymoney.

Newtowncrommelin was unique among all these villages. In 1824 Nicholas Delacherois Crommelin Esq. of Carrowdore Castle in County Down obtained a grant with which he purchased a townland and rented a second in addition to one he already had. These he grouped into a parish and proceeded to build a village, to which he gave his name. The village included a Presbyterian meeting house, a church, three schoolhouses and a 'very large double-gear mill and kiln'. Fairs were established – no less than twelve in the year. Unfortunately the project attracted the wrong people, namely 'a class without any capital whatsoever' and 'of whose habits as to industry and honesty nothing whatever was known to the proprietor' and so all of it, so full of promise, came to naught. By the end of the 1830s Nicholas Delacherois Crommelin's dreams were in ruins.

The people in these villages were mostly descended from Scottish Presbyterians who arrived in great numbers in County Antrim in the sixteenth and seventeenth centuries and had principally engaged in agriculture and hand-loom weaving. During the recession of the early nineteenth century many went to Scotland to help with the harvest, and returned home at the end of the season. Others emigrated, never to return. The flow of emigrants was stemmed for a few years after 1833, when the *Lady of the Lake* passenger ship foundered on a voyage from Belfast to Quebec with the loss of many lives including a number from the Ballymoney and Ballymena area. Of the remainder of County Antrim's fairs, the most important were held at Ballymoney, Ballycastle and Bushmills. Ballymoney started off with three in the year: the others had four. In the case of Ballymoney and Ballycastle they were so successful that eventually there were around a score in the year in each town. The number held in Bushmills increased to twelve.

Ballymoney had three old fairs held on 5 May, 10 July and 6 October and successful markets held at least twice a month. These were said to be well supplied with yarn, grain, pork, butter and all the necessaries of life, together with linen webs of every description. One of the markets is remembered in a poem entitled 'The Load of Kale Plants'. As well as selling cabbage plants the writer (who remains unknown), was in search of a wife:

O sweet Ballymoney of fame and renown
I went to the fair, that being held in the town
On the fifth day of May, in the year forty-five
A very fine day for the bees for to hive.

Being young and undaunted my fortune to advance,
I went to the fair with a load of kale plants,
And up the Main Street, before Robinson's Mart
I lowered my cart with a proud beating heart.

There were pamphreys and Dutch, and curleys so sweet,
And rousing drumheads that grow up like a leek.
There were cow kale, pull early boys, eat while you're able
And pickle for dressing the gentleman's table.

Now my plants were all sold, I wished them long life,
I have nothing to do but look out for a wife.
The ladies I'll view, I'll mark all their points,
I'll not take a wife that is stiff in the joints.

The first that I met, she wore a silk gown,
With long yellow hair, and her curls hangin' down,
Says I to myself, 'My girl, you're a swizzer,'
I stood her a tay, where we got the good measure.

Hiring Fair in Ballymoney. The girl on the left (holding the bundle) is for hire.

Horse Fair on the Fair Hill, Ballymoney.

And then I presumed for to kiss this young dame,
And there I presumed for to ask her her name,
Well indeed then, kind sir, and my name is McCloy,
I'm the peat cadger's daughter, from the town of Armoy.

Early in the nineteenth century Ballymoney had a factory at Ballynacree Skrin which spun the coarse yarn used in making corn bags; also a large distillery and brewery which ensured the continuing success of the grain markets. Few houses in the main street had side or back entrances in those days, resulting in animals (including cows and horses) having to pass through the halls or kitchens of houses to reach their byres or stables. Manure was removed by the same route. However, the town was surrounded by good land, used extensively for dairying and fattening purposes as well as general mixed farming. This is evidenced in the diary kept by the young Alexander Erskine of Dunaverney around a century later. His record of the year's events are reminiscent of the opening words of *Ecclesiastes*, chapter 3, that in the husbandry of the land, as in life, there is to every thing a season, and a purpose to everything under heaven:

   A time to be born and a time to die; a time to plant and a time to pluck up that which is planted.

   The year was 1911. Even before the old year ended, ploughing had begun on the Erskine farm for the coming season. Alex believed that for each week before Christmas that the land

Tom White with Anne and Dorothy Erskine.

Courtesy of Dorothy Arthur

was turned over the result was an extra hundredweight of grain come next harvest time. The year began with repairing old drains and making new ones; also facing and topping hedges – all labour intensive work achieved with the aid of slasher, spade and shovel. When the frosts came, work in the fields stopped and Tom, the hired man, concentrated on the yard work while Alex and his brothers worked on the outbuildings – repairing roofs, replacing ill-fitting doors and anything else that required attention. A broken floor board was fixed in a cart and a faulty cart shaft replaced with a new one. Horse collars were repaired and new back-ropes, chains and britchin bought. Anything that could not be repaired was replaced. A plough and saddle harrow were purchased from Alexander Hill in Ballymoney at £3 15s and fifteen shillings respectively. They spent three shillings on a bill-hook and half-a-crown on blades for a turnip slicer.

February began with taking weeds off potato ground and carting them away to make ready for ploughing. Snedding and carting turnips occupied much of the rest of the month, together with threshing corn and planting a new thorn hedge in a march ditch [property boundary]. The corn was usually threshed one day and cleaned the next, unless the second day happened to be a Sunday in which case the cleaning was done on Monday. The threshed straw was built in huge stacks a short distance from the barn, until such times as it was needed for bedding or feeding. Corn was either sold in Ballymoney market or carted to the mill at Stranocum to be ground into smash for winter feed for the cattle. Some (mostly bruised) corn was fed to the horses. The best of the chaff was filled into bags and sold to make mattresses.

Work on drains was continuous on any well-run farm. Altogether ten drains were repaired that year in the long field – about ninety perches [one perch was 5½ yards] in all. A sheugh that was holding up the drainage of a field was also cleaned out. It was heavy work but Tom, the farm hand, was young and strong and never demurred at any job that he was asked to do. The Erskines valued him highly.

Alex, the eldest of three brothers, left the others cleaning corn, carting turnips and ploughing potato beds on the tenth of the month while he took himself off to a ploughing match at Leaney just outside Ballymoney. It was a dry, bright day and the ground was in good fettle for the event. The nineteen competitors were divided into two classes – one for chill and the other for swing ploughs. Local man James McCahon was a popular winner in the swing plough class, taking home the Milltown Mills cup for the third year running. The ploughing match was one of several functions undertaken annually by the Ballymoney Farming Society since its inception way back in 1835.

The Tatty cow calved a white bull calf on the twelfth and the black sow farrowed on the fourteenth, producing thirteen pigs – seven belties (pink mottled with grey) and the rest bright pink. The next day Alexander went to the letting of lands by auction at Stranocum. According to his diary everything went very dear, with land being let for grazing at £2 an acre and land for oats making £6 an acre.

Income in the early months of the year came from the sale of crops and livestock. A bull fetched £22 1s 3d, a fat bullock weighing 8cwt.1qr.18lb and with a girth of six feet sold for £13 4s 6d and two pigs brought in £4 5s. Potatoes sold at around half a crown a hundredweight, corn at eightpence a stone and straw at 1s 10d a hundredweight. The milk cheque for the month of January was very small at 18s 1d but increased when the cows went out to grass, reaching a peak of £7 19s 10d in July. Towards the end of the half-year term (12 May) the price of potatoes rose to four shillings for the popular Up-to-Date variety. Other varieties being grown included Skerries, Duchess of Cornwall and Golden Wonder.

March was an exceptionally dry month, allowing the work of threshing, ploughing and lifting potatoes from pits to forge ahead. The small potatoes were saved for seed, the larger ones were boiled for the pigs (and the household) and the rest sold. A yearling bull was bought at the spring sale at Balmoral for £33 12s. It was a big price but it was a subsidy bull and the brothers knew that come November they would be paid a premium by the Government for keeping him for the convenience of the farmers round about. By the end of March the work of carting, ploughing, cross-ploughing, grubbing, harrowing and drilling was well ahead, and planting began. Load after load of manure was drawn to the field and spread manually with a graip along the drills. Artificial fertiliser (super phosphate) was sown by hand on top of the manure, and the potatoes – which were carried in a bag rubber [an apron made out of a hessian bag] – were planted directly into this, about twelve inches apart. As well as using small potatoes for seed, large ones were cut in two retaining at least two eyes in each section to make sure a plant would grow. Ten ridges of the variety 'Up-to-Date' were also planted that year.

As it turned out, the good weather continued well into the month of April making 1911 an excellent year for putting in crop. It was also good for lambing the ewes. Alex always bought his flax seed and grass seed in April though he had no intention of sowing it until the following month. Two bags of M.B.M. flax seed were purchased at £4 10s and a quarter of Perennial and a stone of Timothy grass seed at £3. A stone of clover seed (Alsike) was purchased at a cost of eleven shillings for mixing with the grass seed.

On 10 April £2 was paid to Lady Harberton for a rood of bog, rented for turf cutting. The Garry Bog was close to the Erskine farms and provided them with all the fuel they needed for the winter. Mid-April saw the start of sowing the corn, followed by the spring harrowing of the flax ground and the tilling of potato ground at the cottar house. The last of the potatoes were planted on the twenty-sixth and cabbage plants were set in the same drills so that they ran in neat rows, spaced far apart across the field in the opposite direction to the potatoes. Work was interrupted on the eighteenth by the death of a relative and only essential jobs like feeding and milking were done until after the funeral. By this time the weather had turned showery but there was enough fair weather to facilitate the planting of more cabbage and the preparation of ground for sowing flax and turnips.

The first of the flax was sown on May Day, followed by moulding the potatoes and the start of the turf cutting. When the peats were cut they were then spread out on the bank to dry. After a couple of weeks they were built into

Pigs were killed and made ready for the curers before they left the farm.

Courtesy of Peter McGuckin

Courtesy of Dorothy Arthur

Renée Erskine pulling flax. During busy times everyone had to lend a hand.

loose piles of a dozen or so to catch the wind and dry out further. Later they were built into still bigger piles and carted home between other jobs as the year progressed. The pig butcher arrived on 3 May and killed six pigs. One was kept for the use of the family and the rest were sold as pork in Ballymoney the next day, together with six tons of potatoes and 23 cwt of straw. Three fat cattle, a bullock, two sheep and three crowl [ill-thriving] pigs were also sold in the run-up to the May hiring day. The rest of the time was spent putting in the remainder of the flax, spreading manure, sowing turnips and cutting peats.

The twelfth of May was always a watershed in the farming year. On that day in the year 1911 Mary A. Rainey, Thomas White and Alexander Hill were paid the remainder of their wages for the previous six months. The next day Thomas (Tom) was re-engaged for the sum of £7 10s, Alexander was re-hired at six shillings a week and Mary was replaced by a new servant girl – Maggy Bellingham also at £7 10s. Everyone took the day off to attend the hiring fair in Ballymoney, though Alex managed to find time to prepare ground for turnips before he went. The town at that time had several industries but really owed its success to agriculture and its thriving markets.

Tom White had left school in the summer of 1908 and hired with a farmer at £3 for six months. Little enough you might think, but when he was offered half this amount to continue for the winter term he decided it was time to look for work elsewhere. He would go to the November fair in Ballymoney and try his luck. Hopefully his reputation as a good worker would have gone ahead of him. His slim build, kind face and thick auburn hair appealed to Alex Erskine, who was on the lookout for a willing lad to dig sheughs in the Spring Bog. Tom knew the work would be hard but he was not afraid of that, and the prospect of a good home and a wage of £5 for the half-year was very attractive indeed. It was the beginning of an association with the Erskine family that was to last the rest of his life. Now here he was, eighteen months later, back in Ballymoney, only this time he was here to enjoy himself. He couldn't have been more content. He gave of his best, and he knew he had a job for life if he wanted it – and his wages had gone up to £7 10s! He must be the luckiest man on earth.

Tom really enjoyed that Fair Day. The weather was glorious and all the familiar sights were there. Maggie Ramsey was at Cromie's corner selling confections of all descriptions – especially Peggy's Leg, a sticky yellow concoction made to her own recipe. Shooting galleries, delph sellers and clothes sellers were doing brisk business on High Street. A small crowd surrounded Mousie O'Neill and his three performing white mice. In the throng Tom spotted William Stewart, a

The Erskine brothers. From left: Alexander (who wrote the diary), Robert and William.

Mowing corn with a tractor and cutting bar. The man on the right is using a tilting rake to lay off enough corn to make a sheaf. The one on the left is tying stooks.

Courtesy of Dorothy Arthur

James Baird bringing home the turf from the Garry Bog.

well-known figure about town and easily recognisable in his bowler hat. William was always on the lookout for workers for his dairy farm or perhaps even for his grocer's shop. He also needed a shepherd for a mountain he owned near Limavady. A fiddler from Armoy stood outside a pub playing 'The Rose of Tralee' and ballad-singer Alec Knox was singing the only song he knew – 'Master McGra' [the greyhound Master McGrath]. Happy Jamie accompanied himself on the hurdy-gurdy as he sang 'Where is My Wandering Boy Tonight?' The Malone brothers had travelled from Ballymena and were selling apples at sixpence a bucket from their trap, while the pony munched bruised corn and hay out of a nose-bag slung over the end of the trap shaft.

Badges were the whole rage that year and were selling like hot cakes. Word got round that they could be bought for tuppence at Sam Gamble's sweet shop in High Street. Tom bought one in the shape of a sheepdog and, imitating his contemporaries, pinned it on his cap. By late afternoon when the serious business of the day was over, the young ones (especially the girls) walked the streets – up Church Street and Victoria Street, round by Linenhall Street, down High Street, back to Church Street – round and round they went calling out cheerfully when they saw someone they knew. When they tired of that they could go to a dancing class where they could learn to dance the Quadrille, the Lancers or the Four Hand Reel. There was great rivalry amongst them as to who could wrest a badge from one of the boys' caps.

Robert Erskine with the bull bought at Balmoral.

This is their day, their faces show it;
They're brave weel-like, an' man they know it,
An' mony a match that's made this day
Is clinched in kirk afore next May.

from *The Hirin' Fair* by John Clifford

From past experience, Tom knew that the second half of May would be occupied almost entirely with cutting peats. As it turned out the hot weather continued, and apart from a few half-days scaling (spreading) dung, sowing turnips and moulding potatoes he was in the Garry Bog all the time. The brothers left him in charge on 26 May while they went off by train to Balmoral Show – a distance of forty-six miles. The good weather brought out the crowds from both town and country and they had a great day.

June came in hot and dry – great for the peat, but bad for the corn which desperately needed rain. However thistles were flourishing in spite of the drought and had to be painstakingly removed using wooden pullers specially made for the job. The brothers took time off on the first day of the month to vote at the elections for Ballymoney Rural District Council. The next day finished the turf-cutting and Tom was then sent to scour a sheugh on their side of a ditch that marched [bordered] a neighbouring farmer. At about the same time a man was engaged to repair and re-cradle a well that had fallen in. An unexpected late frost on the eleventh gave the potatoes a set-back in the bogs below the railway, just when they had finished hoeing and moulding them.

The flax crop was by now well forward and it was necessary to clear the hay off the dam fields in readiness for the spreading. On 17 June the weather broke with thunder and heavy rain – the first for twenty-two days. Other jobs that month included thinning and hoeing turnips, and of course the inevitable spreading and rickling of peat. There were still some old potatoes left in the barn and before they could be used every one had to be disbudded individually by hand. The brothers had decided that at some stage before the winter two new sheds should be built, one for housing a cart and the other for turnips, and on the last day of the month a load of sand was purchased in readiness for the day they would find time to begin. They would do the work themselves. Five loads of quarry dust were purchased at the same time. This could be scattered on lanes or even spread over bogland to improve the texture of the soil.

July began with cleaning out a flax dam. Much of the month was taken up with carting home and stacking peats and looking after the potatoes which still needed hoeing to keep down the weeds. As July was the main month for blight, they were also sprayed several times, just in case. To do this the wings and tail-board were taken off the cart, and the sprayer, a frame surmounted by a horizontal wooden barrel, was lifted into it. The spray – 8lb of blue stone [copper sulphate] dissolved in a crock of water and 10lb of washing soda dissolved in a bucket – was then passed through a wooden strainer into the sprayer barrel full of water. A couple of thick ammonia bags were thrown loosely over the hole on top to prevent spillage. The spray was released by being pumped by hand through nozzles on a boom at the back of the sprayer as the horse progressed along the drills. A fine spell of weather during the second week of July ensured the cutting, tying and stooking of the grass seed and about a week later, when the seed was ripe, the stooks were carried carefully to a corner of the field, where they were built in huts and where they would remain until they found time to thresh them. A tarpaulin was usually spread alongside during threshing and the stooks placed on it so that any ripe seed that happened to fall was saved.

But the most important job of all during July was to make ready for the flax pulling. To this end the dam meadows were cleared of hay. As the weather had turned showery the hay had first to be made into laps. This was done by rolling the hay over the arm and laying it down, rounded side up, in such a way that the rain ran off and the wind blew through the middle. On the next good drying day the laps were shaken open and built into small cocks at one end of the field. The ground was then raked clean. Bands for tying the beets (sheaves) were usually prepared beforehand. These were made out of two lengths of rushes knotted together at the flowering end. Finally, dams were checked and thoroughly cleaned out in readiness for retting. On the last day of July the flax pulling began. Work concentrated on the flax for the next few weeks, though they could not entirely forget about the hay and potato crops. August was the month when the hay-cocks were drawn to the stack yard where they were rebuilt into larger stacks, thatched with rushes and tied down with rope against the storms of winter.

The flax produced a good crop that year, though the stems were a little short due to the dry weather. When it was ready for pulling, extra hands were engaged at threepence a stook. It was tedious, back-breaking work, though traditionally convivial, as family, neighbours and hired hands banded together to make the most of it. The beets were counted at the end of the day and each man paid accordingly. The warm, peaty water rotted the stalks in a record time of seven days that year and then the most malodorous job of the farming year began – that of throwing the slimy, smelly beets onto the edge of the dam so that the excess water ran back in. All the carbolic soap in the townland could not remove the stench of the rotting flax from their aching bodies. The beets were then carted across the field and laid down in rows about five yards apart. The spreaders came behind, lifted a beet onto their left arm, unloosed the band and walking backwards, spread it thinly on the ground, the rows almost touching. The rush bands were kept and after a couple of days it was tied into beets again and eventually stacked in barts, to be sold later in Ballymoney market or drawn directly to Hamilton's scutch mill in Stranocum.

As soon as the flax was finished, work began on threshing and cleaning the seed hay. After threshing, the seed was put through a jigger in the barn to remove the weed seeds before bagging and selling it. Towards the end of the month repairs were made to a reaping machine in readiness for cutting the corn. These included making a new shaft and spending eight shillings on a new driving rod.

A sick cow due to calve turned out to be the first of several animals to fall ill with the dreaded red water. Alex knew that the cattle on his land were susceptible to this, especially in the early summer and autumn when ticks abounded. The disease was spread by the tick first biting an infected animal, then biting a healthy animal, passing on the infection in the bite. It required the immediate attention of a vet, or both cow and calf could be lost.

If August was the month for flax, September was the month for corn. Extra workers were again engaged, this time at two shillings a day. Their job was to lift the loose corn behind the reaper and tie it into sheaves, which were then propped together in fours and tied at the top with a straw band to form stooks. The continuing dry weather ensured that the work of harvesting was kept to a minimum and within a few weeks forty-four huge stacks stood thatched in the stack yard. Alex and his brothers then turned their attention to the grass seed. Thirty cwt of Perennial were bagged and sold in Ballymoney Market at thirty shillings a cwt. Some ewes and a lamb were sold for £3 7s. Towards the end of the month the last of the peats were carted home from the moss.

October saw the digging of the potatoes; again back-breaking work involving many hands. The gatherers worked in twos; bobbing up and down as they threw the potatoes into two-handled wicker baskets. It took two to carry the full basket to the pit and tip it on the end of the ever-lengthening heap.

They finished on a wet Saturday but did not complete the thatching and covering of the pits until a few days later. It was important to do this before the winter frosts set in. Towards the end of October they found time to begin work on building the new cart shed. They worked at it off and on for the next month. The last two days in October were wet and were spent snedding mangolds and levelling a dyke between two fields.

In November the cattle were brought in from the fields and housed for the winter. The County Committee of Agriculture paid the £12 premium due on the subsidy bull purchased earlier in the year. Payment was also received for two pigs. More pigs and a cow were sold in December, together with seven bags of oats. The year 1911 was winding down. Another season had already begun.

> *I take my fiddle down and my Mary smiling there*
> *Brings back a happy memory of the Lammas Fair*

No book about fairs would be complete without a mention of the best known fair of them all – the Lammas Fair at Ballycastle, immortalised in song by John Henry MacAuley of that town. The name comes from the Old English *Hlaf Maesse* (Loaf Mass) meaning the festival of first fruits.

This fair dates back to the fourteenth century (or earlier). We know that Randal McDonnell received a charter from James I in 1606 for holding fairs in several places including Ballycastle, but fairs were held there long before. It is on record that Gillaspick McDonnell was gored to death by a bull at a celebration of public games which took place at a fair in Ballycastle in 1570. In the early days the fair lasted a full week. When the railway opened in 1880 it reduced to four days and to two around 1910. It was held towards the end of the month, and not at the beginning as its name would imply. Traditionally the first day was devoted to the sale of cattle, horses, sheep and pigs, and the remainder to enjoyment. This is summed up in an article in *The Coleraine Chronicle* of 30 August 1862:

> *This Donnybrook of the North commenced on Tuesday last, when business and not fun is the principal element. There was a large number of small 'shelties', a vast number of sheep from Rathlin and a pretty good show of black cattle. Business was pretty brisk and good animals changed hands at remunerative prices. The fair was continued on Wednesday, when the town was crowded with well-dressed country folk of both sexes. Amusements of a class characteristic of this fair were duly patronised. The fair lasted until Thursday, though to those who have seen previous fairs, the last appeared rather thinly attended and the fun neither so fast nor so furious.*

Ballycastle Hiring Fair, Co. Antrim.

Courtesy of Ian McCullough

Years ago people came from miles away just to attend. They came over the sea from Islay and Raghery. The Islay fishermen came in their luggers [small vessel with sails] to sell their dried fish, stayed for a week and took back with them such things as bricks, oil lamps and hand-made boots. The Raghery (Rathlin) men came to sell their sheep and cattle. The Islay connection died out before the First World War but to this day the Rathlin folk still come to the fair. Locals went down to the sea front at night to join them in music and dancing, for the visitors lived and slept on their boats and entertained themselves while they were there. Dancing also went on in the public houses and in various halls throughout the town. A visitor to the fair remembers two hill farmers arriving at one of the dances, 'Farmers came, you know, the sheep men off the mountains; an' they would a' brought their dog to the dance. They brought their dog to the fair an' then they brought him to the dance.'

In those days the town thronged with cattle and cattle dealers, pigs, Cushendall ponies, roulette men, old clothes vendors and showmen of all descriptions. There was an Indian fire-eater who chewed tow [fibres of flax] soaked in paraffin – then set a match to it. Clouds of smoke came from his nose and mouth. Another man danced on broken glass in his bare feet. A third could balance a cart wheel on his chin. Buck Alex (all the way from Belfast) appeared from time to time with his tawny African lion. Eli the Jew came with his gaming stall.

The Lammas Fair coincided with the quarterly hiring fair, which was one of seventeen fairs being held in the town at the turn of the twentieth century. Hiring started about ten o'clock and went on for most of the day. The saddest sight at the fair was the little group of workhouse boys who had barely reached their teens before they were sent out to earn a living. Up until about 1920 they were easy to recognise, with their shorn hair, hob-nailed boots and coarse woollen clothing. (Were they perhaps even glad to escape the austerity of the workhouse?) Girls were usually placed in service privately and did not often stand in the fair. Girls from further afield, especially those from Donegal, arrived in their bare feet, carrying their footwear in their bundles until they came within sight of the town. They then dusted themselves down, straightened their clothes and washed their feet, before pulling on their shoes and stockings in readiness for hiring. The usual place for doing this was at a spring well, known as 'The Spout' which was situated at the head of the town, on the Coleraine Road. The custom of washing feet took place at a number of fairs. The same Spout watered horses, washed potatoes and supplied the surrounding houses with water for all their domestic needs. Hiring is known to have taken place in Ballycastle as recently as 1948, though officially that was the year it should have ended.

Centuries ago Dunluce ranked as 'a town of considerable size', with an annual fair held on 12 November. In those days it was the seat of the County Assizes, and had its own courthouse, jail, dungeon and even a gallows on a nearby hill. Fairs were held there regularly until the 1700s, when they transferred to Bushmills because of the gambling, rioting, and sundry other vices that were perpetrated at them. Whether or not the behaviour of the people improved when they went to Bushmills is a matter of conjecture.

The main crops grown in the area were potatoes, grain and flax. The most important time of the year was the harvest. Often workmen formed themselves into a group (called a boon) and travelled from farm to farm to help with saving the crop. At a really busy time the women of the house pitched in too. The poem 'The Lint Pullin' sets the scene:

> When I was young and pulled at lint, I was handsome, spry and trig;
> I always kept in temper wi' the lass was on my rig,
> And if the pullers chanced to kemp [race], no matter wha was late,
> I ay took special caution that my lass was never beat.

County Antrim

I once went down by Bushmills way, for they had a boon on there;
It's not for the greed of gear I went, but for the spree and tear;
For young ones then I would have you ken would fair jump at a chance,
And they would work the li'e lang day, at night to get a dance.

The servant girl that was in the house, she was neat, genteel and fair;
She had twa bonny rosy cheeks and a head o' curly hair;
Besides she had that winnin' way that would your favour gain,
And I felt my heart a-warmin' for that maid called Mary Jane.

When we landed on the head-rig the maids they got their choice,
Each to pick their partner from among the men and boys;
And when we started on the foot my heart did jump wi' glee,
For Mary Jane was on my rig for she had picked on me.

You see, I was the stranger there, I had no room to talk,
But them that has the knack can pull as fast as some can walk;
I looked across at Mary Jane and says I, 'We've got to pull.'
She threw her bonnet down the field and answered back, 'We will.'

I did the sweeping across the rig: she did the breakin' in,
And every time we pulled in front, I made her tak' her win;
And though both right and left of us, they were pressing us very hard,
We were the first two at the head, we had beat them by a yard.

We had scarcely pulled the others out, when the bell rung six o'clock;
We were a' fatigued an' wearied and glad to hear the knock.
My comrade, lingering at the gate, it's unto me did say:
'If they pull as hard the morrow, Rab, in the rig wi' you I'll stay.

I helped her fill her creel that night; it was for the morning fire.
I asked her would she like for life with me to come and hire.
Says I, 'You'll have to work gye hard and your wages will no' be big.'
She says, 'We'll pull thegither [together], Rab, the way we pulled the rig.'

Bushmills owes much of its success to the Macnaghten family, who spared no expense in improving the town. In 1828 Sir Francis Macnaghten built a market place on the main street. It included two huge grain stores, each three storeys high, and a commodious slated shed for the sale of grain in wet weather. This was enclosed in a walled yard with two gates opening onto the street. It was said at the time that few parishes possessed a greater advantage, namely a good market within four miles of a good harbour (Portrush) from which grain and butter could be shipped weekly to England or Scotland. Some grain was also shipped from the quay in Portballintrae. Bushmills had several corn mills and flax mills, not to mention a spade mill and the ever famous distillery. Twice weekly markets were held for the sale of meal, potatoes, grain and yarn. A linen market was attempted in 1833 but did not succeed. The four

Courtesy of Ian McCullough

Fair Day in Dervock.

original fairs increased to twelve in the nineteenth century and from then on were held regularly on the fifteenth of each month. The weekly markets continued to flourish. Sir Francis added a handsome clock to the market entrance in 1874, though he was by then leasing out the market rights.

Successful fairs were held throughout the centuries at Dervock, Armoy and Mosside. A market was held on the fair day at Dervock and Armoy. Dervock was noted for its horse fairs as distinct from other types of livestock offered for sale. It is likely that hiring took place at all these places. It certainly took place at Mosside for *The Coleraine Chronicle* of 27 May 1876 stated:

> *The Mosside (Co. Antrim) Annual Hiring Fair was held on the usual stance on Monday last (22nd May). There was a large attendance of parties desiring to be hired and many employers were on the ground. Wages reached much the same as in other hiring fairs held during the last few weeks. There was a good show of cattle, and those exhibited were in low condition owing to the backwardness of the grass. Strippers sold at from £9 to £11; two year olds from £6 to £9 and one year olds from £3 to £6. Sheep were scarce and sold readily at about 9d. per lb. There were no horses or fat cattle shown. The fair altogether was below average.*

Two fairs were held annually in Stranocum around 1835, but they were even then in decline. Fairs were held also at the Giant's Causeway, Ballintoy, Cushendun, Cushendall, Glenariff (Waterfoot), Carnlough and Glenarm. The Giant's Causeway held one for years every thirteenth of August purely for amusement. It was said to attract a great assemblage of well-dressed country people who spent their time dancing, eating and drinking in tents, or strolling about the rocks and cliffs. Ballintoy held four annually, at which Highland ponies, cattle, meal, yarn and flax were the principal articles sold. In addition to the usual corn and flax mills in the area, employment was found in the three salmon fisheries, the best known of which was at Carrick-a-rede, where a rope bridge was constructed in 1850 to accommodate the fishermen going to their work. Cushendun is notable because many of the Highland ponies sold at the fairs in the surrounding countryside were imported through its harbour. At the turn of the twentieth century it had seven fairs of its own, held on the first Wednesday of each month from February onwards. It is likely that these were established many years before.

Cushendall had eight fairs, the same number as were held there fifty years previously. At that time potatoes, oatmeal, dried seaweed, yarn and a little coarse linen were the main commodities sold. Farmers in the main preferred to sell produce such as pork and butter in Ballymena and Ballycastle, where it fetched a higher price. Publicans in Cushendall tried to liven things up on Fair Day by setting aside rooms and employing pipers or fiddlers to provide music for dancing, but the parish priest declared that such gatherings were sinful and ordered that they be discontinued. However, a little card playing and some cock fighting went on quietly in spite of the priest. Formerly sheep, cattle and ponies were sold at the old Fair Hill beyond the summit of High Street but that was abandoned in later years in favour of the village streets. There is little doubt that hiring took place at the quarterly fairs held on the fourteenth of the month, for the *O.S. Memoir* of the time records that, as in Ballycastle, young women could be seen walking to within a short distance of Cushendall with their shoes and stockings in their hands, prior to washing their feet in preparation for presenting themselves at the fair.

In the early nineteenth century Glenarm had two fairs, described as 'inconsiderable', and Carnlough had four. By the end of the century Glenarm had four and Carnlough six. Glenarm was a post town and since the Coast Road had not yet been constructed, the mail was carried on horseback once a day from Ballycastle. The Coast Road was made in the 1830s 'to ease the hardships of life for the Glensfolk who could only with difficulty take a cart to market in summer and in winter could be isolated for weeks.' The opening of the new road transformed their lives. Instead of marketing their produce by boat across the sea to Scotland or around the Irish coast, they could now market it in Larne or any of the neighbouring towns. The lot of the Glensfolk had at last begun to improve.

THE POTATO

Sublime potatoes! that from Antrim's shore
To famous Kerry, from the poor man's store
Agreeing well with every place and state-
The peasant's noggin, or the rich man's plate.
Much prized when smoking from the teeming pot,
Or in turf-embers roasted crisp and hot
Welcome, although you be our only dish;
Welcome, companion to flesh, fowl, or fish;
But to the real gourmands, the learned few,
Most welcome, steaming in an Irish Stew.

(written around 1800 by an unknown author)

COUNTY ARMAGH

Well 'twas gettin' on past the heat o' the year
When I rode to Newtown fair;
I sold as I could (the dealers were near)
Only three pound eight for the Innish steer
An' nothin' at all for the mare.

Armagh has many claims to fame. Queen Macha was born within its borders. Saint Patrick began his labours there in the year 445. Brian Boru visited it and liked it so much that he chose it as his burial place in the eleventh century. It has also been acclaimed for its orchards and its linen.

Markets and fairs were held for centuries in almost every town and village in the county. Armagh, Portadown and Lurgan were good for the sale of produce and livestock. Newtownhamilton (Newtown) was best for hiring. Tandragee, Lurgan and Armagh had excellent brown linen markets. These were attended by linen drapers who bought the unbleached cloth for their bleach greens. The cloth was woven in their homes by tenant farmers and their families. Landlords encouraged this, seeing in it a good way of making the rent: although the work had a high labour content it had a high value end product. Rents fell due on the first day of November. Tenants were also expected to work a certain number of duty days during the year. This ended when tenants bought out their holdings so that landlords lost their hold on the farming community. Under the Landlord and Tenant (Ireland) Act, 1870, the Government paid the landlord a fixed sum for each holding and the tenant made good the debt to the Government in the form of land annuities which were paid twice a year.

The fair in Armagh City was perhaps the oldest in the county. Hugh Roe O'Neill petitioned Queen Elizabeth in 1587 and was granted permission to hold a market there every Tuesday. When the Plantation of Ulster began in the seventeenth century a patent was granted to the archbishop 'for a market where a fair has been held since time out of mind'. He was also granted permission to hold two additional fairs (Bishop's fairs) – one on Saint Patrick's Day (17 March) and the other on Lammas Day (1 August). He was at the same time granted two fairs at Carnteele (County Tyrone), one on 15 August and the following day and the other on 8 September (the Nativity of the Blessed Virgin Mary) and the following day. In 1634 another fair was established in Armagh, to be held on 29 June and there was a fourth held in September.

These weren't the only privileges granted to the archbishop. He had the right of pillory, tumbrell and thewr; i.e. he could decide the punishment meted out to offenders. He could appoint coroners, clerks of the market and masters of assay as well as establishing Courts of Piepowder, and he could collect tolls. At a later date he was allowed to hold two fairs at Tinan (Tynan) one on 13 April and the other on 15 June; also a Friday market.

In 1821 the market rights were leased to a group of local inhabitants for the sum of £1700 on the understanding that any surplus profit would be used for the improvement of the city and its market places. Tolls ranged from a half-penny for a lump of butter under 10lb weight to sixpence for a nurseryman's cart with flowers or plants. There was no charge for a hand-basket of eggs or fowl.

The Flax Market, Armagh in 1913. There were 130 carts present on the day the photograph was taken.

Each commodity had its own selling place. Flax was sold in Irish Street and linen in Dobbin Street. When the linen market declined, Dobbin Street became the market place for poultry, eggs and butter. The weighbridge and the markets for pork, grain, grass seed, hay and straw were at the Shambles in Mill Street. Live pigs were sold in Gaol Square. The four fairs granted in the seventeenth century were held regularly throughout that century and the next. In the nineteenth century they increased to twelve and were held on the first Thursday of every month for the sale of horses, cattle, sheep and pigs. Horses that didn't sell in Armagh were taken to the next fair in Moy. If they didn't sell in Moy they were walked to Kilrea.

Of the little group of villages to the north of Armagh City, the best known were Charlemont, Loughgall and Blackwatertown. Charlemont, which takes its name from its founder Charles Mountjoy, was incorporated as a borough by James I in 1613 and held two fairs from then until the 1830s. Cattle, provisions and yarn were the main commodities sold. However they were badly attended because of their proximity to Moy, where large monthly fairs were held. They ceased in the mid-nineteenth century. Fairs once held in Loughgall suffered the same fate.

Blackwatertown had a weekly market every Monday during the grain season when merchants bought grain (and potatoes) for export through Belfast and Newry. The usual route was via the River Blackwater, Lough Neagh and the Lagan and Newry canals. The lighters carried timber, slates and coal in the opposite direction. During this time monthly fairs were held but they were badly attended, and like those in Loughgall and Charlemont they died out around the middle of the nineteenth century.

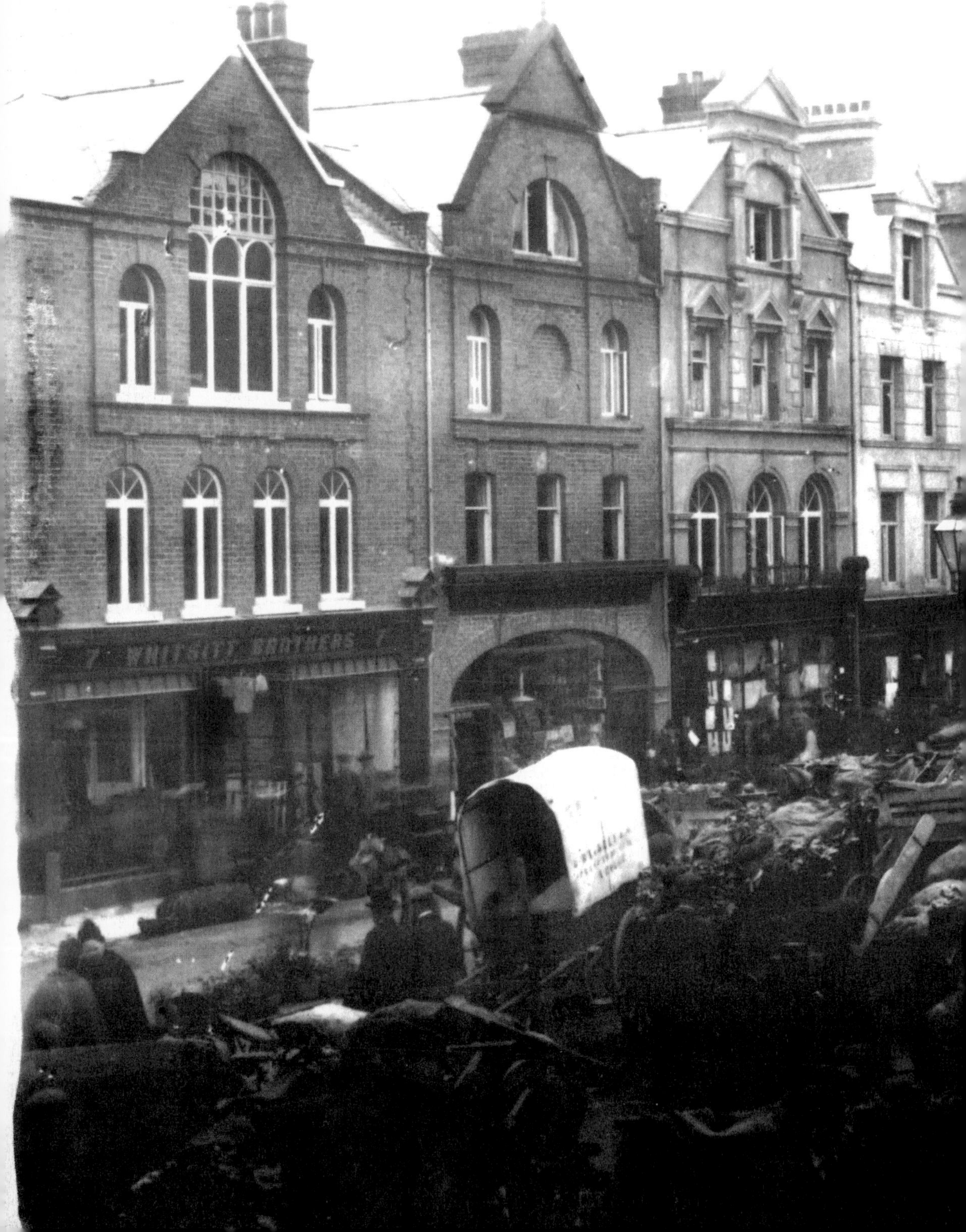
WHITSITT BROTHERS

Market Street, Armagh circa 1908.

Killylea(gh), Tynan (Tinan) and Middletown all had fairs. Killylea had none until around 1800 when monthly cattle fairs began. Although the cattle were described as inferior, fairs survived well into the twentieth century. Tynan and Middletown, on the other hand, had much older fairs. In the seventeenth century the archbishop of Armagh was given a Friday market at Tynan and the two fairs mentioned earlier. On the last Friday in the month a so-called Great Market was held: it was very large, almost assuming the proportions of a fair. These markets were probably held near the old cross which at that time stood in the churchyard, like that in Dromore. The cross fell into ruin at some stage, but was rescued, restored and moved to its present position in 1844. A second cross was moved to Tynan Abbey. There were two other crosses in the abbey grounds. The cross in the village is thought to have been a termon or boundary cross but may have been used also as a market cross. The Surveyor of 1835 certainly thought so for he stated:

> *The remains of an old stone cross formerly used as a market cross are still visible. The inscription is defaced but two hideous little figures resembling idols may be discerned.*

(Copy of Statistical Report by Lieut. C. Bailey 4 May 1835. Vol 1 *Ordnance Survey Memoirs of Ireland*, Parishes of County Armagh, 1835-38.)

Middletown had six fairs throughout the eighteenth century and twelve in the nineteenth, together with a general market held every Thursday and two grain markets which supplied the needs of the local distillery. The grain markets stopped suddenly in 1850 when the distillery failed. However, farmers' wives in the surrounding countryside made excellent butter which they put up in meskins and took to the markets in Killylea and Middletown. Much of this was bought up by dealers who exported it through Belfast and Newry. Eggs were sold in the markets too.

Keady came to prominence towards the end of the eighteenth century with the arrival of the stage-coach as a means of transport. The Dublin–Armagh stage passed through the town six times a week, three going in one direction and three on alternate days going the other. No doubt it patronised one of the town's twenty-five licensed hostelries. The Surveyor of 1838 described Keady as 'having the appearance of a handful of houses thrown into the valley without much regularity as to size, materials or relative position' and the market house as 'small and insignificant'. However there were at the time successful weekly markets and a fair on the second Friday of every month. Hiring was also a feature, but the serious hiring took place a few miles away at Newtownhamilton. By 1870 a new market house had been constructed and markets were being held three times a week, one for butter, eggs and pork and two for grain. The weighmaster at the crane in those days was Laurence McShane. Laurence was also Keady's grain merchant. The Callan River which flowed through the town provided the power for the corn mill situated beside the market house, as well as the many other mills scattered across the countryside. James Greene, a native of Keady, remembers the markets well:

> Barney the gasson sold fish. He drove a white horse and cart from Omeath to Keady selling herrings. He wore a blue-and-white checked apron with long pockets full of coppers. He started to sell at Robinson's Crossroads about a mile outside of Keady on a Thursday evenin' shoutin', 'Herns alive.' [Herrings] [He] then sold roun' the town and put the horse

into Carver's yard that night; took the cart out an' sold them along the mill wall the next mornin'. He sold them at sixpence a dozen an' counted them by placin' them between his fingers. He always claimed to have an extra one in the count. He wud say, 'An' there's one for the gasson.' Carts sellin' plants gathered there too. The apple sellers gathered roun' the monument.

You cud have bought delph too an' second han' clothes. Trousers was one an' six or two shillin's an' a coat half-a-crown. Men wore putties to keep their trousers clean. After the war you cud have bought putties at sixpence or less. Keady was a good market. Pigs were sold in Davis Street; cattle in the Square or any of the streets roun' about; horses in Chapel Street.

James Greene.

But it was to Newtownhamilton that James went when he decided to hire for the first time. The farmer who hired him lived between the two towns on the Armagh-Monaghan border. The year was 1925:

I hired in Newtown. It wasn't far from Keady – about six mile. I went on my own. My father was dead. I was the third youngest of eleven. You stood there. They were all over the place, strangers and farmers and everything. Farmers wud a come from roun' be Armagh an' Killylea an' the Dyan to look for a man. They wud go about watchin'. They cud nearly tell a man that was useful for a bit o' work. Then when the hirin' was over the young ones went down to the pubs and had a bit of a sing-song. There was twenty-seven pubs in Newtown that time. Tom O'Neill's in Blaney Street was a favourite, at the fut of the hill. That's where the boys went, weemin too; the Crossmaglen men and the Cullyhanna men. It didn't take much drink till do them. Two or three bottles of stout wud set a fella drunk. They weren't used till it, ye see. There was more Crossmaglen men hired (and weemin) than any other people I know. The girls hired for farmwork the same as the men. They had arms on them like strong horses. Crossmaglen and Cullyhanna the len'th of the Dundalk border – a tarrible people hired from that district. There was a cattle fair that day too, at the Commons, and sheep and pigs.

The first man I hired with was John Douglas of Aughnagurgan. He didn't know me and I didn't know him. His house was on the very border. It was a big slated two-storey house and a cart shed on the end of it. The stable an' the barn laft [loft] was all in the one wi' the house too. It was a big range of a house. The brothers an' sisters used to come home to help wi' the harvest.

I used to go to Newtown Chapel of a Sunday. I got the afternoon off. I had to milk before I went and be back to milk in the evening. You fell in wi' people from roun' about. John Douglas was a Presbyterian. He went to Clarke's Bridge Meetin' House.

It wasn't so bad if you got a good house. I foun' out Douglas's wasn't counted a great house for grub. There was a man lived in a neighbour house the' called Barney Laverty. An' I was doin' the lane wan day – clippin' the hedges an' cleanin' the channels an' things like that, an' Barney says to me, 'Young fella', how are ye gettin' on?'

'Not too bad at all, Barney,' I says.

An' he says, 'How are they treatin' you for mate?'

'Well, Barney now,' says I, 'I cud be doin' wi' more.'

'I know that,' says he. 'It's counted a bad house for food. But,' he says, 'If you "put the hammer" [pressure] on them at the right time, you'll have no bother. I know they think a good deal of you. I know that.'

Well one day we were ploughin' an' it come till dinner time an' it was a Friday. Now I didn't ate beef that time on a Friday. An' I was that hungry I could a' ate a whole cart an' the cribs an' all. I was that hungry after ploughin all mornin'. An' I looked over an' there was a salt herrin' on my plate, an' they were atin' beef. Well, Barney Laverty had sort of put a bit of spirit in me. I says, 'What's that?'

She says, 'Sure you don't ate beef on a Friday.'

Says I, 'I don't, an' I'll not ate it, but I'm not atin' that.' I tell you the sweat was runnin' aff me wi' anger. Says I, 'Haven't you plenty of eggs, an' butter, an', says I, 'I cud ate that.'

An' she turned away all in a huff an' she give me the eggs an' ever since that day that I put the hammer on them, I cud get anything I wanted. They didn't like givin' you eggs, for they were makin' a few coppers on them you see. She'd bake soda bread right enough, an' the bread man come once a week. She wud've been sparin' too wi' the milk an' butter. They sowl [sold] that too, d'ye see.

I used to ate raw turnips, especially the wee young ones. Them was quare [good] stuff. An' an odd time they kep' pigs. An' if I was boilin' spuds in the boiler for the pigs, them lovely big spuds, I used to take a wee lock [amount] o' salt out (I wasn't askin' *her* for it, like) an' you cud have a good feed of spuds. An' another thing, if you got a hen layin' in the manger, you were sure to cop that egg; or outside annunder [under] a whin; raw eggs, the boys all ate them. Every man I knowed that was hired always ate raw eggs. I stayed there three years. It was a good house only I wasn't gettin' enough to ate at the start.

It was a big farm, about fifty acres. He had fourteen cows. That was a cheque every month; an' calves an' dry cattle in the field, heifers and bullocks. I had to cut cabbage and turnips in the wintertime. Then he took cattle to the fair, either Newtown or Keady. There were no cattle lorries at all that time. You walked. You'd meet some other man an' they'd all go together. That left plenty of help to go into gaps an' places where cattle run. If he run into a field on your side you had to do the running and bring him out again. I seen me running from the Water House at Darkley; you know that's a brave long hill down. The bullock was scared an' broke away. He was runnin' like a racehorse. You know a baste when he gets out, he can run! An' they all had to wait till I got 'im back. An' I got in front of 'im an' got 'im turned. I was out of breath, nearly droppin'.

There used to be ceilidhing houses. I used to go to a man the' called Henry John Laverty. He was a wee oul thin man, lived wi' the daughter. The house would be full wi' all 'aged' men. There was no electric. There was an oil lamp wi' a back on it hung on the wall. Keady Fair night was a good night to go. So was Newtown. The fair night was the main night for a bit o' craic. There was only one man could read an' that was Charlie McColville, a big tall man. He read very slowly. Charlie had a farm o' lan' below this house. As soon as Charlie come in Henry John would say, 'Were you in the fair the day?

What sort of a fair was it? What was cattle like?'

'Dammit, there was a good rise on them the day.' If it was only ten shillin's it was powerful. Then, 'Did you get the almanac?' *Old Moore's Almanac* give things about moons an' fairs an' things. Charlie had to houl it up till the lamp till see it. They'd ask him questions: 'What about the weather?', 'Does it give the winner of The National?' an' things like that. Then there was another house I used till go till – Mills's – over fernenst [opposite] Douglas's. I'll tell you about that too.

In days gone by you couldn't commend a woman better than to say that she was a powerful worker – in or out of the house. That meant out in the fields alongside the men. The downside was that women had sometimes to carry butter anything up to ten miles to market because the horses were needed in the fields. James Greene's neighbour at the first place he hired, Ann Jane Mills, fitted into this mould. But Ann Jane didn't let anything get her down. She made her own fun, often getting the better of the men in doing so. James Greene reminisces again:

There was a farm over fernenst Douglas's an' sometimes if I finished early I wud go over. There was seven brothers of them, big rough men they were, an' the sister Ann Jane. She wrought the skin aff her bones keepin' them men in feed. She baked a ten stone bag of flour every week, an' she was the best maker of tea I ever seen in my life. I said it was the water. She had a good well at the side of the house. I never got tea anywhere like it. She always made it in a tea-drawer – a tay-drawer★ – not a tay-pot.

She looked after the cows an' young cattle. Any young cattle they had, she fothered [foddered] them. She was goin' from daylight 'til dark. She used to wear clogs and you would hear the rattle of her comin' across the street. I'd go over on a summer's evening an' if she was milkin' she'd hear you comin'; an' she cud skite that milk straight from the cow's teat an' hit you fair up the face. Sure as a gun. An' she'd laugh till she'd drop aff the stool, at gettin' you as soon as you come in. She cud hit you between the eyes. And she had a dog wud'a ate ye. The brothers was big rough men. Some of them wrought on the roads. She was a big heavy woman, wrought from daylight till dark.

Then Sammy, one of the brothers, said, 'We've a big day comin' up at the hay an' we'll have plenty of help.'

They had no hay-floats at the time. It had to be lifted off the cock wi' a fork an' threw on a cart. They had nine horses an' nine carts nearly all belongin' to the neighbours. Then it was all built into one big stack. I was on the stack all day. I never was as tired in my life. Ann Jane made mate [food] for all them men. But there was a fella called Stewart Ross and he was a terrible talker. When the men all sat down an' he'd be startin' his dinner he wud start to talk. But the rest were fly. They'd ate away for they were very hungry. There wud be plenty of spuds, cabbage, bacon – no scarcity – an' plenty of milk. An' Ann Jane wud start liftin' the plates one after the other an' scrape them intil a bucket. An' he wud har'ly have two bites out of it wi' talkin'. But she passed no remarks, just went on an' lifted them all. It fair put 'im from talkin', I'm tellin' you.

Then sometimes they wud have a ceilidhe in the barn loft that night, especially after the flax pulling. They'd have taken a barrel of stout into the field, draught stout. That was emptied out with a ladle into pint tins. They'd nearly be singin' in the fields. They'd clean

---

★ vessel made of tin and used by manual workers for making tea. It was placed over an open fire and boiled before the tea was poured. Similar to a billy-can, it had a spout on the left hand side.

Market day, Keady. The building on the left (with the arched window) was the market house.

up the barn, knock the cobwebs off it, put a lock of planks roun' it to sit on an' that was great enjoyment. There was singin', dancin', fiddlin'. They'd dance Setts, the Mazurka, the Waltz. Somebody wud get up an' dance a horn-pipe, or sing. I mind [remember] me singin' in Barney Laverty's loft. I nearly always sang 'The Bradys of Killane':

The weather it was cold and rough, right in the wintertime,
There was roads to clane, and sheughs till drain, to mix and scatter lime,
You'll have to be a good servant and do the best you can,
For if you don't you'll not be long wi' the Bradys of Killane.

I went into my bed that night, upon it I did roll,
Oh the fleas they made a bold attempt my kidney for to hole,
They gathered round me in thousands my poor hide for to tan
And I soon found out the fleas slept none in the Bradys of Killane.

About three o'clock in the morning I heard an awful row,
I looked out through the window, saw something like a sow.
She said, 'Come get a bucket and something quick for Nan'
For the old sow knew her master was The Brady of Killane.

I went in for my breakfast, there was nothing I could see,
But a pack of hungry children, 'Leave something there for me.'
They tortured and tormented me, that cursed crooked clan,
Oh they'd shout and roar and call for more at the Bradys of Killane.

I worked down in the fields all day till me hand would har'ly shut,
And only the skin was brave and tough the bones would sure have cut.
I watched and prayed both night and day that the Lord would send a van,
For to take me from that cruel spot called Bradys of Killane.

[This song is also sung as *Bradys Of Strabane*.]

There was no shoes that time, just thick knitted stockings an' big heavy boots. An' a girl wud get a hoult o' ye. She was that big an' strong, ye couldn't get yer arms roun' 'er; an' she wud throw ye about like a cork. I'm tellin' ye. An' everybody wud cheer. There was quare [good] craic that time. I'm tellin' ye.

Newtownhamilton, situated in attractive upland country called 'The Fews', was by far the best market town in the South of the county. It was founded by one of the Hamiltons in 1770 and no doubt fairs and markets began at that time. By 1838 Newtown was described as a good town with around two hundred slated houses and the rest (about forty) thatched. The markets were held on Saturday and were well supplied with 'all kinds of meats and wearables'. The last in the month was also Fair Day. Stallions paraded through the streets before the fair, with their manes and tails plaited and intertwined with ribbons. The markets took place around the market house in the centre of the town (a big feature was the sale of cabbage plants from the Loughgall area) but as James Greene said, the fairs were held at the Commons, a piece of ground at the junction of the Markethill and Armagh Roads. The last fair was held in 1961. It was very poorly attended.

The months of May and November brought hiring day, which drew droves of young people from the mountain areas round about and also from Counties Louth, Monaghan, Roscommon, Longford, Antrim and Down. Hiring must have taken place on more than one day, for it was said at the time that 'servants when on going to their place if they find it not so agreeable as they expected then they come the following market day to look out for another place'. This was fraught with risk. It was in Newtown that a man hired with a farmer, regretted it before the day was out and hired with another. The first refused to take back the earls. The case went to law and the man was fined. He refused to pay and was jailed.

Terence Quinn from Crossmaglen was another of the many who found their way to Newtown. The year was 1909. Until that day he had been attending Glasrumman School, but he had taken a dislike to the new master who subscribed to the 'Spare the rod' theory. 'If you have tears,' he would threaten his terrified pupils, reaching for the cane as he spoke, 'prepare to shed them now.' At other times he would sit down and open a newspaper, every so often darting a sharp look over the top to try and catch someone out. Terry and his pal had been thinking about leaving for some time but the arrival of this new master decided it. They set off that fine May morning and walked the seven miles to Newtown, taking up a position along with some other boys in the Market Square. Stall holders were already doing business when they arrived. A ballad singer was singing:

> It wasn't the men from Shercock
> Or the men from Ballybay,
> But the dalin' men from Crossmaglen
> Put whiskey in me tay.

At the mention of Crossmaglen, Terry and his pal looked at each other and smiled.

One big fellow who had been there before was airing his knowledge. 'There'll be no hiring 'til eleven at laste [least] but you're better off gettin' a place on the stan,' he announced to no-one in particular. Terry was quite surprised then when he was approached by a small stout man who was so out of breath that he was puffing and blowing all the time. Sweat was running down his jaws, wetting his collar. Terry hired with him for £3 12s and discovered afterwards that he was known to all as the 'Spit' Gibson. Terry's job was to look after Gibson's forty head of cattle, twenty pigs, six milch cows, two horses and an old grey mare. The job held no terrors for him as he had done similar work at home. There were also twenty dozen fowl which were looked after by Gibson's two nieces. Many a time Terry would have liked a boiled egg for breakfast, but every egg was counted and sold to Thomas Doyle of Markethill to provide cash for the day-to-day running of the house. Terry's breakfast consisted of oatmeal porridge and a mug of buttermilk, along with what they referred to as 'a rider on the mug'. This was a piece of bread cut to about one eighth of an inch wider than the rim of the mug and always in imminent danger of falling in. Terry hired for seven years at as many farms, before being persuaded at the age of nineteen to look for work in Scotland. That was the end of hiring as far as he was concerned.

Team of horses with swing plough.

Annie McCreesh also hired in Newtown. She was just fourteen and she remembers her first hiring as if it were yesterday. Here is Annie's story:

> At that time there was really very little money and parents had to let their children take whatever they could get in the line of a job. They couldn't afford to keep them at home. I happened to hire fairly convenient with a man called Pat Hughes about four miles outside Keady on the Castleblaney Road. Pat was a stonemason. He lived in a big white-washed house with two rooms downstairs – a kitchen and another room. It was quite old-fashioned really. The fire was down on the floor and a big ash pit underneath it and bellows that you could blow to light up the fire. It was a big open fire with old black pots that you hung on a crook.
>
> My job was to look after Pat and his brothers who were elderly, and also their old mother. There were two rooms upstairs. The brothers used one and me and the old woman used the other. When Pat brought me he said to her, 'Mother, I brought you home a wee girl.'

Courtesy of Ian McCullough

Hiring Fair in Newtownhamilton. The lad with his hands in his pockets is for hire. (second right at bottom of picture) There are several interested farmers nearby. The three women watching on the far right are probably the family of the farmer (wearing a hard hat) standing behind the boy.

'Pat,' she says, 'did I not "rare" enough o' childer?' (She had brought up eight.) But she was very good to me. I cooked for her and cooked for the men and kept the house clean.

She had cards and she would say to me, 'When you get that done we will have a game of Old Maid.' That passed an hour for her. She died when I was only there a month. I was in bed the night she died. They woke me when she was about to depart. I was really frightened. After she died Pat brought a nephew of his home to keep me in company. He was called Patrick after his uncle. He was about six and I used to take him to Drumhearney school. I grew very fond of him.

About that time I had an older sister hired in Keady town. She used to come out on her bicycle to see that I was alright. Then Pat bought me a bicycle and the two of us used to ride home together. It was about eleven miles. I did it often. The roads were really bad at that time, rough with loose gravel. Sometimes we had to get off and walk. We walked it in winter for we were too scared of the bad roads to take the bicycles.

Then I took it into my head that I wanted to see more of the world. I left Hughes's and went to what they called the Big Fair Day in November. That was the time the workers all came home for a week. They had their money and everything was rosy. That was a great week altogether. There was dancing and fiddle playing and singing – my house tonight, yours tomorrow night, somebody else's the next night. Word got round. It didn't matter

Pulling flax. The flax had to be pulled (not cut) to ensure that the fibres were as long as possible.

if you had nailed boots. It was only a cement floor. Nobody looked for any big feed or anything like that. You ate soda bread, butter and jam. Everybody did their party piece. All they were out for was the night's fun. Then there was the flax pullin' nights. My sister Maggie got word that there was a flax pullin' night comin' off near our place at home and the two of us set off and cycled the whole way up till Newtownhamilton – home to Camlyball in fact. You had to have a light on your bicycle but I had only a glimmer and comin' up under the trees there along the Dundalk Road this policeman shone his light out, so we jumped off.

He says, 'Where's your lights?'* I was cheeky so I said, 'Behind me liver!'

'Well,' he says, 'there's one sure thing, they'll not be behind your liver when I'm done with you!'

And for God's Sake he asked us our name and where we were going. We told him and he, by the way, wrote it down but there was never a word about it. That's the only time ever I was in trouble. Anyway we came all the way home to Camlyball, saw my mother, and any of them that was goin' to the dance was ready. We took our bicycles and there was a near-cut across the fields and we carried our bicycles till we got to the road. When we arrived at the house sure for goodness sake the dance was in full bloom. We danced all night and had supper an' all and went straight from there back to Keady when the dance was over. It must have been about seven o'clock in the mornin' when we got back. The church bells were ringin'. Maggie went to the place where she was workin' and I went on by myself out into the country and got me good clothes off, never went to bed or anything.

I'll never forget that day. There was a big churnin' to be done and at that time it was a big high churn and a staff and plunge, and for goodness sake sure I was hardly fit to lift

*Lights – slang for lungs

it up and down to get the job done. I worked all day and I'm tellin' you I was glad to see bed that night after all that.

Of the other places that Annie hired two stand out in her memory. One was R.W. Bell's of Hillsborough, where she spent several happy years and during which time she met Patrick (Paddy) Taggart (featured in the 'Down' chapter) whom she was later to marry. The other was a place at Newry where she got the fright of her life. To reach her room above the dairy she had to go up a stepladder and through a trapdoor. The window of the dairy was invariably kept open to keep the milk cool, which worried Annie as no one had got around to putting a wire guard on it. One night she woke with a start to the sound of dishes rattling below. She lay still, terrified, and eventually the noise stopped. The next morning, she discovered that a cat had come through the window in the night and helped itself to some milk. The noise was made by the movement of the dish as the cat licked it clean.

In the south of the county lay at least half a dozen places which had fairs or markets at some stage in their history. Crossmaglen was the largest, though it was described in 1830 as being 'of late origin'. Nevertheless, it had at that time a weekly market for the sale of butter, eggs, fowl, grain, and grass seed; also good fairs which survived until the next century. Fair Day usually ended with fighting and the settlement of old scores, when many received beatings which they 'never got over till released from their earthly sufferings.' Crossmaglen had an extra large Market Square which contained a small market house and a weighbridge. Ballsmill, a few miles away, had just one fair in 1888, held on 26 May. It is likely that it had more at an earlier date.

Jonesborough had fairs which ceased about 1865. When they ceased in Jonesborough they improved in Forkhill and the number held each year increased from four to twelve. Fairs were also held in Cullyhanna, Ballybot and Camlough. They did not survive beyond the 1860s in Cullyhanna. Those in Ballybot increased from four to twelve in the nineteenth century but died out early in the twentieth. The most successful of the three were in Camlough, where they were held regularly on the third Monday of every month for nearly one hundred years. The October fair was known locally as the Foal Fair and the main feature was the sale of mares and foals. When a foal was sold it walked, accompanied by its mother, to the farm of its new owner. Mostly the mare returned immediately to her original owner to have another foal the next year, but just occasionally a farmer bought mare and foal, which stopped both from fretting.

In the centre of the county lay the towns of Richhill, Hamiltonsbawn and Markethill, all of which were once thriving towns in their own right but were eventually overshadowed by the larger towns nearby. Richhill was founded by the Richardson family in the seventeenth century, when it was reported to have the best market in the county for linen cloth. In the eighteenth century it was said that 'the inhabitants of Armagh came to Richhill to purchase their wearing apparel and victualling'. By 1838 it was reduced to a small market dealing in yarn only and by 1888 that too had gone and the couple of hundred weavers left in the area were acquiring their yarn from other markets such as Portadown and Tandragee. The decline in the market was blamed on the Quaker community which boycotted the town after one of their members was killed in a riot there.

Hamiltonsbawn was founded by a John Hamilton in 1619. The same built a strong bawn and settled twenty-six British families at that time, but the bawn was destroyed by the troops of Phelim O'Neill in 1641 and the property eventually came into the possession of the Achesons, one of whom was raised to the peerage as Lord Gosford. Both Hamiltonsbawn and Richhill had fairs and markets. Richhill had never more than four fairs and Hamiltonsbawn had just two, held on 26 May and 26 November. According to G.H. Bassett in 1888 'good farming country surrounds Hamiltonsbawn, and to this fact is due the maintenance of old-established fairs twice a year, and hiring fairs, when nearly all the villages of the county situated near large towns have lost these much-prized helps to prosperity.' They continued until the outbreak of World War II.

Hamiltonsbawn was also where the action took place in Tom O'Reilly's poem, 'The Hiring of Dan Magee':

> *I am an honest farmer's son, my name is Dan Magee*
> *I was born and reared in a wee townland not far from Tandragee.*
> *At fifteen I was straight and strong, for that age fairly tall,*
> *I saw my father's shoulders bent, my mother's frame grow small.*
>
> *Says my old man to me one day, 'I've reared you well till now '*
> *You can drive a plough and harrow, and neatly milk a cow.*
> *The family's young, you're now a man; it's getting too much for me*
> *We'll talk it o'er with Ma to-night and see what you must do.*
>
> *That night we talked till the embers died and at last did all agree*
> *That I'd attend next Hiring Fair, try what my luck might be*
> *I'd need a pair of working brogues, strong socks, a shirt or two*
> *For heavy days in the sleet an' rain, an oul' coat of me da's would do.*
>
> *Hamiltonsbawn was the nearest place for a lad like me to go*
> *And I left one morn for my first sojourn as the cock began to crow.*
> *I stood in the fair in the cold still air, and the farmers passed me by*
> *My soda farl had long since gone and my bottle of milk was dry.*
>
> *At last when hope had almost fled and my courage ebbed away*
> *A man came over, sized me up, and then to me did say,*
> *' If you can milk, an' mow, an' drive, my lad, I think you'll do'.*
> *And as I could answer yes to all, he says, 'Well, what say you?'*
>
> *Now Willie McCann was a dacent man should I never meet another*
> *But Liza Jane was a daughter of Cain — or Tam the divil's mother*
> *She had me up at the skrake of day an' out at the sun's first light*
> *Six cows to milk and the byres to clean before I touched a bite.*
>
> *Poor Willie, he did the best he could to make up for the heartless Jane*
> *By giving me pokes of tobacco and a few pence, now and again,*
> *But his kindly deeds were wasted — Once bitten you're always shy,*
> *And I swore there'd never be another Jane, not till the day I die.*

Now my long half-year of torture came at last to a welcome end.
I bade good-bye to Willie and left him as a friend.
But the back of me hand to Liza Jane and all my sympathy too
To the poor unfortunate divil who'll take my place in the queue.

The area around Markethill was also Acheson territory. Nineteen Scottish families were settled there during the reign of James I and markets and fairs were held throughout the seventeenth and eighteenth centuries, increasing to twelve in the nineteenth and twentieth. An old farmer reminisces:

Fair day was always the third Friday. The' driv' the cattle down out of the country lanes down into Markethill an' sold them in the streets. The cattle used to stan' wi' their heads up agin' the wall. An' the horses an' carts were there wi' pigs an' sheep. They run the horses to let people see what sort o' shape they were in. There weren't many horses – just one or two. I remember gettin' a calf give to me, a white bull calf. I put it in a two hundredweight bag an' set it in the back of the trap an' brought it home an' reared it. I was thirteen years of age. That was about 1934. There used to be stalls an' strongmen. There was a man had a big board of nails an' he lay down on it and got somebody to stan' on his bare chest.

The markets for fowl, eggs and grain were held on Monday; butter and eggs on Friday. Friday was also the day that manufacturers' agents brought linen yarn to the town for the weavers. Dean Swift is believed to have visited Markethill in 1729 as the guest of Sir Arthur Acheson.

The territory around Tandragee (variously called Tanrygee and Tanderagee) formerly belonged to the O'Hanlons but was taken from them for their part in the Rebellion of 1594–1603. The highwayman Redmond O'Hanlon was perhaps the most notorious member of the family. Redmond was a rapparee [bandit] and was known as the 'terror of the Fews' for the way he plundered and terrorised the people of the countryside. But his discretion eventually outran his valour and he was murdered by a member of his own gang. He is reputed to lie buried in the old graveyard at Relicarn near Scarva. The O'Hanlon lands were confiscated by James I and granted to Sir Oliver St John who rebuilt the castle and settled the town. Sir Oliver was also granted rights to fairs and markets. However, the O'Hanlons returned in 1641, destroyed the church and castle and killed Sir Oliver. The town prospered in spite of these disasters, with fairs and markets continuing throughout the eighteenth and nineteenth centuries. In 1835 there were twelve fairs and excellent weekly markets which were abundantly supplied with linen and the usual animals and farm produce. In addition thirty-five cart loads of pork were sold and the sale of flax averaged £6,000 per week during their respective seasons. By the end of the nineteenth century the markets had gone except for a few people who sold butter. Later lords of the castle included Colonel and Lady Olivia Sparrow, Lord Viscount and Lady Mandeville, and the Duke of Manchester.

Contrary to reports at the time, most landlords treated their tenants well as stated by the Ordnance Surveyor of 1838:

Lord Mandeville as a landlord deserves the highest praise. He gives his tenants lime to whitewash their
houses. He lends money to farmers of small capital to labour and crop their land and takes their labour in

return for payment. He keeps a surgeon to visit them, supplies them with medicines and a dispensary and maintains numerous schools in this and the adjoining parishes in which his estates lie for the education of their children.

Yet another landlord is praised in the following verse:

Mountnorris has its monthly fair,
It has its school and house of prayer,
And fair improvements too we hope
While lives our landlord, Captain Cope.
On Ganges banks he once did roam,
A British soldier far from home;
But now lives here in our green isle,
And makes the honest farmer smile.

Mountnorris owes its existence to the erection of a fortress during the rebellion mentioned above, in which both the O'Hanlons and the O'Neills took part. It was named in honour of a commander called General Norris. It too acquired fairs at an early date but they did not survive beyond the nineteenth century. At one point it was better known for the disturbances which took place there than for the business done.

Poyntzpass got its name from Sir Charles Poyntz, who commanded the Elizabethan army which defended the pass between Down and Armagh. The surrounding area was inhospitable bog and forest,

Poyntzpass around 1920.

Picture courtesy of Cecil Allen

which in the sixteenth and seventeenth centuries was constantly under attack from the O'Neills. From the eighteenth century onwards it benefited from the proximity of the nearby Newry Canal which was used for the export of farm produce – especially grain. The arrival of the railway the next century was a further boost. Monthly fairs were held in Poyntzpass until the twentieth century. Although the mart at Poyntzpass 'has since closed local man Cecil Allen remembers:

> Fairs were held in the street 'til the 1950s. I remember farmers comin' with cattle. There's an iron rail was put up to keep them away from the windows. It's still there. Sheep were in pens. When it was over they used to brush the street and wash the footpath. Nowadays [2003] sheep are auctioned here at the mart on a Thursday night and pigs on a Saturday – fat sows, fat pigs, pork pigs – no cattle now.

The best market town in the county was Portadown. Trading there dates back to 1631 when Michael Obins and his mother Prudence secured a patent for a fair and market. The Obins family brought with them fourteen English families. Around the same time the first bridge was built across the Bann.

In 1814 the Obins estates were sold to the Sparrow family of Tandragee and some years later Millicent Sparrow married Lord Mandeville, who later became the sixth Duke of Manchester. Some of these people are remembered in the street names of Portadown today. Although the Duke had a patent for fairs and markets in the town he never collected any tolls. In 1878 the town commissioners bought the market rights on a lease lasting nine hundred and ninety nine years. They then built new market places and levied a charge on the traders using them. The markets, including a fair green situated off Shillington Street, comprised in all about seven acres. Markets were held every Saturday and from the nineteenth century onwards a fair was held on the third Saturday in every month, together with three old fairs held on Easter Monday, Whit Monday and 13 November. Portadown was the main centre for selling the hundreds of black cattle which grazed the meadows on either side of the Bann. They were sold at the fair green or in the nearby streets. Farmers always sold a cow with a full udder as this helped the sale. Sometimes the new owner milked the cow before setting off for home. If the locals timed it right they could go home with a free can of milk. Hiring took place on the first Wednesday of every third month. Attempts were made to start a horse fair in Portadown but without success.

An abundance of produce and livestock arrived into the town on their allotted days to their allotted places and the sellers were charged a small fee. In 1888 the charge for selling a cow was two-pence; one penny for a calf or pig; young pigs in a cart a half-penny. Sellers of butter paid from a half-penny for under 10lb weight to three ha'pence for over 20lb and those selling eggs paid a penny per hundred. Charges for poultry ranged from two-pence per dozen for hens to four pence per dozen for geese and turkeys. A load of apples cost the seller a penny while a load of root vegetables, hay or straw cost two-pence. No charge was made on the sale of grain but a penny was levied on a bag of grass seed. It was a common sight in those days to see a grass seed merchant remove his hard hat and shake a small sample of seed on the crown to test its purity before buying. The black surface of the hat showed up flawed seed immediately and the price was adjusted accordingly. Rather than take a bad price the farmer would sometimes take the seed home again for further cleaning. The price might even rise before the next market.

Market Street, Portadown on Market Day.

Fruit and vegetables were sold in Market Street; crockery, rope and tin-ware in High Street; new-laid eggs – white, brown, bantam or lovely blue duck eggs – in the market in Mandeville Street; squealing pigs in Woodhouse Street and so on. The Saturday market was a great source of entertainment for town and country folk alike, and nothing was left untried in the line of side-shows that could make the day more enjoyable. Second-hand clothes sellers excelled themselves with their banter and sales talk.

In spite of the thousands of weavers in the cottages in the surrounding countryside, and (later) in the factories, the town never had a good linen market. This was offset by the excellent markets in Armagh and Lurgan and to a lesser degree in Tandragee. However all of this came to an end in the first half of the twentieth century. When the linen mills closed, the premises were utilised in other ways. For instance Watson Armstrong's weaving mill was used as an ordnance factory during the war and afterwards as a pottery by Wade Ireland Limited. Many of the goods produced by the latter are today much sought after by collectors – their famous whimsies [miniature ceramic animals] for example.

The town grew rapidly in the eighteenth and nineteenth centuries with the opening of the Newry and Lagan Canals. These gave Portadown direct links with Belfast and Dublin and for a time with Scotland and Wales. By 1836 merchants in the town owned eighteen boats which imported and exported thousands of tons of merchandise annually. Iron, coal, timber, slates, flour and oatmeal were imported; grain was the main export. In addition ninety tons of pork a year on average went to Belfast on carts. These returned loaded with such things as tea, sugar, hardware and cotton and woollen goods.

Boatmen and their families lived on board their boats. They paid their dues to trustees who were to see to it that the money was used for the good of the town, namely to keep the quay in good repair and to make sure that the town was clean and well lit. Their efforts were frustrated by a private individual who built a larger quay but charged the same amount in dues.

With the arrival of the railways in the middle of the nineteenth century, Portadown was not only the main port on the canal between Newry and Lough Neagh – it was also an important junction on the Great Northern Railway. It was not just a market town: it was also a manufacturing town with 3,000 employed in its mills and factories. Spinning and weaving went on at the same time in several thousand homes in the countryside. Many of the cottagers had apple orchards, especially to the west of the town towards Loughgall. At the height of the season anything up to 200 cart loads of apples arrived into the market on a Saturday.

But pride of place in manufacturing goes to Lurgan. The original proprietors of the town were ousted by John Brownlow (a Nottinghamshire gentleman) who brought with him forty English settlers and their families in 1610. The town and castle were burnt by rebels in 1641 and lay in ruins until the reign of Charles II when rebuilding began. By 1725 Lurgan had a sizeable community and 'a fine parish church with a shingled spire'. By 1800 it had around four hundred houses, two of which were shingled with bog oak and the rest slated or thatched.

Two patent fairs were granted to John Brownlow by King William after the Battle of the Boyne, one to be held in August and the other in November, each lasting two days. There was also a good weekly market held around the market house in the main thoroughfare which was broad enough to accommodate both business and traffic. Market tolls were abolished in Lurgan around 1850. The market for grain, grass seed, pork, potatoes, vegetables, fowl, butter and eggs was held on Thursdays. In 1846 the general market changed from Friday to Thursday to avoid clashing with that of Belfast. By then the town had added monthly fairs to the two old fairs already mentioned making fourteen in all.

With the exception of Belfast no town in Ireland increased as rapidly in population and wealth as Lurgan. This was due mainly to the development of the linen industry. The manufacture of linen was introduced to the area by William Waring in the reign of Queen Anne (1702-1714) and from then on the town went from strength to strength. Waringstown (the home of the Waring family) was also celebrated for its linens and cambrics.

The sale of webs of linen soon became a feature of Lurgan's weekly market. In the early days business was done in the open street, the buyers paying for and receiving the goods afterwards in hotels. Before long the need for a linen hall was felt and one was built near the church. It was replaced in the early 1800s by a larger building which was said to be thronged every Friday with weavers who exposed their webs on long tables provided for the purpose. At that time there were at least 18,000 hand loom weavers employed in enterprises wholly or partly directed from Lurgan. They lived mainly in Armagh, Down, Antrim and Tyrone. With the introduction of power loom weaving in 1855 the linen markets declined and in 1865 Lurgan's linen hall was demolished.

The north of the county (more specifically Annaghmore, Tartaraghan and the Montiaghs) was almost exclusively bogland from which turf was extracted and used extensively for fuel. During the nineteenth century the road from Annaghmore to Armagh was said to 'suffer at all seasons of the year from the constant traffic of turf carts.' At the same time lighter [flat-bottomed barges used for canal and river transport] loads of turf were being sent from the Montiaghs via the River Bann to Portadown and via the Newry Canal to Madden Bridge, Scarva and Poyntzpass for distribution to a wider area.

This was by no means exclusively for domestic use. Vast quantities were needed by the linen bleachers for boiling their cloth and by farmers for burning their lime and bricks or drying their agricultural produce. Magheralin and Moira also drew their fuel from the Montiaghs and in return sold limestone which could be mixed with bog or stable manure and used as fertilizer. This could be purchased already mixed in the Loughgall area at ten pence a barrel. Some people gathered rushes to make mats, rushlights and seats for rush-bottomed chairs. These were sold in local markets. The mats were used on stairs and as covering for earthen floors.

A system of farming popular in Armagh long ago was that of heating the boglands so that they would yield good crops. Peat fires were lit around the ground about to be planted. The remaining surface was sprinkled with hot ashes and the crop sown in the warm earth. The heated land forced vegetation and growth, ensuring a good crop of oats or potatoes.

There are many versions of this popular song. Bawn (or Bawnboy) is in Cavan though the song was by no means confined to that area. It is entitled 'The Rocks of Bawn'.

Come all ye loyal heroes and listen unto me,
Don't hire with any farmer till you know what your work will be,
For he will rise you early from clear daylight till dawn
And you never will be able for to plough the rocks of Bawn.

Oh, rise up, gallant Sweeney and give your horse some hay,
And give to him a feed of oats before you start the day;
Don't feed him on soft turnips, take him down to yon green lawn,
Or he never will be able for to plough the rocks of Bawn.

Oh, my clothes they are all torn, and my shoes they do let in,
My heart is always trembling now for fear they might give in,
My heart is nearly broken now from clear daylight till dawn,
And I never will be able for to plough the rocks of Bawn.

My curse upon you Sweeney boy, you have me nearly robbed;
You're sitting by the fireside now, your feet upon the hob.
You're sitting by the fireside now, from clear daylight till dawn,
And you never will be able for to plough the rocks of Bawn.

I wish the Queen of England would send for me in time,
And place me in some regiment all in my youthful prime;
I would fight for England's glory from clear daylight till dawn,
And I never would return again to plough the rocks of Bawn.

COUNTY DOWN

In thrift and industry it has no superior. Although a large proportion of the inhabitants profit by the extensive employment of capital in the linen and other industries, there is no county in which a greater effort is made, intelligently, to secure satisfactory results from land cultivation.

from George Henry Bassett's *County Down One Hundred Years Ago*, 1886

The industry and thriftiness found on farms in this part of the province in 1886 is still as evident in the County Down of today. In those far off days it was by far the greatest flax-growing county in Ulster. It grew more potatoes than any other county although only third in order of size. The county can also claim the first Ploughing Society which was set up in Bangor in 1816. This was followed by the formation of a number of farming societies, many hosting an annual show. Subscriptions for membership ranged from one shilling to one pound depending on the size of the applicant's farm.

One of the more important towns from the farmer's point of view was Newry which had markets and fairs as far back as 1613, when Arthur Bagenal was granted permission to hold a market every Thursday 'with tolls and commodities'. Amongst other things he was to have a custom or toll of six gallons from every butt of wine (called sack) and three and a half gallons from every hogshead of wine sold. The patent also granted two fairs in the year, each to last three days; and at Greencastle (of which more later) a weekly market and one fair in the year. The town of Newry was destroyed in the rebellion of 1641 but soon recovered – due in no small measure to its port and its strategic position servicing the counties of Down, Louth and Armagh.

The town's markets continued virtually uninterrupted over the years and were well supplied with brown linen, farm produce and fish, including oysters and other fish caught in Carlingford Lough. During those years the markets were held on the streets and the Market Square was filled with huckster's stalls.

The town had an important butter market which drew business from counties Armagh, Tyrone, Monaghan, Cavan, Down and Louth. Lord Kilmorey built a butter crane there in 1808. Threepence was charged for each cask weighed and twopence for each crock. A butter taster was appointed whose duty it was to taste the butter in each cask or crock and mark it according to its quality. Most of the butter was exported to Liverpool.

By this time three excellent coaches and the day and night mails passed through the town regularly together with several 'cars' each capable of carrying up to fourteen passengers. The mail coach made a twenty-minute stop in Newry for breakfast, during which time the horses were changed in readiness for the long haul to Dublin. The full journey took twelve hours. The town had the added advantage of being accessible by sea and canal and got another boost in the middle of the nineteenth century with the arrival of the railways.

By the end of the century there were five market places enclosed in various parts of the town. There was a market house (no doubt replacing an earlier one), several hotels, an assembly and news room and a bridewell (gaol). By then it had a population of around 16,000 and its fairs were held monthly. Its manufactories included three flax spinning mills, two linen weaving factories, an apron factory, five flour mills, two iron foundries, two mineral water factories, seven tanneries, stone polishing mills, coach-building, cabinet furniture making and salt works. These helped sustain regular markets which were by then held every Tuesday, Thursday and Saturday in King Street, Mary Street, Needham Street and Market Street. They encompassed the sale of grain, grass seed, pork, sheep, pigs, flax, hay, straw, potatoes, fruit, plants, hides, fowl, meat, eggs, butter and vegetables. The town was particularly noteworthy for its market in feeding stuffs, especially hay and straw. These found a ready market with the small farmers, who converged on the town from the surrounding mountain areas to buy fodder and bedding for their cattle. Hay was needed also for the town horses which pulled the vehicles of the bakers, tanners, coal merchants and undertakers to name but a few.

Almost as important to farmers were the quarterly hiring markets held 'after the Scottish pattern' in the Mill Street, Hill Street and North Street areas. Farmers arrived into the town in traps and carts putting their horses into yards at such places as the Victoria Hotel and Terry Murphy's in Monaghan Street for the duration of the fair. Bargaining for labour was conducted on much the same lines as buying and selling cattle. Men and boys stood at the hay market in Hill Street or the old butter market. Women and girls usually congregated at the corner of Upper Mill Street. Nearly all were Roman Catholics but some parents preferred to send them to a Protestant house – firstly because no manual labouring work was done there on a Sunday and secondly because a Protestant farmer was more likely to send them to mass regularly. A Roman Catholic farmer would consider that once a month was enough for a servant.

The first Thursday in May and November was known as Loosing Day – the day that workers left their old jobs. Then followed a week of entertainment and dancing and on the next Thursday they went back to the fair either to re-hire with their old masters or to hire with someone new. Hiring also took place on the third Thursday. Any farmer who was known to have treated a servant harshly or unfairly during the half-year was likely to get a trouncing from the Mullaghbawn boys before he went home.

One of the noisiest places on the evening of the fair was Edward Street Station from which excited and nervous young people were setting off into the great unknown. Mothers wept as they parted from their children for the first time. Third class carriages were packed to overflowing while first and second class carriages were usually empty and kept securely locked. Sara Savage of Poyntzpass captures the mood of one young hireling in the words of the poem, 'Hiring Day':

1   *I couldn't look behind me*
     As I left the cottage door.
     It was parting from the wee ones,
     That made my heart so sore.

2   *My mother took my bundle;*
     We were heading for the fair,
     And the crowd was nearly gathered,
     Agin we landed there.

3   *We heard a lot of bargaining –*
     We stood about till late;
     'Twas for some a ready market,
     But others be to wait.

4   *Then a man spoke up fornenst us*
     As he eyed me up and down,
     'Is the wee chile up for hirin',
     Or just in to see the town?'

5   *'A widda's chile,' says Mother,*
'Sure she be to go and earn,
The more she's young she's willin',
And won't be hard to learn.'

6   *Soon the wage was settled,*
And the earnest in my hand.
Says the master, 'Now it's hometime,
We'll make it while we can.'

7   *My mother was beside me,*
As we jostled through the throng;
Says she, 'I be to leave ye –
Now, don't be thinkin' long.'

8   *Her plaid my eye could follow,*
On the journey as before,
Then turning from the station,
Sure I saw her shawl no more.

9   *There's many a change since them times,*
For its three score years come May,
But I never was as lonesome,
As on that Hiring Day.

Paddy Taggart was one of hundreds of young people who hired in Newry in the 1920s. As he stood with his mother in North Street along with her two sisters and their families who were also hiring, he couldn't help feeling excited at the prospect before him. He has vivid memories of that day:

There were these weemin steppin' about carryin' baskets on their arum [arm], wicker baskets wi' lids. They were goin' into the butter market and they had walked maybe miles.

So then there was a man came over to me and he says, 'Are you a son of John Taggart's?'

I said, 'I am.'

And he said, 'Who have you with you?'

And my mother stepped forward and he said till her, 'What would this boy have till get? We could do with a lad like this. When I heered who he was, that's why I'm so interested in him. I'll give him nine poun' for the six months.'

My mother says, 'Now, it'll not be in this fair the day. I think you'll give him ten.'

And didn't he say owin' to the case he

Paddy Taggart (aged 16) and his mother on Hiring Day.

would give me ten. And then he took us down to Mickey Boyle's pub at the fut o' Mill Street. My mother didn't touch drink but she took a mineral and I took a mineral and he took a half-un o' whiskey himself.

When he got up to go he give me five bob and he says, 'You know where I live (Connolly's blacksmith's shop) an' when you're goin' home you can stop. If not, come in the mornin'.'

So of coorse when I was goin' by it he was out watchin'. He would be afraid you wouldn't go you know. Good enough people, dacent people. And me and this blacksmith – he was a son – we slept together, shared the same bed, the best of a fella', and died young. So I was up there 'til November. I wasn't involved in the black-smithing, just the farmin'. He had a big farm there (...) everything in the line wi' workin wi' horses too – runnin' up spuds, grubbin' turnips an' things like that. The crop was in then, d'ye see. That was the third Thursday in May. Then it would run on 'til the second Thursday in August (the quarterly fair) and if you had a bad place you were eligible then to leave. On the third Thursday that would be hirin' day again.

A blacksmith's was a place where people gathered. It was a warm place. It was all horses that time – no tractors – horses comin' through the day, and ploughs. And then at night all the oul ones would be in, young ones too – no weemin. There could be a dozen people there. And there was no wireless, no television – nothin'. They would stan' there in the dark an' talk an' the oul men would smoke clay pipes.

The worst year, I remember it well, was 1932 – spuds a shillin' a 'hundred' (hundredweight) – an' this day in Newry the weemin was there wi' their sons and daughters. Honest to God, they would nearly a' give them away to get them fed. I hired in Warrenpoint that year at the Yankee Bar, an' he had a dairy too and milked twelve cows. I had nothin' to do wi' the bar of coorse.

He bought turnips. These turnips come in cartloads an' they would tip them up in the shade [shed] an' you would go out in the mornin' an' pulp these turnips for the cows. Then the cows were milked an' that milk was strained and she (the man's wife) would measure the milk out – wee small kens [cans] and I would deliver the milk roun'. There was wan about a quart, and then a pint and a half pint.

You would be up about six o'clock. You would get your breakfast about nine. The pubs opened that time about ten and he would want to have all redd up about that time to get the pub open. Then I would be away up in the fields switchin' at hedges or somethin'. I had no watch or nothin'. He would say to me, 'There's a wee factory down there and you'll hear the whistle of it goin' an come up for your dinner.' Then you would be home – it would be dark round about half four and the cows had to be fed and milked again. But it was harder in winter. The farmers hadn't the money to pay you. They were sellin' – the bullock that's makin' £400 now, you would have got him that time for eight.

Then there was a servant girl in it, and that girl was paid off for not being in at ten o'clock at night. I thought that was a tarra! So when I left there I went home for a week. That week, the boys and girls, they would'a rid miles on bikes just to go to parties. But there was more boys and girls struck up (a friendship) at the hirin' than anywhere. God, sure that's where a whole lot of them met!

Well anyway, the next man I hired with was Willie Quinn up the Antrim Road in

Courtesy of Norman Foote

The Dickey Farm at Moyrusk, Moira.

Lisburn. He had a poultry farm an' then he bought lan' and started up dairying and kept a boy and girl. I was treated alright there – a dacent man. The houses where you hired, it all depended on yourself. If you were nasty or bad with them, they would get real nasty with you. It's just like meetin' the police on the road. If you get nasty wi' them they'll get nasty wi' you. The money that I had for that six months now was £13. That was about 1933.

They all grew spuds, cabbage, turnips and that's what the boys and girls were fed on that time. A woman wouldn't be runnin' to a butcher's shop every day. Many a time I took salt an' spuds for my dinner and a drink of buttermilk.

Anyway it come up to the time that I would be leavin' an' Quinn said, 'I'll give you ten bob a week.' And I said, ' I have promised to go till a man at Moyrusk an' I'll be gettin' brave wages off that man.'

That man sent for me, and that was Tommy Dickey. I went up the Sunday before, and the father was sittin' on a bucket turned upside down in an outhouse. He had a baird [beard] on him down to there [indicates a spot near his waist] and I asked him, 'Is this where Tommy Dickey lives?' And he jumped up and he says, 'Tommy Dickie doesn't own this place. I'm Thaney Dickey and *I* own it.'

I says, 'Is Tommy about?'

'Tommy is about, but maybe he wouldn't be able to do your business. There's a fella' to

87

Tommy Dickey.

come here to see him. He's lookin' to come to him for the next six months but,' he says, ' I don't think you're him.'

'Well,' says I, 'barrin' he has two comin', I'm him.' So Lord, I think I see Tommy comin' splayin' down the street, an' he says, 'How are ye doin' Paddy? Was he goin' to hit you?'

'Oh no,' says I, 'but he let me know that he was the boss here anyway.'

'Och,' he says, 'give him no heed,' and neither I did. Mrs Foote was there (his sister) and she was a great turn, but bate up wi' pains – married to Tom Foote. Boys, I'm tellin' you, Tom was some grower of strawberries!

Anyway Tommy says to me, 'I've had desperate hard luck wi' boys here. As a matter of fact we have had no boy for the last six months at all. I'll tell you what happened. I went to Newry and I hired a fella from Hilltown an' he came down here alright and the second day he went down to a field to face [trim by cutting back growth] a hedge and when he got his ten o'clock tea he disappeared after it. Then the following Thursday I went to Newry again and I hired a boy and when I had hired him and all, a man come over till 'im and asked 'im what he was gettin'. He says 'Thirteen poun'.' An' the man says, 'If I'd seen you sooner, I'd a give you fourteen.'

And he says, 'You're not too late yit. I'll take fourteen.' So Dickey lost him. The other man knowed this lad you see, and he gave him fourteen. So Dickey toul me, 'I'll give you fifteen.'

'I'll be here on Thursday week,' I says.

'We're a bit stuck for a man here and I want this place white-washed an' cleaned up, for it wasn't done this couple of years,' he says. An' the oul man turned out to be great crack. So I stopped wi' Dickey six months an' I lived in a loft outside. That was the usual. You would put a bit of a boord [board] in a corner and they gave you a bit of a blind and that was your wardrobe. I put it up myself. You had a wee lookin' glass. It was the same everywhere. I hardly ever slept in a house.

Then dang it, I got word that Hugh Stockman wanted to see me and I went up this Saturday night. I had just about a fortnight to do at Dickey's and when I went up Stockman was choppin' sticks on the street in the dark. He had a hurricane lamp. And he shouts at me, 'Who's there?' And he says to me, 'You're wi' Dickey. I wonder would you come to me next term.'

I says, 'I've already toul Dickey I'm l'avin' [leaving]. I'll change to anywhere. I always worked at the cattle trade.' Dickeys, d'ye see, daled in cattle too. The oul fella daled in cattle and Tommy daled in horses. Tommy would go to the Moy fair and he might buy three or four horses, maybe buy a young horse and break it in. Ah, Tommy was a tight fella.

Mrs Stockman – she was a Bradbury from The Maze. Her brother had a brickyard there: Johnny Bradbury. Hugh's father owned the Racecourse Farm but when Hugh got married he bought a house and land on the Antrim Road in Lisburn, but he still daled in cattle. Anyway Stockman used to say to me, 'I'll be away now in Cavan next week, Paddy. If anybody's lookin' me I'll not be home 'til Friday night.'

A man called McGurnaghan come to me and said, 'The first wee heifer you get, tell Hugh to send her out, and I've two springin' heifers here for him. God, this wee heifer come in – she was a lovely wee heifer, not too big, and she was calved. And Stockman says to me, 'I gave £18 for that heifer. Tell McGurnaghan she'll be nineteen. If she's not suitable have her back here on Monday night and I'll take her to Allams on Tuesday.'

So anyway I set off (to McGurnaghans) wi' this wee heifer on a rope. McGurnaghan took an awful time walkin' roun' her. I says to him at the last, 'Do you want to draw [try milking] that heifer or not?'

He says, 'She's not here (his sister) to draw her, an' she would want to see her milked. I don't think I'll have her.'

'Then,' says I, 'If you don't like her there's no use in botherin'. There's no use in you an' me lossin' [wasting] our time.' I'd both seen him and heered him and I'd come to the conclusion that he wasn't interested. Says I, 'Who knows what time that sister of yours'll be home. I think we'll call it a day.'

At the heels of the hunt Isaac Logan bought her. He was another dealer – daled in store cattle – and he toul me to l'ave her up with another farmer called Dan McCann.

McCann says to me, 'Do you work for Stockman?'

'I do,' says I.

'I was lookin' a couple of dropped [newborn] calves,' says he.

'If you come the morra there's four or five thonder,' says I. Dammit he landed up the next day and he says, 'I think I'll look at these calves.' He went into the house that they were in, and he says, 'What price are they?' Says I, 'The heifer calves is twenty-five shillin's and the bull calves is a poun' and you can take your pick.' He went into the house and chased them out (to get a better look at them) – three bulls and two heifers. 'Will you take five poun' for the lot?' says he. Says I, 'I will not. It's not enough.'

'What will they be?' says he.

'There's two heifer calves there and they'll be fifty shillin's and the bulls'll be poun's apiece [each].' says I. He looked at them again and he thought and he says, 'Aren't they dear?'

'Now,' says I, 'If you think they're dear, don't you take them because,' says I, 'they'll be sowl [sold].' And wi' that another man walked into the yard and says, 'Have ye' any calves?" And McCann spoke up and he says, 'No, they're sold.'

Says I to the second man, 'Don't you go away for a minute now,' an' we went into the byre and there was a cow calvin'. So I says, 'You're not far aff your pad yet. There's a cow calvin' there. You'll not be able to take it wi' ye the day but if it's a livin' calf you'll get it.'

Then McCann said, 'What way'll I take these?'

'Have you any bags?' says I.

' Aye,' says he, 'but they're only 'hundred' [hundredweight] bags. You couldn't put them calves into 'hundred' bags.'

'Now,' says I, 'If you have the bags I'll put them intil it.' So he went till the car and he came in wi' five or six 'hundred' bags and I put them in an' tied them roun' the neck. He says to me, 'I worked wi' cattle for ages an' I never seen a calf in a bag before.'

'Well, I tell ye,' says I, 'If I had a shillin' for every one I put intil a bag, me an' you could have a quare night's drinkin' the night. I'll tell you that.' He says, 'I never seen them in a 'hundred' bag before.'

'That's the way they nearly all l'ave here,' I says. So we put them intil the car, a couple in the boot and some inside on the back seat. They couldn't come to any harm. He would be home in twenty minutes anyway.

I was at Stockman's thirteen and a half years. Stockman was a real cow daler. He even bought for a dealer in England called Myles Broadbent. I left there then and went to John Mercer in Hillhall, then Charlie Stewart in the Moira Road, Hill Stewart, Clifford Boyd in Hillsborough, Wrights in the Old Hillsborough Road – I suppose I was thirty years round Lisburn and Hillsborough – travellin' round Flatfield, Hillhall, Broomhedge, The Maze. There's not a part of it I don't know. You know I done a helluva hirin' in my time!

Although far behind Newry in size and importance Banbridge, as well as being an important linen town, had good markets, fairs and hiring fairs. Under a patent dated 1767 the Marquis of Downshire had power to hold a weekly market and five fairs annually. However it is certain fairs were held there before that date. In those days the market house stood in the middle of the main thoroughfare but it was demolished in 1834 to make way for the cutting linking Bridge Street and Newry Street. A new market house was then built by the Marquis at the corner of Scarva Street and Bridge Street. Butter and eggs were sold nearby. The general market was in Victoria Street.

The market rights were transferred to Town Commissioners in 1881 when the markets for pork, flax, grass seed, fowl, butter, eggs, hay, straw, grain and turnips were taken off the streets and moved to more suitable sites within the town. Eggs, pork and butter were bought by dealers and transported to Belfast in carts for export to England. Cattle and sheep were sold on the first Monday of every month and a day was set aside in the months of January, April, June, August and November for the sale of cattle and horses only. Banbridge was known far and wide for the quality of its horses, being second only in importance to Moy. Two thousand horses were sold there during 1834, together with three thousand cows, six thousand pigs and two thousand sheep. Many of Belfast's working horses were purchased in Banbridge. Just before World War I foreign horse dealers were seen at Banbridge and other fairs. One, a German called Vanderbelt, would sometimes buy as many as six hundred horses and ship them back to Germany which was at that time preparing for war. No one seemed to notice that he was buying up all the best horses or to realise that these would be used amongst other things for pulling cannons.

For around a century Banbridge's poor were looked after in the workhouse in Linenhall Street. They both grew and consumed the vegetables produced in the eleven acres of land surrounding it. At one time they wove coarse cloth, no doubt also for 'home' use.

Newtownards was another good market town. It was founded by Sir Hugh Montgomery in 1606 at which time 'there was not a cabin in or about the place'. Fairs were established and a market house built around this time. The original market house and fair green were situated just beyond the old Town Cross near to Hugh Montgomery's house. The cross bears the Montgomery Coat of Arms and the date '1636' – also the Arms of other leading families of the day. What we see today is really only the pedestal of the cross in the shape of a small octagonal building which once served as a chamber for the Watch, and as a repository for the safe-keeping of the drunk and disorderly. It has a weather vane on top surmounted by a lion.

A market cross was a focal point in any town and was used not only for making promises and sealing bargains but also as a platform for making announcements of interest to the townspeople. When Charles II was proclaimed king for instance, it was announced in Newtownards from the market cross. According to legend claret flowed from the spouts around it in celebration. Trumpets and drums sounded too and bonfires were lit in the streets that night. Market crosses existed in a number of places (Dromore, Limavady and Coleraine, for instance), but Newtownards has the only one of its kind to survive. The town suffered as a market town from its proximity to Belfast. To overcome this, co-operative shops were set up around 1800 to encourage people to spend their money locally. One hundred people invested £1 each in the co-operative to sell the commodity of their choice – groceries, delph, etc. People were appointed to do the selling, and profits were distributed half-yearly. The shops were regulated by 'people of respectability and clergymen of different denominations.'

A few years later Newtownards was described as 'a neat town, generally clean, although neither watched, paved, lighted or cleansed.' The present town hall (once the market house) dates from around 1763. It is a handsome building at the north end of the Square. Its eastern end was once used as a potato and grain store and the western end for the sale of fresh meat. The weekly market has always been held on Saturday. Fairs at which horses and black cattle were sold were held on the second Saturday of each month throughout the nineteenth century and beyond. In addition three old fairs were held in January, May and September. Hiring died out in the town shortly after World War I though normal markets and fairs continued for many years. Although two out of three families were at that time spinning and weaving, the cloth produced was used at home and there was no linen market in the town. Anyone with surplus cloth took it to Belfast. However, as in Banbridge, Newry and many other towns, the workhouse offered boys training in agriculture on the workhouse land and doubtless some of them eventually found work on farms in the area. Others received instruction in tailoring and cobbling, as did able-bodied paupers. Girls were taught knitting, sewing and other domestic tasks.

Comber had four fairs but no market or market house throughout most of the eighteenth and nineteenth centuries. However stall holders of some kind must have turned up at fairs, for they were charged fourpence halfpenny for an open stall and sixpence for a covered one according to the Ordnance Surveyor of the 1830s. Tolls ranging from twopence for a sheep or pig to sixpence for a horse were also charged. At that time the Comber area was regarded as good corn and flax country and there were numerous mills throughout the countryside. A report was published in the *Northern Whig* following a tour of inspection by a Peter Barnard in 1823. It stated: 'In no part of Ireland or the Netherlands that I have visited have I seen flax in the field of so good quality as that grown in the immediate neighbourhood of Comber.'

By the end of the century the town had monthly fairs and a market for hay, straw and potatoes but efforts to establish a general market did not succeed. The fairs reduced to four again

Old cross, Newtownards.

Market Day in Newtownards. The cart is loaded with potato baskets.

sometime between the two World Wars. By then farmers were marketing their produce in Belfast. It would seem however that the town once had a market for yarn – according to words once penned by an unknown poet:

A maid goin' to Comber her markets to l'arn,
To sell for her mammy three hanks o' fine yarn,
She met with a young man along the high-way
Which caused this young damsel to dally and stray.

"Sit ye beside me, I mean you no harm,
Sit ye beside me, this new tune to l'arn,
Here is three guineas your mammy to pay,
So lay by your yarn 'til the next market day."

They sat down the-gither, the grass it was green
And the day was the fairest that ever was seen,
"Oh the look in your eye beats a mornin' in May"
"I could sit by your side 'til the next market-day."

Many seaside towns were market towns too – Kilkeel and Warrenpoint for instance had markets and fairs throughout the nineteenth- and into the twentieth century. In Kilkeel the action took

Market Square in Comber. The group on the left are striking a deal over a horse.

93

place in the Market Square and from there to the market house in Kilmorey Square. Cattle, sheep and other animals lined Greencastle Street as far as Mourne Presbyterian Church on the last Wednesday in every month which was Fair Day in the town. General farm produce such as potatoes, oats and flax were sold in the markets. There was also a market for brown linen. Customers came mainly from the local area.

Warrenpoint on the other hand attracted people from Armagh, Louth and Down (anything up to six thousand in summer) and the scene of activity was the Square and Duke Street. Much of the produce was bought by agents who exported it to Liverpool via the steamers belonging to the town's port, which had developed during the eighteenth century and was used for the export of cattle, poultry, eggs and oysters. The harbour at Kilkeel was used extensively for exporting potatoes, oats, native timber and granite. The main import at both places was coal. Like Bangor, Warrenpoint had one of the earliest farming societies (formed in the 1830s) which met once a year to organise a ploughing match, cattle show and grain show. Rostrevor and Dundrum had good fairs too which were held continuously from the seventeenth- to the twentieth century. In the case of Dundrum they probably began with the Normans in the twelfth century. Dundrum was also noted for its Great Markets.

However, none of these compared with the great fair at Greencastle. 'The Ram Fair', as it was called, is thought to have started in Pagan times, was revived by the Normans in the twelfth century and again by Arthur Bagnal under patent granted by James I in 1613. There were, for a time, two in the year, the main one being held on 12 August. All roads led to the fair, and the sea also was dotted with

Norman Keep, Greencastle. Fairs were held nearby.

© Green Collection, Ulster Folk and Transport Museum

boats and yawls coming from the Louth shores. The custom of enthroning a ram on the castle walls as a symbol of the fair and giving him the title 'King of the Benns' was introduced by the Normans and kept up until Greencastle's fairs ceased early in the twentieth century. From his vantage point no doubt the ram could see the extent of the fair, which was said to stretch for miles in every direction. To farmers the main business of the day was that of selling their animals. In the old days a grassy plain stretched along the shore and this provided the 'green'. Nowadays a narrow lane called Fair Road leads down to the beach and what is left of the old fair green.

The setting was idyllic with the Carlingford mountains across the lough on one side and the backdrop of the Mournes on the other. The people arrived from day-break, mainly on foot but also in farm carts, donkey carts and any other mode of transport they could find, bringing with them geese, ducks, hens, turkeys, baskets of eggs and so on. They were joined by vendors of such things as noggins, trenchers, churns, butter pats and wooden spoons; also the inevitable large quantities of whiskey and poteen. There were tents galore, almost all of them with a 'resident' piper, fiddler or fifer. Prizes were given for the best dancers of jigs, reels and hornpipes. There were fortune-tellers, jugglers, and performers of every description to distract and entertain all day long. And always the sound of music was in the air as the young folk danced the hours away.

Who has e'er had the luck to see Greencastle fair
A Mourne man all in his glory was there.

The Ards Peninsula had its own market towns. Most of them (with the exception of Carrowdore) were also ports of varying degrees of importance. Portaferry had the best markets. Donaghadee was the busiest port. Others included Kircubbin, Greyabbey and Ballywalter.

Portaferry had excellent fairs and for a short time a small linen market. In addition to the monthly fairs held on the second Tuesday of each month it had two patent fairs dating back to the seventeenth century. They were held on the last day of July and the first day of December.

In those days it was the custom in Portaferry to pay £1 premium to the person who brought the last horse to the fair. Smaller premiums were paid to the person who brought the last sheep, cow and pig. No doubt many farmers and buyers came from the Strangford side of the lough, for a ferry was making the journey back and forth thirty times a day as far back as 1837. Fares ranged from one- to threepence. About a mile north of the town there was a quay which was often used as a safe harbour for vessels travelling between Belfast and Dublin.

Kircubbin's markets began in the latter half of the eighteenth century thanks to the Right Honourable Robert Ward who encouraged trade and built a market house in 1795. However although it had fortnightly markets and quarterly fairs, the village at that time was better known for its straw bonnets than its agriculture. The straw was brought by boat from England and the finished bonnets were exported to England, Belfast and Dublin. Women also did flowering (embroidery), this work being imported from Scotland. By the middle of the nineteenth century twelve additional fairs had been established and were held regularly on the first Monday of the month until well into the twentieth. By then the main exports were grain, beans and potatoes and the imports were coal, salt and Indian corn.

The ruins of the abbey founded for Cistercian monks by Affreca, wife of John de Courcy in 1192 proclaim the ancient origins of Greyabbey. The first Plantation owner was James Hamilton who acquired the lands in a grant from James I early in the seventeenth century. James also

Donaghadee Harbour, once used extensively for shipping cattle to the mainland.

granted a port to Greyabbey 'with pilotage, anchorage, keelage and other privileges'. However an insufficiency of water decreed that the port was little used except by a few sloops discharging coal onto carts. Fairs established at that time survived to the end of the nineteenth century but were never considered of much importance.

Places like Ballywalter, Carrowdore, Donaghadee and Bangor had fairs too though never more than two in the year. Thousands of cattle and horses were exported through Donaghadee except for a period at the end of the seventeenth- and beginning of the eighteenth century when Charles II placed an embargo on the import of Irish cattle into England. Donaghadee was a favourite point of departure. From there a short sea crossing brought them to Portpatrick and dealers were quite prepared to do business in such towns as New Galloway and Dumfries as they passed through on their way to Carlisle. In 1790 over 17,000 beasts were carried across to Portpatrick, mainly cattle but including horses and other animals, together with a considerable number of passengers. Some departed from other ports such as Bangor. Bangor also had a sizeable livestock trade and their usual destination was Portpatrick. Passengers used to complain about the smell of the animals which travelled on the same boat.

Holywood was said 'to have the advantage of the short distance to Belfast where there is always a ready market.' Places like Knockbreda and Ballymacarrett, then mere villages, fell into the same category. Holywood once had four fairs held on the first Monday of February, May,

August and November at which the usual farm animals were sold, though the fairs were said by the surveyor of the 1830s 'to be held more for pleasure than business.'

Downpatrick, once known as Rathkeltair, was a place of considerable importance. Saint Patrick arrived there in the year 432 and founded the abbey which over the centuries has been plundered and attacked time and time again. The town was also attacked by John de Courcy in the twelfth century at which time it was described as but a collection of wattle and daub dwellings grouped round a monastery on a hill. Its markets almost certainly date back to that time, for coins minted in Downpatrick and bearing de Courcy's name have been found. The broken cross at the Cathedral is thought to have once stood near the market house at the centre of the town. If so, it is probably the remains of a market cross – another indication that markets existed in Downpatrick before the Plantation. It was at the market cross in Downpatrick that Edward Bruce proclaimed himself king in 1315. However he was defeated and slain in battle at Dundalk within three years.

The town has always depended largely on the wants and needs of farmers. Hundreds found employment in weaving. The linen woven in the area was marketed in the town itself. In the early years it had four fairs one of which was held on Saint Patrick's Day. By 1837 there were six, held in January, March, May, June, October and November. Later they increased to twelve and then to thirteen, with two being held in the month of May when farmers needed extra cattle to eat the grass which was always lush at that time of year. Tolls in the early days were due to the Lord of the Manor who had been granted the patent to hold them. Sixpence had to be paid by anyone with a covered stall and fourpence for a stall belonging to a hatter, shoemaker or broguemaker. Fourpence was also the toll due on a pack of wool, sack of apples, load of earthenware, carcass of beef, cow, ox, bull, mare or horse. Twopence was charged on hogs and swine. The charge was one penny to anyone selling a web of woollen cloth, a hide, cake of tallow, crock of butter, load of cheese, fish, soap, oysters, lemons or timber. The sale of a lamb or a web of drugget cost a ha'penny. On week-days (as opposed to fair days) the tolls were greatly reduced. By the end of the nineteenth century these charges had disappeared and the markets improved accordingly. There was also by then a fair green on which fairs were held once a month. Boats could navigate the Quoile almost to the town, but with difficulty, and most chose to use a quay about a mile downstream. Potatoes and grain were exported; timber, coal and slates imported. Lime was brought by sea from Larne and often as not sold at the quayside.

A few miles north of Downpatrick lay the village of Kilmore where four fairs were held annually. However by the early 1800s these had died out and it was described as 'a wretched place containing a Roman Catholic chapel and thirty-five houses, four of them almost ruins'. Nearby Crossgar however was by this time clearly 'on the up' thanks to the efforts of a Mr Thompson who then owned it. In 1829 Thompson built a market house and established weekly markets and monthly fairs where cattle and all general commodities were offered for sale. The lower part of the market house was used for weighing and the upper part as a carpenter's shop and grain store. The fairs flourished and were held regularly until the middle of the twentieth century. Crossgar's markets were noted for the quality of the butter, eggs and fowl sold at them.

Of the remaining towns Killyleagh, Dromore, Castlewellan, Rathfriland and Ballynahinch all had fairs. Most had four in the early years, increasing to twelve in the nineteenth century, except Killyleagh which had never more than four at any time. All had hiring fairs. Killyleagh had a busy harbour through which butter, grain and potatoes were exported. Coal, lime and timber were imported. The town had just two hiring fairs in the year held on the eleventh days of April and October. They stopped years ago (according to G.H. Bassett in 1886) because 'there was too much drinking and fighting and not enough people wanting to hire'. It is likely that young people were by then finding employment in the town's two spinning mills and earning more than the few pounds that farm servants were earning at that time for six months work.

Dromore (according to the manuscript notes of Harris's *History of Down*) had in 1557 no buildings, only some old thatched houses and a ruined church. Part of the town's old tenth-century cross was at that time being used as a seat for the stocks. The church was later rebuilt and the cross returned to the vicinity of the church where it had originally stood as a market cross. Dromore was one of a number of places to be granted permission in the seventeenth century to hold a Saturday market and Bishop's Fairs near the cathedral 'where the great cross now stands.' A bishop in those days had wide-ranging powers. He could appoint coroners and clerks of the market. He could collect market tolls and establish Courts of Piepowder to enforce fair practice in trading. He had the right of 'pillory, tumbrell and thewr'.

By 1821 the town had 363 inhabited houses (mainly thatched) and a population of 1,860. The Lagan provided the power for a number of mills and as elsewhere in the province linen

Creighton's flax mill on the Lagan above Dromore. Inset: The old stocks of Dromore were once used to enforce fair practice in trade.

'Old Ulster' pig for sale – Castlewellan fair.

was woven in hundreds of individual homes. The Market Square had a court house with a market house underneath in which meal and potatoes were sold, and shambles nearby for the sale of meat. By 1885 there was a new market place and a new town hall. Markets were held on Wednesdays and Saturdays and there was a fair on the second Saturday of each month. Dromore was by this time a manufacturing town with up to a dozen factories giving employment to hundreds of women and girls. There would have been few women seeking work at that time in the town's two hiring fairs.

Castlewellan was famous over the years for its sheep and cattle fairs which attracted butchers from as far away as Belfast. It once had a small market in brown linen and linen yarns as well as the usual farm produce. Hiring fairs were held on the first days of May and November when prospective hirelings could be seen standing at the market house. According to tradition, Maggie's Leap outside Newcastle was named after a girl who jumped across the chasm on her way to market with a basket of eggs on her head. There were no markets in Newcastle so presumably Maggie was taking her eggs to either Castlewellan or Dundrum. Good monthly fairs were also held at Mayobridge and Hilltown from about 1850 onwards.

Courtesy of Terry Eakin

An auction takes place in 1906 in Rathfriland. The building central to the picture was the market house.

Rathfriland was once one of the best inland market towns in Ulster. All approach roads led uphill to the Market House and weighbridge in Church Square. Each item of produce arrived on its allotted day – pork, oats and grass seed on Tuesday, flax and fowl on Wednesday and so on. The first Wednesday in each month was also the fair day and at the appropriate time it was hiring day as well. On that day a collection of sheep, cattle, donkeys, goats and dogs arrived into the town (on foot) and before long the dealing began. It was a serious business culminating in the words 'Houl out yer han', signifying that a deal had been made. The handing over of a luck penny and the sound of smacking palms completed the transaction. Looking at them it was hard to believe that those farmers had probably left home at about three in the morning and walked twenty miles or more, depending on the waywardness of their animals as they passed field gaps and road ends along the way. Poultry arrived quietly, lying in twos in the bottom of a cart with their legs tied. Ducks protested occasionally usually by quacking loudly in chorus. A dealer from Ardglass appeared on market day and sold herrings from a spring-cart. His voice could be heard above the general din 'Herns alive. Herns alive. Alive an' kickin'. Sixpence a dozen an' an extra one for the cat. Herns alive.' There were all the usual stalls too and a handful of pedlars, musicians and tramps making the most of the opportunities the fair offered.

No town enjoyed its markets and fairs as much as Ballynahinch. Every street had its scene of bustling activity. Cattle and sheep were sold at the fair green, pigs appropriately in Pig Street

100

and beside Smylie's pub in Meeting Street. Horses went to Dromore Street. The October fair brought droves of foals and 'six-quarter-olds' (aged eighteen months). The latter were broken approximately a year later. There were good young horses too, old horses and shelties. Farmers came long distances to the November fair to sell a few cattle and buy a horse for ploughing. When the month of May came round, that horse was sold and calves bought to eat the grass during the growing season. This cycle continued year after year. The price of the horse bought the calves and the price of the calves bought the horse with hopefully a few shillings profit made at each deal.

One dealer from Loughinisland wouldn't have missed Ballynahinch fair for anything. On one occasion he took pigs to Ballynahinch market and ended up forgetting about the pigs and selling his horse.

I daled in horses back an' forrad you see. (About 1940) I'd brought a litter of pigs into Ballynahinch – suckers [just-weaned piglets] – and I loosed the horse out of the spring-cart up at the market you see. Well I came down to James Cardwell's yard to put the horse in and this fella stopped me and he says to me, 'Boy, would you sell that horse?'

Says I, 'I would certainly.'

'Well,' he says, 'I'll be back in ten minutes. There's a man'll buy this horse aff ye.' So I put the horse in the yard and just had all done when him and this other man landed. He says to the other man, 'That's the horse and I think he's a good enough horse.'

'Arthur, now that's a good enough horse definitely,' I says. 'I can stan' over him.'

'Well,' the other man says, 'What do you want?'

I says, 'I want sixty-five poun' for him.'

He says, 'Would sixty not do you?'

'No, it would not. No.'

We argued a while and then Arthur says, 'Jack, you may divide that fiver with him.'

Then I remembered. Says I, 'Listen now. I have a litter of pigs to sell and I've the spring-cart with me.'

'Well,' Arthur says, 'That's all right. In that case we'll lift the horse the morra mornin'.'

And Arthur went away aff and this man says, 'Come on an' we'll get a bottle o' Guinness here.' And James Cardwell had a wee back room. And we were maybe fifteen minutes. We had a drink or two an then another one. And another one. And there was a boy come runnin' in. Says he, 'You're a-wantin' up the street badly. There's a man stannin' waitin' on you.' So up I went an' this man says to me, 'Wait 'til I see yer man. Bringin' pigs intil Ballynahinch an' goin' to a pub an' drinkin'.' I says, 'Listen. I've the horse sold an' I can sell the pigs.' So I did too.

Then one Saturday mornin' I went to look at this black horse. And a helluva good horse he was. I says, 'Is he a good working horse?' He says, 'He is. He come out of a hearse in Rathfriland.' And a good horse he was. I kept him three months and then I sold him till a farmer outside Ballynahinch. Edward Carlisle they called him. He was a dalin' man too. And the next thing happened was about a month after it oul Billy Poole in Ballynahinch – he was an undertaker – he called me into the bar.

He says, ' Come in here boy. I want to speak to you boy.'

Says I, ' What's wrong?' I knew he was angry you see. He says, 'What was wrong that you couldn't a toul me you had the black horse? We have a horse here that's goin' 'down the hill' a bit, an' when I heered about you sellin' that horse till Eddie Carlisle – a black horse! And when I foun' out where he come from!'

I says, 'Listen. I didn't know anything about the horse. The only thing I was told about the horse: he come out of a hearse, a place in Rathfriland; a place where they were givin' up the business.'

He says, 'I woulda give you any money for that horse if you'd asked me!' It took two black horses to pull a hearse you see.

Hiring in Ballynahinch took place in the Market Square; also in Railway Street and in later years beside the war memorial, the crowd often spilling over into other streets. The hirelings were easy to pick out with their shabby clothes and well-worn boots. Farmers on the other hand often wore britches, leggings, a collar-less shirt fastened at the neck with a stud, long overcoat and soft felt or hard hat. By mid-afternoon farmers were on their way home. The atmosphere became noisier and jollier as the evening wore on. Drunkenness and fights were common. A newspaper report of 1938 headed '*Court Cases in Ballynahinch*' tells of two brothers from Annsborough who were charged with being drunk in charge of a horse and cart on their way home from the fair. A police sergeant heard the horse coming at an unusually fast rate. He discovered the driver leaning in a recumbent position over the reins and paying no attention whatsoever to the horse on the road. Another occupant in the cart was lying back with his legs dangling over the tailboard. The driver said he had had four half-uns (hot) that day. He wanted a drop more when he reached the Barrack. He was fined forty shillings and his brother was fined fifteen shillings. There were also prosecutions that day for illegal betting, selling sausages containing too much preservative, poor school attendance and drinking meths. The meths drinker denied the charges stating that he had bought the meths to rub on a cow's udder. He had got drunk he said on a five naggin bottle of wine!

Killinchy had one of the smaller fairs. Those held in 1837 were described as being 'badly attended and scarcely any cattle bought or sold.' The dates on which they were held coincided with the quarterly and half-yearly hiring fairs so they may originally have been held for that purpose. Long ago the people of Killinchy burnt kelp and sent it to Liverpool where it sold at three to nine pounds a ton depending on quality. Most of the produce of the area however, including fish, wheat and oats, was marketed in Belfast. Oysters were sent to Lisburn where they fetched one shilling and sixpence a hundred-weight. Killinchy's fairs had almost died out by the end of the nineteenth century.

Not so in Saintfield, which always had good fairs. The town started off with six increasing to twelve throughout the nineteenth century and into the twentieth. On the last Wednesday of every month blue and orange painted carts containing litters of pigs arrived into the town and parked, up-ended, at the bottom end of the wide main street. The pigs were displayed in a box beside the cart. Horses were sold at the upper end and were put through their paces in the roadway. In its heyday (at the turn of the twentieth century) buyers came from the United Kingdom, France and Austria in the knowledge that they could buy a good horse in Saintfield. Cattle and sheep were bought and sold around the corner on the fair green. Hiring took place at the fair green too. Shops were kept busy especially that of Minnis Bros. which was ideally situated about half-way along the main street. Frank Minnis sold feeding stuffs, groceries, hardware and other household items of interest to farmers and their wives. In 1886 Frank was also performing the duties of postmaster. At one time there was a horse thresher and corn mill behind the shop premises offering yet another service to the farming community.

Several blacksmiths, drapers, grocers, butchers, coal merchants and nine spirit retailers made up the bulk of the other businesses in the town, together with a saddler, an auctioneer, a boot and leather merchant, a hotel keeper, a watchmaker and two newsagents. At M.M. Priestley & Sons you could have bought anything from a hat to a garden shed or artificial manure. If you needed the services of an undertaker he could have supplied you with a one, two or four horse hearse; an oak, birch or black coffin, a shoulder scarf, mourning band, ribbons and gloves. The R.I.C. Barracks was staffed by Sergeant Loftus and four constables. Three physicians cared for the sick while five clergymen and a priest looked after the souls of the folk in the surrounding countryside – together with the 769 villagers counted in the census of 1881.

Many other villages enjoyed success too. Most had fairs and markets at some stage over the years. It is likely that hiring took place at some of them. The more important ones were held at Dromara and Hillsborough – also in the west of the county at Moira, Gilford, Scarva and Loughbrickland. Most of these had charters from an early date. *Watson's Almanac* records that Scarva and Loughbrickland held fairs in 1745. Hillsborough and Dromara are not mentioned although Moyses Hill had been granted permission to hold fairs in these places more than a century before. His charter allowed him to have a market every Wednesday in Hillsborough and a monthly fair from March until November; also a fair at Annesbury (Dromara), with tolls and profits. He was to appoint a corporation in Hillsborough consisting of a sovereign and twelve burgesses and freemen. The corporation was to have power to appoint as many freemen as it thought proper, taking five shillings from each. The aforementioned burgesses and freemen had permission to make and sell wine without licence and the liberty to tan leather within the borough. The territory mentioned was formerly owned by the Magennis family but forfeited by them after their part in the rebellion of 1641. Loss of territory was to be expected in such circumstances.

Loughbrickland, Scarva, Gilford and Moira can all lay claim to having been market towns and had fairs at some stage in their history. Those at Loughbrickland did not survive the eighteenth century. Scarva held fairs (but never more than four) which prospered from the seventeenth to the twentieth centuries. Moira also had four and a good market which died out around 1880. Although the markets ceased, fairs continued in both places until the twentieth century. Both benefited throughout the years from nearby canal and rail transport. The main cargoes were farm produce and fuel (generally peat in one direction, coal in the other); also lime in the case of Moira.

Although Gilford had a weekly market and twelve fairs in the second half of the nineteenth century they died out when farmers began to take their produce to the more prosperous markets in Portadown and Banbridge. Large numbers of cattle were sold in Dromara while cattle, pigs, sheep and a few horses were at one time sold in Hillsborough. Fairs continued in both places until well into the twentieth century. Local farmer Morgan Greer reminisces:

In Hillsborough the fair was held at the top of the main street and round the corner as far as Park Street. You brought maybe five or six cattle and turned them to face the wall opposite the Shambles, mostly stores around a year old. Dealers – they would have helped each other. One fellow would have bid you so much. Then another would have bid you

The junction of the Lisburn and Ballynahinch Roads in Hillsborough around 1924.

© Irish Linen Centre and Lisburn Museum Collection

so much less and tried to convince you that you were asking too much to make you bring the price down.

Cattle made an awful mess on the street especially at the time of year when they were coming off the grass. It would have been up the walls and everywhere! There was a surveyor lived at the top of the street – Sam Stewart I think he was called. He used to keep his place very tidy. He used to put out barrels with planks across to keep beasts away from his door. But once Allam's got going in Belfast that was the beginning of the end for country fairs. That was about the 1920s. Allams would have been selling cattle 'til nine and ten at night. People were a long time 'til they accepted the change but it came eventually.

Dromara had a market for linen yarn and Hillsborough a small linen market at the turn of the nineteenth century. Dromara's market was celebrated for its butter which was bought by dealers, taken to Belfast and exported to Liverpool. Hillsborough market was never really successful owing to the nearness of Lisburn and ceased altogether sometime before 1880. Fairs were held in both towns until the outbreak of the 1939-45 war. It had a good potato market for a number of years but eventually that too ceased. The Hill family had a reputation for generosity. They never collected tolls in any of their villages. At one time Hillsborough had an estate office where eighty thousand pounds in rents crossed the counter every year. Much of this was passed back to the tenants in wages and charity.

Dromara did not have the luxury of a hotel but Hillsborough was on the coach route to Dublin and post horses, chaises and cars could be obtained at the Corporation Arms (later called the Royal Corporation) at the top of the Main Street. The market house was close by in the Square and the Shambles was only a matter of yards away on the Dromore side of the village. The countryside round about was good farming land and most farmers kept hired help.

Matt Kelly was destined to settle in the Hillsborough area though he had never ever intended working on a farm and he was to work at a number of other jobs first. His first job on leaving school was feeding flax into the crimpers in a flax mill but that ended when the mill closed down. Work was hard to find in the 1920s and he was lucky to be offered a job in a corn mill, even if it was only shovelling the hulls into the furnace that dried the corn. That ended when he decided to go to a football match one Saturday afternoon instead of turning up for work. After that there was nothing for it but to try his luck in a hiring fair. Matt takes up the story:

> I was just sixteen at the time. The quarterly fair was coming up in February. I got my bundle under my arm and walked it to Newry. It was a big come-down. It meant sleeping away from home for the first time and I didn't fancy it. I hired that day with a man called Joe Dodds at three poun' for three months and went home with him that day in the cart.

Tea in the corn field. The machine shown is a binder which cut the corn and tied it into sheaves - a big advance on the old mowing machine. From left: Derek Gilmore, Ernest Brown, William James Blair, Albert Branagh, Isaac Patterson.

Courtesy of J.E. Blair

He was a Protestant and I was a Catholic. I asked him, 'Will I get to Mass of a Sunday?'

'That's all right,' he said. He lived at a place called Desert about five mile out of Newry. He had about twenty or thirty acres af land and kep' two horses. At that time he was considered a big farmer. He was a very decent man and a sergeant in the B Specials. I had my own room in the house with an iron bed-stead and a feather mattress and a good bolster to put my head on. On the first morning I tidied myself to go to Sheeptown Chapel. I was just going out the door when Joe called out in a sharp voice, 'Where are you going, boy?'

'I'm going to Mass, Joe.'

'Come back here. You're not going out of Joe Dodds's house that way. You know where the polish is. Get them boots cleaned.' That was the sort of Joe Dodds. He didn't want anybody going from his house that didn't look respectable. Anyway I stayed there just three months. I wasn't getting enough money so back I went to the May hiring.

Matt was typical of most hired workers in that he made the most of whatever situation he found himself in, realising that it would be foolish to bite the hand that fed him. He hired at several places after that, some good and some bad. At one place he had the temerity to mention that the porridge was too thin for him to sup. The next morning he could stand his spoon up in it. At another the bedclothes weren't changed during the six months he was there. At yet another he could see the stars through the roof of the barn as he lay in bed. However, he was usually so tired that he slept soundly even when the rain poured in.

It was a different story when he hired at Hayes's at Soldierstown, for there the servant men had their own room above the kitchen and Gertie the maid attended to the beds every day. Matt had never in his life seen such luxury. He knew he was in a gentleman's residence when he saw, for the first time in his life, a chamber pot under the bed. Not that he would have dreamt of using it! He continues:

It was a lovely place. There were just the two of us staying at the time though there was another man who lived with his wife in a house in the yard. The household consisted of old Mr Hayes – he was a big hefty man – and his son Dick who was very tall. Then there was an old uncle who used to give me after-shave.

It was just a general farm with cows and bullocks and lots of pigs. I remember makin' hay at it – tossin' it up with a fork, then puttin' it into laps or rucks. When it was ready it was brought into the stack-yard on the ruck-shifter. Then in the middle of the yard there was what they called the round-house. It was a covered-in place and the horses used to walk round it. That was where the thrashin' was done. Och, I liked Hayes's – but I didn't like the pigs. So I left.

I hired at a few other places in that part of the world but eventually found myself in Newry once more. The year was 1930 and it was to be the last time I hired at a fair. This time the man that came forward was from McKee's Dam outside Hillsborough. I was puzzled as to why the man was coming to speak to me for he had a lad with him that he had already hired. But he needed another lad for a neighbour, he said. I decided to give the neighbour a try. His name was Mercer – William (or Willie) Mercer. He lived with his widowed mother who was ill and couldn't do very much. He and I did the cookin', made the butter, took the eggs to market. He had just one horse and Wards, his cousins across the way, had three. I sometimes ploughed in Ward's field with Mercer's horse and one of their horses and then ploughed in Mercer's field with the same pair of horses. Man I just loved to take hold of the handles of the plough and walk behin' them two horses and the steam risin' off them at the start of a day's work. You always tried to make sure your furrow was clean and straight. You took pride in the way you did things them days.

After a time Mercer's hadn't enough work for me and I finished up working full-time for Wards. They were very good to me too. Old Granny Mercer (Mrs Ward's mother) used to darn my socks and do my washin' and there was no trouble about going to church or anything like that. Of course they were staunch Presbyterians and great churchgoers themselves, though two always stayed behind to look after the house and yard. You would have seen the other nine heading off to Hillsborough on bicycles every Sunday morning.

About that time I met a man called Sam McComb who taught me how to kill pigs. Sam's tools consisted of a kettle for the hot water, a stunning hammer, a set of knives and a sharpening steel. The steel always hung like a sword from his belt. The two of us killed pigs all over the country. One of the places we killed was at Jack McClure's. (It was Jack that hired me that day in Newry for Willie Mercer.) Jack worked on the railway but he would have killed four or five pigs at a time and kept one for the family to eat off all winter. Then I got to know his daughter Annie. The problem was – her father didn't allow her to go with boys so we had to meet in secret. He would have raised an awful row if he had found out. After a while Annie and me decided to get married. I borrowed £3 to have a suit made with a tailor in the Listullycurran Road. When I was shavin' on the mornin' we were to be married I was thinking about Annie. She was goin' on the bus to Lisburn Market with her eggs an' butter. I was wondering how I would face her father afterwards. The arrangement was that I would follow on the bicycle and we would meet Canon O'Boyle at the chapel at eleven o'clock. Everything went according to plan and we came home man and wife. Annie's father wasn't as cross as we expected. I suppose he could do nothing about it anyway. In the end Annie's father forgave us and gave us the piece of land to set up home but Annie was always afraid of him and quaked at the sound of his voice 'til the day he died.

One of the more unusual places to have a fair was at The Maze for the duration of the July races. In the good old days races were held every day for a week alternating with Downpatrick every second year. Those at The Maze were often attended by two of the warders of Hillsborough Fort – dressed in full regalia (white buckskin breeches and waistcoat, black gaiters, scarlet tunic and black cockade hat with a white plume). They made the journey on foot, passing the chapel known as Reilly's Trench, then taking to the towpath of the canal at Halliday's Bridge, exiting at Kesh Bridge and passing Maze Presbyterian Church and old schoolhouse on the last stage of their journey. The custom ceased sometime between the wars. In all probability their presence marked the attendance of members of the Downshire family or their guests at the races. This was a throwback to the days when a contingent of twenty Castlemen escorted the Downshires to church.

Bryansford, Narrow Water, Clough, Seaforde and Killough may be quiet today but all of these places had at least one fair around three hundred years ago. In those days Seaforde had six so it must have been as full of promise as a gold mine. They reduced to two at the end of the

Matt Kelly and Annie McClure around the time of their marriage.

nineteenth century and died out altogether soon after. Killough (then owned by Lord Bangor) had four and benefited from having a good pier from which oats, potatoes and wheat were exported for many years. Bryansford had never more than one fair at any time. The fairs at Narrow Water and Clough may have existed long before the others as each has a castle with 'roots' in the thirteenth century. The Duke of Ormond built the present castle at Narrow Water in 1663 on the site of an old castle built by Hugh de Lacy in 1212. It is surrounded by a bawn thought to have been built by the Magennis family, who occupied it in the centuries between. The most successful of all these fairs were at Clough which held one in 1938 long after the rest were no more.

To finish: a story about one of the county's most famous sons. Just beyond Hillsborough in the townland of Taughblane lived farmer Johnny Murphy who in 1938 purchased his first tractor – a wee grey Fergie. Johnny was ploughing one day when he became aware that he was being watched from the field gate. The stranger hurried to reach the head-rig first, holding up his hand in an authoritative way and indicating that he wanted Johnny to get off the tractor. It was none other than Harry Ferguson, who had stopped on his way home from his garage in Belfast to see how his latest customer was handling his new machine. Harry lost no time in jumping onto the tractor and ploughing a few yards before stopping to make a minor adjustment to the plough. He then continued to the other end of the field, turned with the skill of an expert and returned to where Johnny stood, giving him a few words of advice before proceeding to his father's farm at Growell near Dromore.

Courtesy of Robert Murphy

Johnny Murphy on the tractor on which Harry Ferguson demonstrated his ploughing skills. In this picture the tractor is fitted with spade wheels to give the tractor a better grip when moving the hen-house to fresh ground.

As he drove through the countryside Harry Ferguson might well have reflected on how long it had taken to mechanise such a fundamental industry as agriculture when the Industrial Revolution had taken place nearly a hundred years earlier. Incredibly his enormous contribution to the world of agriculture has never been fully recognised although a plaque marks the house where he was born.

BIRTH PLACE
OF
HARRY GEORGE FERGUSON
ENGINEER & INVENTOR
1884-1960

Courtesy of Joe Warnock

Birthplace of Harry Ferguson, Lake House, Growell, Dromore.

COUNTY FERMANAGH

In those days there wasn't any mode of travel as is today. A horse was used, and the bicycle was the main way of travellin'. If you managed to get to the stage where you were able to buy a new Raleigh bicycle at £5 you were looked upon as exceptional.

Tommy Ovens, Brookeborough

Fermanagh is virtually cut in two by the River Erne which links the two island-studded lakes of the same name. Of all the islands the best known is Devenish, with its round tower and other architectural remains. The central and most important town is Enniskillen but each district had its own towns and villages, all of them interesting in their own way.

To the west of the county lie the villages of Belleek and Garrison, one world famous for its fine Parian china, the other almost unknown except by the fishermen who fish the waters of Lough Melvin for trout. Other villages include Derrygonnelly, Monea and Churchill. The village of Churchill declined when the new mail coach road was built along the lough shore, as it was no longer on the main road from Enniskillen to Ballyshannon. All were once famous for their fairs, but while those at Monea and Churchill had been reduced to just one by the end of the nineteenth century, the others flourished and were still held monthly until fairs ceased in 1960.

The original Plantation families were the Humes and Dunbars who brought with them settlers from the Scottish borders. The Humes built their bawn and castle (Tully) and founded their village near the present village of Churchill. Their territory stretched westwards as far as Belleek. Sir John Dunbar's territory stretched from Lough Erne, through Derrygonnelly (where he built his bawn) to Garrison. It was his second son who founded the village of Garrison and built a barrack there, thus giving the village its name. Roads, if they existed at all in those days, were difficult to traverse and Lough Erne was the main highway: much use was made of barges and heavy flat-bottomed boats called cots. When the Planters built their castles therefore, they often built them convenient to the water's edge. The shores of the Lower lough alone must have had at least five, constructed by such families as the Blennerhassetts, the Dunbars, the Humes, the Caldwells and the Archdales.

There is no evidence of a village at Derrygonnelly before the Plantation but the site is so ideal that a settlement of some kind probably existed there before then. The nearby Sillees River would have provided a ready supply of water for domestic use. It certainly provided the power for a number of mills. In the far-off days there were houses on both sides of the river but there was no bridge by which it could be crossed. When necessary people crossed it by a ford.

There were no fairs in the village before 1800. The nearest were held at the end of Stratore Lane on the road to Knockmore. These ended when a battle took place between Orange and Green factions at the fair of July 1810. After this the then-landlord (General Archdale) was granted permission to hold a market in Derrygonnelly every Saturday and gave land in the village, known as the Commons, for a fair to be held on the twenty-fourth day of each month.

Thomas John Ovens (Tommy) knew Derrygonnelly well. When he was about to leave school in the early 1920s his teacher recommended him as a suitable person to serve his time in

Charles Parke's shop in the village. Tommy was to live with the Parke family for three years. In those days most shopkeepers farmed too and Charlie Parke was no exception. Tommy takes up the story:

I was livin' in Belleek in those days. Derrygonnelly would have been seven Irish miles away; seven long miles. [an 'Irish mile' was roughly 1 ¼ statute miles] Life was hard and practically everything you ate with the exception of tea and sugar was produced on the farm. You had your own pig which you put in the salt and you grew turnip and cabbage. If you were so inclined there was plenty of game; and trout, bream, salmon and perch in the Erne. My father was a keen fisherman and fond of having a shot. But then again you waited at certain times of the year 'til the cattle were sold to get your shoes. And if the cattle didn't sell you waited 'til the next fair. It was quite common for children to go to school bare-footed even sometimes in the month of March. When I was ready to leave Drumbad Public Elementary School my teacher recommended me to Charlie Parke to serve my time to the grocery trade. In those days shopkeepers were farmers as well. That meant there were byres to be cleaned out. You had to do your share of that. If it was a good day and the creamery was over and things were quiet on a summer day the village practically closed down. Anybody that was able-bodied went to help with the hay. We had no machinery in those times. You had a machine for cutting the hay but after that it was all forks and rakes.

Fair days in Derrygonnelly were great occasions; but the hiring fair was the highlight of the year – the two hiring fairs. Money was scarce and labour the other way round. They came from the mountain areas with probably a small farm and two or three cows; and you had in those days a large family.

Hiring day affected me in that on that day there were no meals cooked in the kitchen although where I worked was known as one of the best food houses in Derrygonnelly. None of the shop boys sat down to eat a meal (on hiring day). You slipped into the kitchen. The kettle or teapot was sitting on the range. There was plenty of homemade bread, butter, jam. There was no time to make dinner or sit down for a meal. You could slip into the kitchen for five minutes or so and go back in an hour if you felt hungry again. I lived in; no payment of course, I was what was known as servin' my time. But you got your keep and you were comfortably bedded and well fed. That lasted three years. Even when you had your time served it was very difficult to get a job. You were quite willing to stop on another year whether you got wages or not.

Fair Day meant extra business. We opened the shop at eight o'clock. Cattle (mostly Shorthorns) would have been already coming in along the street. People were movin' about. Some of them had been up very early and walked the cattle to the fair. Dealers sometimes met them outside the town and tried to buy them before they reached the Fair Green. Mostly though, dealing went on all morning with them slapping hands, dividing, arguing about the luck-penny, spitting and finally slapping hands again before a deal was finalised. The animals would then be driven into someone's yard. Some would have been sold for dairying, some for breeding or fattening. Others would go for mince or sausages. Quite a number would be headed for Enniskillen station on the first stage of their journey to Scotland.

If it was the spring of the year you put certain stuff out in front of the shop – netting wire, shafts, hay rakes, pitch forks. You wheeled out two or three or four different types of seed corn on a hand truck; grass seed too. You rolled down the tops of the bags so that people could have a look; scythes, scythe blades and scythe stones too. Then in winter it was lamps, brushes, buckets – whatever was a-usin'.

Then at a certain time of year farmers brought in their eggs to the shop. The woman of the house packed them in a basket. Now these eggs – it was a barter business. No money changed hands. You counted the eggs and the woman got her groceries. If she got ten shillings worth of groceries and she had ten shillings worth of eggs that was the deal completed. If you owed her a shilling or two you gave it to her and vice versa. We had one man came in with a donkey and brought twenty dozen eggs with him. He came from Rossmore in the direction of Boho. He and his wife packed ten dozen in each creel and they were packed in hay. Two people had to lift these on and off at the one time. They were hung on what I understand was a madrig. A madrig was [a saddle] made of straw and on top of that there was a piece of wood that fitted on top of the donkey's back. They strapped that on. On each side there was a wooden peg about an inch or an inch and a half in diameter. (The same type was used for taking the turf out of the bogs.) When we had the eggs counted we packed them in straw in a three hundred- or six hundred case and sent them to Enniskillen by horse and cart about twice a week. They went to egg packers who shipped them across the water to wherever the market was at that particular time.

There would have been five or six men working out in our yard on a fair day; throwing on a bag of meal – and a bag of meal was two hundredweight at that time. It took two to throw that on. There would have been one or two horses out there too, tied to a post in the yard; maybe belonged to a customer. We didn't stable horses but the horse was happy enough to stand there if we threw him a han'ful of hay now and again.

It was all counter trade at that time. Tea was weighed. Sugar was weighed. Sugar came in two hundredweight bags – 224lb. A lot of it came in carts. Tea came in chests which varied in weight and varied in the different types and qualities of tea you bought. Tea retailed at as little as one and sixpence a pound. You'd all that to weigh up and you tied it with string, and you had to be competent enough to be able to put a knot on your twine and only cut one end. In those days waste was one of the things that would not be tolerated. One thing we used in those days was snuff. Snuff was a standard order on those coming into the shop. There was practically no tinned stuff – maybe a few tins of pears at Christmas; and Christmas time was only Christmas day.

At the May Fair you could have bought straw for thatch and scollops for pegging it down; cabbage plants too and you would hear cart loads of young pigs squealing. At that time they were taken off the sow at eight weeks and sold for fattening. They squealed (or grunted) and darted into a corner if anybody put their hand into the cart to move them about a bit to get a better look. Farmers always lift a pig by the ear and the tail to judge the weight of it. That makes it squeal too. This all took place on the main street.

Now let's get back into the shop again; and along with all the other things, we sold boots and shoes. Wellingtons in those days weren't heard tell of. The best boot that you could sell a customer cost around twelve shillings or twelve and sixpence. And that was a full kip [leather made from the skin of young cattle] leather boot with a tip on the heel and a toe-plate on the toe and three row of hobnails round the sole of it. That sole would be half an inch thick and the good boot was what was known as 'pegged and sewn and screwed'. Then there was what was known as a whole-back and a split-back. The whole-back was made with the one piece of leather and you could have bought that with or without a toe-cap. The split-back was made with two pieces. Those were made across the water. There was a boot known as a 'Hold-fast' and there was another one called 'Times-test'. That was the brand name and they were about the best boot you could buy. And you got replicas of that heavy boot for boys going to school. They cost around five shillings. Ladies' boots were lighter of course and had a long leg. Farmers bought a lighter boot for church or going to fairs.

Tommy Ovens – served his time in Charlie Parke's shop in Derrygonnelly

You sold bread which came in from Enniskillen – and American bacon. It was known as American clear-backs. That came to the shop in a wooden box made of inch timber, wired, because there was no lifting gear as nowadays. That was tipped off on the side-path and was eventually turned over and, with some help, got into the store. It was packed in salt and every morning and especially on a fair morning it was the job of one of the assistants to go out with a big scrubber and brush the salt off. Then it was brought in and put on a special counter. You took your knife which was kept sharp and cut it in two and set one piece on top of the other with the cut sides next your customers. There was no such thing as a bacon slicer. A speciality at that time was home-grown beans and American bacon. Sometimes if a farmer hadn't a pig ready for the salt at home he would have bought a lump of that to tide him over.

In all villages you got these travelling salesmen. There was a character that sold ladieswear – all types of ladieswear. And a well-dressed fella in those days often ended up with a navy-blue suit bought on hiring day. And the character that would be fittin' him out would say, 'Jimmy, get that jacket on ye now. There's one that'll fit ye.' And he'd get a hold of the back of the jacket in his hand and say, 'Button it up on ye boy. Button it up on ye.' And of course the lad would button it up and it would be a lovely fit. He wouldn't be aware that the salesman was holding about nine inches at the back of it. But everybody seemed to be happy.

Then you had the character which sold rope; sold harness. He was called Devine and he always wore a white shirt and a hard hat. He took off his jacket of a warm day but he never took off the hard hat, and the sweat would be rollin' off him. He told stories in the middle of all the sales talk. One of his stories was: 'I was in a house the other night and I asked the woman, 'Will ye make me a drop o' tay?' And she says, 'I will if ye houl the chile for me.' An' I was houlin' the chile on me knee an' a man come in an' 'e says, 'Yer doin' well the night, Paddy.'

113

'Aye,' says I, 'I'm houlin' me own.' An' that's when the trouble started!

A lot of hired people tended to attend the same fairs, stay in the same district. If they moved, it would have been across to Scotland. A big lot of Irish people went over there for digging the potatoes, saved up the money, came back and spent the winter months at home. There was the ceilidhes and the Mummers' dances, and the card playing and the concerts and the show people which travelled all over the country. One of the greatest things that we had then, everybody was happy. We have a wonderful world now but people are not happy.

It was a similar story in Belleek and Garrison, where fairs were held on the seventeenth and twenty-sixth of the month respectively. They died out in both places in 1960 and were replaced by marts in 1961. Belleek's fairs date back to Plantation times. Three were held there throughout the seventeenth and eighteenth centuries. The Belleek of that time was a centre of trade with goods such as iron, slates, timber and coal arriving in carts from Ballyshannon en route for Enniskillen and beyond. Some flax, corn and occasionally cattle were carried in the opposite direction. There was also a big trade in turf. Long ago these were transported via the lough in cots and barges. Barges were reckoned to be safer on the lower lough. In the second half of the nineteenth century James Caldwell Bloomfield introduced steam transport. He also started a pottery at Belleek, first making earthenware for everyday use but later making the fine Parian china we know today.

Garrison is known to have held fairs at Niamdh Hill in the townland of Carrigalough before the Plantation but these are not listed in any almanac, perhaps because they were regarded as religious rather than commercial festivals. The last one was held there on 2 August 1820. We do know that by then both towns had a weekly market, a fair green, monthly fairs and probably a market house as well. Tolls were charged in Garrison, for the 1862 Valuation states that they were collected by a William Blair who had a house, land and corn mill in the townland of Carran West on the eastern shore of Lough Melvin.

There are several theories as to how Garrison got its name. As stated earlier, the most likely explanation is that it was named by Captain John Dunbar when he founded the town in the seventeenth century. At the same time he set up an ironworks and built a barrack there 'to protect the people of Belleek from surprise attacks from 'the fighting men of Connaught.' Another suggests that King William halted his army there and erected a barrack after the battle of Aughrim. Either way there is still a Barrack Street in the village and Edward Blair's farm on the banks of the Kilcoo River was known as Barrack Park when he sold it, together with his house and corn mill, in December 1895. At that time Edward (son of William who collected the tolls) had in his employment James Kerins and Lizzie Clarke. James did farmwork and helped in the mill during the four months in the year that it was in operation, and Lizzie acted as housekeeper to his wife Elizabeth and nursemaid to their two baby daughters. In those days if a farmer sold his farm and moved to another, it was usual to take his hired help with him and James and Lizzie flitted with the family. Lizzie had been hired no further away than Belleek so the move from the furthermost corner of Fermanagh to County Down must have been quite an adventure.

The farm and all that remains of the old mill in Garrison are now owned by local farmer Tommy Kerr. Tommy's father bought the mill from an Englishman who had in turn bought it from Edward Blair in 1895. Tommy remembers the mill in operation – but only just. He was taken along there by his grandfather when he was a small boy. He also recalls the fairs:

I do remember the corn mill. I do surely. My grandfather took corn till it. I remember the fairs too. There would have been cattle sold; not many sheep. This is not sheep country. Goats and horses and pigs – suckin' pigs. It used to be carts at that time with pigs you know. People bought them for fattening. Then the fat pigs mostly all went to Ballyshannon. Ballyshannon was the market town in them old days in all this country. The farmer roun' here that was buyin' suckin' pigs; they sold the fat pig in Ballyshannon. I remember second-hand clothes being bought on the street; an' ropes an' shafts an' delph an' all that stuff. No eggs or butter. Johnstons used to buy the eggs. They collected them from the shops in this country an' they went to Manorhamilton for market day – ten mile up the road there.

There was horses sold in Garrison but the main horse fair in this country was in Enniskillen. That was the big horse fair. There'd be odd times there'd be horses sold here (in Garrison) but the big horse fair was in Enniskillen – always. I worked with horses all my life. I was mowin' with horses when I was seven. We ploughed an' worked with several horses. We never kept them too long. They'd be in the plough this week an' next week they'd be gone. There'd be some fella' lookin' for one and we'd sell him. We bought and sold.

Courtesy of Annette Henry

Edward and Elizabeth Blair.

Tommy Kerr.

Possibly the oldest fair in the county was held at Holywell. It was what was known as a pattern, i.e. a festival associated with the patron saint. These usually lasted two days – one for gathering and one for scattering. Tents and booths were erected for the occasion and they were popularly known as holy fairs. As the name suggests it was once famous for the curative powers of its waters. The last Sunday in July (Lughnasa) was 'station' day when the blind were said to receive their sight and the lame to throw away their crutches. It was also Blaeberry (or Bilberry) Sunday, when large numbers of people climbed the hills to socialise and partake of this delicious fruit. It was generally a joyful occasion with music, singing and dancing. It was also by tradition a day for matchmaking. Holywell is one of the few places to have retained its old market cross. It may still be seen in its original position, though not in its original setting. It lay behind a ditch for a spell when the Belcoo to Garrison road was being constructed in 1847 and marked a grave in the area on more than one occasion. Long ago it was probably at the centre of the market area, marking the focal point in the village.

A market cross was of great significance in days gone by as a swearing object for finalising bargains between traders and even for sealing matchmaking agreements. This was done by the laying of hands upon the cross and swearing that the trade (or agreement) was true. Holywell later held monthly fairs at which livestock of all kinds were bought and sold. Oddly enough I could find no record of these until the nineteenth century (*O.S. Memoirs*) whereas Belcoo is

Holywell's old Market Cross.

Ederny Cross dates from the 7th century.

recorded as having five in *Watson's Almanack* of 1745 and had a market house and fair green by the 1850s. The coming of the railway in 1879 marked the decline of Holywell and the growth of Belcoo. From then on a special train was laid on for marketeers. The markets for pork, butter and other dairy produce improved immediately.

Black cattle, pigs and a few mountain ponies were sold at the remaining fairs in the area – Callowhill (near Derrylin), Stragowna, which was about three miles from Kinawley, and Wheathill, also sometimes known by the Parish name, Killesher. Some cloth and yarn were also sold. These were usually bought by dealers who resold it in such places as Enniskillen and Ballyconnell. Today you might have difficulty in finding some of these places, but if you do find them and stop, local people will show you the old fair green and tell you about the people who used to arrive on fair day and set up stalls for selling their wares, or erect tents in which to sell their whiskey. Callowhill and Stragowna had fairs in the eighteenth century and probably long before. Those at Stragowna died out before 1900 but those at Callowhill (by then moved to Derrylin) were revived and held monthly until the middle of the next century. Hiring took place at Wheathill twice a year until its fairs ceased altogether early in the twentieth century. Often a hiring agreement included a promise on the part of hired workers to devote their free time to spinning.

There were at least six fairs in the villages north of the lower lake, most of them again dating back to Plantation times. They included Irvinestown (once known as Lowtherstown), Lisnarick, Ballinamallard, Kesh, Lack and Ederny. Local farmers would also have attended the fairs in Pettigo and West Tyrone. All but Lack and Ederny had from three to five established fairs in 1745. The most successful of these were at Kesh and Irvinestown, both of which sustained fairs and markets continuously from the seventeenth to the twentieth centuries. Kesh was built by Thomas Blennerhassett and planted with six British families in the reign of Charles I (1625-1649). At the same time he established fairs and a regular Wednesday market. These improved with the coming of the railway which was used for transporting cattle on the first stage of their journey to Scotland. The fairs were dealt a heavy blow when the railway closed in 1945. In fact fairs ceased altogether in Kesh at that time. The best remembered character in the village was Johnny Black, who 'minded' cattle from the time they were sold until they left the town. For this he charged threepence a head. Animals were never released until the threepence was paid.

Irvinestown had similar beginnings, though in its case the lands changed hands several times between 1611 and 1615, in which year they were bought by Sir Gerald Lowther who gave his village the name of Lowtherstown. It changed to Irvinestown when bought by Sir Christopher Irvine in 1667. In the early days Irvinestown and Kesh had four and five fairs respectively each year, but by the nineteenth century they were being held regularly on the fourth and eighth day of every month. In the beginning cattle, yarn and the small surpluses of the farms were the main commodities on offer. By the nineteenth century both places were being frequented by travelling merchants dealing in soft goods and by pedlars and artisans selling articles of husbandry, coarse furniture, household utensils, rope, shoes and fruit. Later a board of trustees was set up in Irvinestown to look after the fairs and markets. They levied a charge on each stall-holder – £1 for anyone selling rope or boots and shoes; five shillings for a stall selling second-hand clothes, half-a-crown if you wanted to sell farm produce and so on. Markets were also established in Irvinestown for fowl, pork, flax, potatoes, corn and other produce. There was a small cloth market. Cattle were sold at the Fair Green, along the Main Street and beside the Methodist Church in Pound Street. A mart was started outside the town when fairs ceased in 1959. It survived a few years but eventually closed down.

The Old Fair Green at Kesh.

The Old Fair Green at Lisnarrick – still a striking feature in the centre of the village.

Of the other villages Ballinamallard and Lisnarick had three and five fairs respectively, increasing to twelve for the sale of cattle and yarn in the 1830s, but they were said to be badly attended in both places and died out altogether around the middle of the century. For all that, hiring is said to have taken place in Lisnarick up until World War I for the purpose of hiring help for hay-making and potato gathering. The centrepiece of the village is its lovely old fair green surrounded on its three sides by tall trees. That of 12 February in Ballinamallard was known as a good horse fair.

Ederny (like Holywell) existed as a meeting place long before the Plantation, possibly because it was on the route for pilgrims on their way to Lough Derg, where on an island Saint Patrick is believed to have had a vision of Purgatory. An old cross, thought to date from the seventh century, stands sentinel on a nearby hill and must have guided the path of many a weary traveller in the distant past. Monthly fairs were held there and in nearby Lack in the nineteenth century. By the end of the century Lack had just one (held on 30 September) while those in Ederny prospered and continued to be held monthly until fairs ceased. Some furniture and other articles for domestic use were sold in Ederny as well as the usual farm produce. However, a mart started in 1960 lasted just a few years.

By far the most important market town in Fermanagh was Enniskillen. Before 1600 the town was ruled by the Maguires who built the original castle, the remains of which are embodied

Market Day, Ederney.

119

in the castle of today. The Plantation and the arrival of William Cole displaced the Maguires, just as the Maguires had displaced the Devines and the Devines others before them. Cole and his heirs were empowered to hold a Thursday market and fair on Lammas Day and they were also appointed clerks of the market and were to keep the toll book. No persons except the freemen of the town were allowed to sell or retail within three miles of it. William brought with him twenty English families as required under the terms of his grant, and on arrival in Enniskillen built a town. This included a church, a cemetery, a gaol and a market house (at the Diamond on the site of the present town hall). On another piece of ground he was required to build 'a public schoole together with a court and garden to the said schoole adjoining.' All this resulted in an immediate improvement to the town, especially to its fairs and markets. It started off with just three fairs in the year but by the nineteenth century these had increased to thirteen, one on the tenth of every month and one on 26 October. Later an extra fair was held on 26 May, making fourteen in all. The Fair Green was in the vicinity of Gaol Square and animals of all descriptions were brought there to be sold, until fairs ceased in 1950. These included black cattle (milch cows, heifers, bullocks); live pigs of various breeds, i.e. Berkshire, Dutch and Irish, the price of which was generally governed by the price of pork in the export market; sheep, usually of Half-Leicester, Irish or Scotch breed; a small breed of ass which was rarely used in draught but in the conveyance of turf, butter in casks, young calves and pigs to market, all of which were transported at one time in creels; also goats and horses. Tommy Kerr reminisces again:

> The fairs was once a month, the tenth of every month. We took three or four horses at a time to Enniskillen. We mostly walked them – cattle too. During the war we walked them. Then there got to be more lorries on the road. Northern Ireland Transport used to draw them. They drew a lot of stock. Where we sold the horses in Enniskillen, we used to call it Gaol Square. Coming from Garrison it was off the main street on the right-hand side. Cattle was sold first and then the horses later. The horses didn't come 'til roughly eleven or twelve o'clock. The cattle would be nearly all gone at that stage. In the old times that was part of the Fair Green. It's partly paled off now for market day – Thursday – flowers and all that kind of stuff.
>
> The old Fair Green was where the first mart went up – on both sides of the road. Then they transferred it out of town; about a mile out the Tempo Road. I still go. There's a sheep sale every week at this time of year (October). But any horses I have to sell now I would sell about home.

Cattle sales included a big influx of animals in transit from such places as Sligo, Leitrim and Roscommon to the ports of Down and Antrim from which they were shipped to southern Scotland. This movement of animals from the south and west of Ireland to the north and east went on for centuries, a drover sometimes spending months at a time on the road with nothing but oatcake in his pocket for sustenance on the way. (This pattern was interrupted at the end of the seventeenth century and into the eighteenth when the English government banned the import of Irish animals in the interests of its own farmers.) Drovers and their cattle were a common sight on Ulster roads even in the twentieth century, though by then many were being moved by rail and lorry.

Creels hung in pairs on a donkey's wooden straddle were still used in Fermanagh in the early twentieth century for carrying turf, eggs and other commodities.

Market Day in Enniskillen was (and still is) Thursday. Long ago the action took place around the market house, with the exception of yarn, butter, eggs and fowl which were sold at the west end of the town. These goods were bought by jobbers who exported the dairy produce through the ports of Newry, Derry and Sligo. Other goods sold included tools and utensils such as spades and riddles, linen, potatoes, beef, hides, meal, plants, salt, hats, flannel, flax, earthenware, fish, fruit and vegetables and the usual produce of the farm. Tolls once collected by the Enniskillen family were later leased to the town Corporation, who charged from a penny to threepence per animal standing on market days, that amount being doubled on fair days.

But all that was about to change. In 1950 James Johnston (known as Jimmy), an enterprising farmer from County Armagh, arrived in Enniskillen and saw enormous possibilities in developing the old Fair Green and the Gaol Square opposite. He purchased the lease on both – rights and all. Fermanagh College now stands on Gaol Square but on the Fair Green Jimmy built a cattle mart and put up pens at a time when cattle marts were practically unheard of outside Belfast. His son Stuart takes up the story:

In those early days the old fairs still ran alongside the marts. (Tempo fair, for instance, continued 'til 1959). There was a bit of dealer resistance in the first instance. They could see that they were going to lose out, but eventually dealers, instead of dealing in the fairs, started dealing in the marts.

121

In the old days all the buyers didn't see all the cattle. By coming through the marts all the buyers saw them all. That was a good thing for the farmer. For a long time fairs still operated in the south and west of Ireland. Dealers bought a lot of cattle in the west of Ireland and sold them in our market in Enniskillen (late '50s and '60s and '70s). In those days they came from all over Northern Ireland and even from Scotland and England to buy Fermanagh cattle – west of Ireland cattle too. A few came from Wales. We sold dropped calves, sheep and pigs too. I did the auctioneering myself. Pigs used to come in carts. We used to have maybe a hundred lots. We sold literally thousands of cattle through the old market in Enniskillen. After they were sold they went to various yards around Gaol Square: there was McLaughlin's yard; Macken's (where the Horseshoe Bar is now); Alice Shannon's. She lived in Belmore Street. Her yard backed on to Frith's Alley, so it was only a matter of walking them down the alley into her yard. She charged threepence from they went in 'til they came out to be loaded onto the train. For perhaps a hundred years they travelled by rail. They actually travelled better by rail. They weren't going up hills and round corners and the driver jamming on the brakes as happens today. After they were gone the Fire Brigade came out to wash the streets.

Animals still weren't identifiable at this stage. They were only identified with a scissor cut on the rump. Each dealer had his own mark. There was no real record of them. Selling by auction was purely an economic thing. It suited the farmer. Then later on health regulations came into place, TB testing and tagging of cattle. There is a record now of every animal in Northern Ireland. You know where it is or where it is supposed to be; when it is born and when it dies; movements to markets; everything is recorded. Nowadays of course it is on computer.

In 1994 the Ulster Farmers' Mart, with Stuart Johnston at its head, moved out of town to the Tempo Road. The new premises are impressive – five sale rings and an exhibition ring for horses. It is today the largest mart in Northern Ireland and farmers come to it from all over the country, anything up to a thousand head of cattle going through the sale ring on a good day. Special and seasonal sales are held on Tuesday, sheep on Wednesday, cattle on Thursday. There are just four horse sales in the year. They are held in March, June, September and a pre-Christmas one held in November or December.

Nearby Tempo was Maguire territory too. According to Pynnar, Bryan Maguire (having pledged allegiance to the Crown) was one of the few Irish lords to hold on to his territory after the Plantation. In 1610 he had '2,000 acres called Tempodessell and 500 of which were his brother's, lately deceased.' The original grant by James I included permission to hold markets, and a Lammas Fair in August, but apparently these did not take off until the eighteenth century. Up until then the village had been called Milltown because of its corn and tuck mills. By the nineteenth century markets were being held regularly on the twenty-eighth day of the month and had assumed the proportions of fairs. The Tempo Maguires died out around this time, having lost their estates through debts and mortgages. It then passed into other hands and eventually to Sir Charles Langham in 1893.

Sir Charles took many photographs of the village, including some of the May Fair of 1900. But the old village green photographed by Sir Charles is no more. Buildings now occupy the Commons which once saw farmers dealing and arguing over the price of cattle, asses and

Courtesy of Stuart Johnston

Enniskillen Mart in the 1950s – it was replaced in 1994 by extensive new premises on the Tempo Road.

goats. The backyards of hotels and pubs which once housed hundreds of animals on the evening of the fair are silent as the grave. No more do horses and donkeys go through their paces at the Diamond or farmers exhibit their pigs and goats on the main street. Gone too the Buttermarket and the acre of ground called the Greenyard, where John Higgins made a living by allowing dealers to put their animals on his grass until such times as they were ready to be walked to the nearest station. Local man John McKeagney explains:

> Tempo was central to a great hinterland of small farmers, all with a few cattle. The farmer would maybe rear three or four calves and after about a year he'd bring them to Tempo fair and the dealers bought them up. Most of them were sold on the Commons which belonged to nobody. You could take them off there afterwards without paying anything. There was a pound near there too. If an animal went astray or somebody bought it and didn't pay for it, it was put in there and you had to pay to get it out. At the other end of town there was what was known as the Greenyard. It was used for storing cattle after they were sold. There was a gateman there to look after them and he charged so much a head for every beast as it went out. That's where the drovers came in. They took over then and drove them to one of the neighbouring railway stations – Fivemiletown, Ballinamallard, Brookeborough. There were ten within a ten-mile radius of Tempo. They galloped them for about three miles. After that they were tired and they were easy walked. They went for fattening to Counties Down, Antrim, Meath and the outskirts of Dublin.

A cattle 'special' used to run from Collooney in Sligo to the boat at Belfast docks. It left with only a few wagons, picking up full wagons at most stations on the way. By the time it reached Belfast there were forty wagons with upwards of six hundred cattle on board en route for Scotland and other places.

There was no hiring fair at Tempo but hiring did take place. I remember a man telling me he was minding a calf on the Doon Road while his mother went to buy something, when a man came up and said, 'Will you come and work for me?' [He was about twelve at the time.] He said, 'You will have to ask my mother.' Eventually his mother came back and the deal was done.

Then there were the eating houses. Adam Nixon's mother told me she used to make soup and teas on Fair Day. She made enough money to last her 'til the next Fair Day. It was that good. Hundreds and hundreds of people were on that street and they all had to be fed.

The people and the cattle have long since gone. The gabled windows of the church, which once looked down on dealers sorting out their animals in readiness for their walk to the nearest railway station, now stare blankly at the sedate back gardens of terraced houses. Gone too are Arthur McKeagney the blacksmith and his kinsmen James and John, who built carts and jaunting cars at the Diamond, and Adam Nixon who turned his front rooms into an eating house on Fair Day.

Neighbouring Clabby never aspired to be anything more than a few houses at a crossroads, one of which was a public house. However two fairs were held there annually throughout the eighteenth and nineteenth centuries.

Fairs were held also in Lisbellaw, Brookeborough, Maguiresbridge and Lisnaskea, again all formerly Maguire territory until that family's involvement in the 1641 Rebellion, when they forfeited their land to Plantation families such as the Brookes. All these villages except Brookeborough had thrice-yearly fairs dating back to around that time (Brookeborough had four). Those held in Lisbellaw were the smallest of the four. They were established initially for the sale of black cattle, horses, pigs and yarn – also butter every alternate Saturday, but people generally preferred to market their produce in Enniskillen. Lisbellaw's fairs died out during the nineteenth century, with the exception of the twice-yearly hiring fairs which continued into the 1930s. The hirelings stood in a row at the market house clutching brown paper parcels containing all their worldly possessions. They came mainly from Leitrim and Cavan, where families were large and poverty rife. Farmers walked up and down with sticks under their arms, sizing them up and wondering if they were strong and able. Parents watched from a distance, only coming forward when someone showed an interest in their offspring. The area around Lisbellaw was great country for turf, much of which was loaded on to cots for selling in Enniskillen market. Some travelled of course by ass and cart or ass and creel. The latter were accompanied by children who generally sold two loads per day, walking anything up to twenty miles in the process. For this they got sixpence, which included the price of the turf. Locally made bricks also travelled by cot, and fetched from seven-and-sixpence to thirteen shillings per thousand, depending on quality.

Four fairs were established in Brookeborough under a patent granted by Queen Anne in 1706 and prospered throughout that century but died out early in the next. A monthly fair was started in 1833 by Sir Arthur Brooke at Coonien (or Cooneen) near a corn mill built by one of his ancestors, but that too eventually failed. However, linen merchants were still attending the markets in Brookeborough in 1835 to buy hanks of yarn. After that the fairs died out altogether

© Langham Collection, Ulster Museum

The old Greenyard at Tempo where farmers and dealers left their animals until they were ready to be walked to the nearest railway station. Could the small figure in the centre of the picture be Oweny Bottley? (see page 129)

until the twentieth century, when they were revived and held monthly until the outbreak of the Second World War.

The Brookes were the leading family in the area. They first settled in Donegal, moving to Fermanagh at the end of the seventeenth century. With them came a new peasantry (English and Scotch settlers) who introduced habits of industry and cleanliness which had not existed before the rebellion. The Brookes grew to love Fermanagh, promoting it at every opportunity and serving their country with distinction both as landlords and soldiers. They were able at the same time to maintain their role as statesmen in spite of persistent pressure from nationalism and the corrosive effects of land reform at the end of the nineteenth century.

Sir Basil [Lord] Brookeborough (1888-1973) for instance, although a born countryman and longing only to farm his ancestral acres, served with distinction in World War I. He applied himself to farming after the war, concentrating mainly on livestock, improving the estate and taking an active part in local affairs including the County Council, the Farmers' Union and the Fermanagh Farming Society. He also acted as chairman of the committee of management of the Clogher Valley Railway Company during the 1930s, not to mention serving as Prime Minister of Northern Ireland from 1944 to 1963. His three sons served in World War II. Two made the supreme sacrifice.

His estate contained an immense area of mountain, and acres and acres of scrubland which provided good covering for deer. Unfortunately this also provided good covering for rabbits – a gamekeeper and two trappers were expected to catch at least eight thousand a year to keep them under control. If anyone was caught poaching or chasing deer he was summoned to see a friend of Lord Brookeborough, and fined anything up to five pounds, depending on his circumstances and whether he had been caught previously. No one was ever brought to court. The money thus collected was given to charity.

Sir Basil is remembered as being friendly towards everyone, particularly the workers on the estate, a fact corroborated by people like Tommy Hance, Joe Crawford and Annie Reid who spent much of their working lives at Colebrooke. In his younger days Tommy lived in a house belonging to the Clogher Valley Railway Company at a tiny station called Claraghy. His wife opened the gates when a train was due and closed them after it passed by. These are their memoirs:

Tommy:

I enjoyed the job every inch of the way. I was there forty years. Lord Brookeborough was a man among men. Although he was Prime Minister he always came home at weekends and took a great interest in the farm. I remember making hay. There was a permanent staff of about twelve though the numbers sometimes swelled to about fifty at a busy time. Captain King (the farm manager) sometimes hired men at the hiring fair in Fivemiletown, but very often they lived in cottages on the estate or lived locally and came on bicycles.

Normally we put in thirty or forty acres of potatoes and a hundred acres of corn. We made about a thousand rucks of hay. During the War we put in extra crops including flax. I was sorry when I had to leave. I felt I had grown into the place. There wasn't a field in it I hadn't worked in.

Annie:

I loved my days at Colebrooke. I was brought in at a busy time – like [agricultural] Shows, spring cleaning, during house parties or if the nurse was away on holiday. I would have helped with the children or in the kitchen or with the washing and ironing. I laundered the riding breeches for the family before Balmoral Show or Dublin Horse Show; washed the horses' tack [blankets etc.] – I even cleaned the harness. I sometimes cleaned the silver or helped in the dining room although that was normally the job of the butler.

They used to have pheasant shoots. They hung the pheasant up by the neck for weeks. They didn't cook them 'til they began to smell high and the tail feathers pulled out.

There used to be great Christmas parties. All the workers on the estate and their wives each got a pound and the children got a present from the Christmas tree. Then we all had dinner and danced after it. There were beautiful paintings, fireplaces, furniture and a big log fire blazing.

Joe:

Captain King asked me to come as yardman, away before the war. I think it was about 1930. At that time there were lots of cattle, pigs, working horses, bloodhorses too. I remember thirteen horses all working in one twelve-acre field and eighteen men planting potatoes.

I used to saddle horses for Master Julian, Master John and Master Henry. They would go out cheerin' an' ridin' like Indians. If a pony threw one of them the other two were sure to do likewise. The ponies would come back like lightning and the children running after them right into the yard. Then they had a wee black pony. It was given to Master Julian when he was a young lad – I suppose about five or six. When it got on in years it wasn't much use so we put it in the cart and we used to draw meal round the fields to the cattle wi' that. Captain John and the other two lads, they thought the world of that pony. When you were goin' out of the field an' maybe tryin' to make up time you would trot a bit an' the boys could hear that any length an' they would give you a slatin' for trottin' the old pony. But what they'd do after they'd give you that slatin', off they'd go in the opposite direction on their own ponies. And when they'd get out of reach you'd give the pony another wee touch an' away you'd go again. An' they'd be listenin' an' they could get roun' an' they'd come out through the bushes at you. Oh the children could tell you off!

I used to take corn an' cattle to Fivemiletown Fair; milk cows or store cattle. Captain King was always there to do the business. It could be Lisnaskea, Enniskillen, Irvinestown, any of them. We bought cattle in those places too an' then walked them home. I walked a drove of cattle till Trillick (twelve or thirteen miles) out over the mountain, got another drove, turned roun' an' walked them home – an' not a ha'p'oth o' help wi' me – not even a dog!

Lisnaskea and Maguiresbridge were Plantation towns and started off with three fairs at that time. By 1835 both had a dozen or more which continued throughout that century and into the next. The markets in both places were said to be 'tolerably' supplied with butchers' meat, pork, butter, yarn, eggs and poultry; also thread, linen and great quantities of grain which went either to Belfast or neighbouring mills in the parish of Galloon. Eggs were bartered by the women in the grocers' shops in exchange for tea and sugar. Grocers then sold them on to dealers at three ha'pence or tuppence a dozen. The dealers sold some in Dublin and exported the rest to Liverpool. Butter was exported through Belfast, Newry and Dublin. Flax went north, particularly to Antrim, Down and Armagh, where the homeweaving industry survived longer than in the other counties.

Maguiresbridge had great horse fairs, the most notable being that of 17 January each year. Wednesday was market day and the first one in each month was Fair Day. In addition the old fairs of 17 January, 20 May and 19 November (granted by patent from Queen Anne in 1706) continued alongside the normal monthly fairs. Maguiresbridge marked the Fermanagh end of the Clogher Valley Railway which linked up with the Great Northern system, giving the people of the area access to wider horizons (Belfast, Greenore, Dublin etc.). It carried passengers, but the main function of the tram, as it was initially called, was agricultural as it was used in the transport of horses, timber, milk, meal and farm produce (also coal) but mainly in the movement of cattle and sheep to and from fairs. Local people sometimes referred to it as the 'black pig'.

Lisnaskea was the ancient capital of Fermanagh in the Maguire era, but was destroyed by them in 1641 when under the ownership of the Balfours, a Plantation family from Fife. The main buildings in both towns (market house, corn market, dispensary, etc. for which credit must go to the Earls of Erne) date from the early nineteenth century. Lisnaskea had one of the several workhouses in Fermanagh. There were others at Irvinestown and Enniskillen. The general market day was Saturday and the market for flax, pork, and fowl was held on Wednesday. The Wednesday nearest the twentieth of the month was Fair Day. Hiring took place at the fairs of May and November and are remembered here by Paddy Cassidy:

The men and women lined up and you sort of had to bid for your man. One man that I know of – he was a small wee man, an' bein' a small man the farmer asked him what he could do. He asked him could he shear corn. An' he said he could cut forty stooks a day! Now there's twelve sheaves in a stook. So listening to the old men, any man that could cut twenty stooks, he was worth his money. But this wee man said he could cut forty! But at May Day you see, you couldn't contradict it. There'd be no call. You'd have to keep him 'til September to know whether he could cut it or not. But they were always good at naming people in the country. After that they called him 'Forty Stooks'. He always held his head up high and before that they called him 'Pat the Man'. He worked at the last with Mr Watt up at the workhouse.

There were at a time three other fairs in this corner of Fermanagh. They were held at Newtownbutler, Magheraveely and Roslea. Newtownbutler got its name from Sir Stephen Butler, who bought it from the original Planter. Like most of its neighbours it was razed to the ground in 1641 but rose again to be the scene of the battle of Newtownbutler which took place near Crom Castle in 1689. It had five fairs in the early days but these almost faded out altogether in the nineteenth century. They revived in the twentieth century to be held on the first Tuesday in each month along with a regular weekly market. The May Fair survived throughout the lean years and was renowned as an excellent cow fair. There is little doubt that hiring took place on that day too. A steady stream of emigrants (mainly Protestants) left for the United States around this time.

Magheraveely had two fairs in the early days but there is no mention at all of these in the nineteenth century. Roslea on the other hand came into its own then. A market house was built, a weekly market established and monthly fairs started on the eighth of the month. Hiring took place there too. The day of the fair is remembered here by Rev. Victor Forster, a native of the area:

Mothers would be out with their daughters and fathers with their sons. It still pains me today when I remember mothers standing on the footpath with two or three daughters, and farmers, roughly dressed, peaked caps over their ears and ash plants in their hands, looking at these girls as if they were cattle – in other words trying to make up their minds if they were capable of doing the work they wanted them to do. But mothers were really more concerned, not with the wages they would get – which was six pounds for six months – but that they would have a clean bed, reasonable food and that they could get off for Sunday morning worship. Many of them were farmers' sons and daughters from the mountain farms between Fivemiletown and Roslea. It was thickly populated and families on the whole were large. There was always plenty of work, for example when they were making turf, and I remember farmers bringing in their loads of turf to Roslea on the eighth of the month. They got five shillings for a large load and half-a-crown for a donkey's one.

One eighth of May, following a band practice three of us went up to this little confectionery store at about nine thirty in the evening and we sat down on a bench at the back of the shop. There came in two young boys who had just been hired for their first six months and one of them ordered a large bottle of lemonade – 'Kirkers' it was those days. Mrs Cummins who owned the shop brought them two glasses to drink the lemonade. They each bought four half-penny Paris buns, consumed the buns and drank the lemonade in complete silence. When they had finished one boy looked over at the other and said, 'Pat, we'll meet here on the eighth of November and we'll have another big brust [feast].' That was a real banquet for them. The three of us had gone in to buy sweets. I was probably about seventeen. I was farming at the time but my friends were still at school.

There used to be a character called Devine who came from Omagh. He had a terrific repertoire of stories. There was this tiny man, I've forgotten his name, but he was known as Oweny Bottley. He wasn't the most handsome of men. He had a prominent Roman nose and wore a very long overcoat which certainly wasn't tailored for him. It was probably given to him by some of the cattle dealers. But this man Devine suddenly spotted Oweny in the crowd and he broke off and said, 'God created man in his own image but in whose image did he create Oweny Bottley!' There were people too selling all sorts of remedies that would cure everything from corns to a sore back.

The Parish priest played his part too. On the Sunday before hiring day he preached a special sermon aimed directly at the boys and girls about to hire. The main thrust of his address was to advise those going into service to make sure they would be free to attend Mass and the Sacraments and at the same time he warned them that whilst being obedient to their masters they should guard against praying with heretics. He also spoke regularly against dancing, hunting on Sunday, wakes and their abominations, runaway marriages and courting in the mountain areas.

The hiring fairs in Roslea were notorious for fighting, rioting and 'people shouting, cursing and staggering along the road.' These were not necessarily of religious origin. A fight could take place for any or no reason apart from the need to release tension. In October an old man appeared at these fairs carrying a sack on his back. He used to call out, 'Old Moore's Almanac – lies and truths.' That night farmers would gather into a neighbour's house and when they had exhausted conversation on the price of cattle and pigs, one would seat himself beneath the oil lamp and read aloud Old Moore's predictions. This would prompt serious debate for the rest of the evening. Such was life in Roslea in the old days.

Fair Day in Roslea in the early 1930s.

Courtesy of Roslea Heritage Centre

COUNTY LONDONDERRY

Drink is the curse of the land. It makes you fight with your neighbour.
It makes you shoot at your landlord – and it makes you miss him.

– Irish Proverb

When James became king in 1603 he little knew that within a few years an event would take place that would change the course of Irish history. The event was the departure from Ireland of the powerful Gaelic lords under their charismatic leader Hugh O'Neill and it was to become known as The Flight of the Earls.

The incident heralded the start of the Plantation. James began by telling the businessmen of the city of London what wonderful opportunities awaited them in Ulster. The 'promised land' stretched from the Foyle to the Lower Bann and included the fisheries of both rivers together with the towns of Derry and Coleraine. Both towns were strategically placed on rivers open to invasion from without, which together with the threat of rebellion from within, made it vitally important that they were fortified and strengthened against attack. The land between the two was at that time populated by 'creaghts' – large pastoral populations who lived in mud huts suitable to a semi-nomadic way of life, easily built and easily destroyed. They spent much of their time with their vast herds of cattle wandering from place to place in search of grazing.

The scheme for the Plantation was the work of three Commissions which sat between 1608 and 1610. In all the counties except Londonderry the settlers were to hold their grants directly from the King. In Londonderry negotiations were conducted by the King and Privy Council who appointed four citizens as a separate commission to work in liaison with Sir Arthur Chichester. The old barony of Loughinshollin was to be added to that of Colerain (as it was then called), to make the new county of Londonderry. The new County was then shared out amongst the London Guilds and Companies to whom it had been granted. These (the Grocers', Mercers', Fishmongers', Drapers', Skinners', Goldsmiths', Merchant Taylors', Haberdashers', Salters', Ironmongers', Vintners' and Clothworkers' Companies; also a number of lesser-known smaller companies) were represented by the Honourable The Irish Society, a group composed of 'six and twenty honest and discreet citizens of London'. The towns of Londonderry and Coleraine together with the fisheries of the Foyle and the Bann were to be the direct responsibility of the Society. Because of their wealth the Londoners were regarded as best able to guard the coastline from the Foyle to the Bann (in view of O'Neill's possible return with an invading force). Their estates totalled about 38,500 acres 'Irish and arable'. Each undertaker was expected to build, within three years, a castle encircled by a bawn for protection against the 'hostile Irish'.

As it turned out the Londoners were far from ideal pioneers. They were in fact reluctant to take on the work and were exasperatingly slow in getting on with it. Some did get to work; others merely glanced at their lands and returned home, while many did not appear at all. Of those who had made progress, the English had concentrated on building, while the more thrifty Scots had started to raise crops. These groups received encouragement from the Commissioners while absentees were threatened with forfeiture. Many Irish however, still occupied their former lands, as the newcomers saw no point in driving out tenants when as yet there were no new ones to replace them. Others lurked in the woods, fought not only with the new settlers but with each other and made raids on the owners of their lost lands.

Throughout the seventeenth century the new landlords set about improving the landscape by clearing trees, making roads and founding towns. The great forest of Glenconkeyne which stretched along the western shore of Lough Neagh was hewn down and the timber prepared for floating down the Bann for rebuilding the towns of Coleraine and Londonderry. All went well until the death of King James in 1625. His successor, Charles I, was determined to obtain more money from Ireland to make him independent of the English Parliament. He imposed new rents and insisted on the colonists obeying his every word. He fined the London Companies £70,000 for occupying lands to which he claimed they were not entitled. This was a dangerous thing to do as the Companies were both wealthy and powerful and in the long run it would not be in his own interests to antagonise them. As it turned out the fine was eventually declared unlawful and was never paid.

The changing political and economic situation made the native Irish rebellious. This came to a head in 1641. Then in 1666 the British Parliament introduced harsh new laws. One was the Irish Cattle Act which prevented the export of Irish cattle and farm produce to England. This struck a blow at one of Ireland's few sources of wealth and it affected Protestant landowners more than Roman Catholic. Driven to find some other source of income, farmers turned to the intensive breeding of horses, a field in which they have been successful to the present day.

The Diamond, Coleraine.

Courtesy of Speedy Moore and *The Coleraine Chronicle*

Coleraine Pig Market.

However, discontent leading to rebellion and war continued for most of the remainder of the seventeenth century. The eighteenth and nineteenth centuries were comparatively peaceful, allowing the Londoners to get on with the job of governing and improving the country.

What the Irish Society inherited in Coleraine, according to Pynnar in his report of 1618, was a town 'in a most wretched state, and that part of the towne which is unbuilt so dirty especially at the market place, that it is nearly impassable'. Derry (of which more later) was but a collection of ruined forts and church buildings.

The market in Coleraine had been granted by charter (three to be held weekly), also one fair in the year to be continued for eight days, together with a Court of Piepowder. Markets of sorts were originally held in the townland of Roselick on the estate of Mark Kerr Esq. but these had petered out. Coleraine suffered greatly during the rebellion of 1641, but continued to hold its markets and fairs. Cattle fairs were once held at Killowen, then a village across the Bann in the Clothworkers' Estate, but these died out while those at Coleraine prospered and increased in number.

The town built by the Irish Society included a church, several meeting houses and other places of worship and 200 timber houses which were enclosed by an earthen wall and ditch. The Society also erected a bridge across the Bann and when this was swept away by floods in 1745, they replaced it with a new one at a cost of £2,050. They founded and built a free schoolhouse in 1705 (rebuilt in 1821). They gave £700 and 35 tons of timber towards the building of a Town Hall in 1742 and a further £200 for improvements to it in 1787. As far back as 1616 they offered £200 towards the building of a pier at Portrush – then a mere fishing station and a known haunt of pirates – if the people of the neighbourhood thought it worthwhile to do likewise. They did not, and it was not until 1827 (211 years later) that improvements to that harbour commenced. By then the cost was £15,000 which was met in full by the people of Coleraine. The townspeople also bought a steamboat for £10,000 to trade with England and Scotland. Exports were mainly dairy and other farm produce. Imports included horses, mares, geldings and Highland ponies.

By this time (the nineteenth century) Coleraine had both a good grain market and a good linen market. The linen market was held in The Diamond every Saturday. There were at the same time markets for butter, potatoes, corn and flax near New Row and one for yarn in Church Street. Cattle were sold in a field to the south of the town, also on Saturday. Grain was sold on Monday, Wednesday and Friday; pork and butter on Wednesday only.

It was around this time that the linen market began to decline and the grain market to improve. A new market place and grain store were opened in 1829 and a charge was levied by the Worshipful Corporation of Coleraine for customs and weighing. The charge ranged from a penny on a sack of potatoes, live pig, or sheep to fourpence on a sack of eels and tenpence on a carcase of beef. By this time the town also had a tannery, a brewery, a soapery, a chandlery and the usual scattering of corn and flax mills in the surrounding countryside. It had a thriving Farming Society which organised shows and an annual ploughing match. It also encouraged excellence by awarding prizes for good animal and crop husbandry.

Hiring fairs were held in May and November. When these began is uncertain but they lasted well into the twentieth century. On hiring day The Diamond was besieged by an army of showmen, hawkers and other catch-penny artists. The east end was monopolised by a Punch and Judy Show. At the entrance to New Row a preacher exhorted the Godless to 'betake themselves to The Fountain of Living Waters' where they might wash and be clean. Nearby the Salvation Army Band played sacred music. Many a courtship was formed on the day of the fair and if the couple hired in places far apart they would arrange to see each other again at the next fair. The usual meeting place was outside the second-hand clothes shop at Stone Row.

One of Coleraine's many hirelings, David Given, was so happy with his lot that he wrote a poem in his master's honour. 'Hiring taught me a lot', he claimed, 'especially the important thing of fending for myself. Sammy Shaw was a good honest man and never asked me to do any work he wouldn't have done himself, and his cottage was truly home to me.' However, he didn't really appreciate the farmer's kindness until one day he decided he would like a change and set off for the fair. He was approached by a rough-looking farmer from outside the town. 'Are you looking for a place, son?' the farmer asked. 'I am,' said the boy. The farmer took a step back and looked him up and down as if he were appraising a cow and asked, 'Have you got your character with you?' (meaning a reference). The boy said that he hadn't but promised to return with it in an hour's time. The farmer agreed and they met again as arranged. 'Good boy. You've kept your promise and come back. And have you got your character?' he asked. 'No, but I got yours and I'm not coming to you.' However, by this time the boy had missed his hiring. After a few days wandering about the countryside he plucked up the courage to return to Sammy Shaw, who welcomed him back with open arms. Years later he composed the following poem.

Courtesy of Speedy Moore and The Coleraine Chronicle

David Given.

On the road from Rasharkin that leads o'er the mountain,
And down through Duneaney, onward to the Main,
There stands a wee cottage by the side of the mountain
Which brings back sweet memories again and again.

'Tis forty long years since lonely I cherished
The glow of the fire, 'neath its roof thatched with straw,
For friends I had few and oft would have perished
Had it not been for the kindness of brave Sammy Shaw.

I being light-hearted and youth was adorning
I craved for adventure and in strange parts to roam.
But fate brought me back in the grey of the morning
To the cottage on the brae that I always called home.

Praise indeed from a hired man!

Fairs were usually reported in the local papers thus informing farmers of the price of livestock as well as the price of workers. *The Coleraine Chronicle* of 13 May 1876 says of the Coleraine Annual Cattle Fair And Hiring Market:

> *What was formerly the chief fair of the year for the sale of black cattle and sheep and the hiring of domestic and agricultural servants was held in Coleraine yesterday (Friday). The weather was splendid and the attendance of substantial farmers and their wives and the almost equally well-dressed crowd of young men and women was immense. The market for 'helps', as the Americans say, and for cattle was large. The hiring fair will show more animation today (Saturday) when it is quite possible the value placed upon the services of agricultural labourers and domestic servants yesterday will be virtually toned down to what employers are content to concede. Stout young men told us yesterday that they thought £9 in the half-year ending 12th November for hands who could do almost anything on the farm was about a high average, £10 for the same period being only in a few instances granted. Boys got from £4 to £6; girls and young women £4 10[s] 0 to £5 5[s] 0 for a similar period...*

The area south of Coleraine was renowned for its weavers, its bleach greens, its lapping greens and drying houses. Credit for this went to the Merchant Taylors and the Scotch and English settlers who 'by their incessant industry and good conduct' raised the parish to its then wealth through the linen trade. In spite of this there were at least thirty badged paupers in the area. The badge, made of tin and stamped AHADOWEY, KILREA or wherever they came from, indicated that they were 'respectable' beggars and as such were entitled to beg throughout the parish. Badging ceased in the 1840s with the advent of the workhouse.

There was a good linen market in Kilrea (a Mercers' town) and one was attempted in Garvagh (an Ironmongers' town) but the latter did not succeed. Each of these towns was but a cluster of miserable huts when taken over by their respective London Companies in the seventeenth century. Their agents first built fortified houses for themselves and then proceeded

Courtesy of Ian McCullough

Fair Day, Kilrea. The building on the left is the Northern Bank. Kilrea Presbyterian Seceding Church is on the right.

to establish markets and fairs and build towns, but again their efforts were hampered by continual attacks and uprisings.

Kilrea started off with weekly markets and just one fair held in September. By the early nineteenth century it had eight fairs. It was renowned far and wide for its 'lively horse markets'. Large quantities of yarn were sold and there was good trade in second-hand clothes. Every second market was a linen market at which coarse narrow webs of brown linen were sold. A corn market was held every Thursday. As time went on fairs increased and were held regularly on the second and fourth Wednesday of the month until they ceased in the twentieth century. The Wednesday market still takes place but today it is held on the old Fair Green in Maghera Street.

By 1830 the town had around 900 inhabitants, many of whom had been weavers but their looms had by then fallen idle. During the next decade the Mercers' Company sank a well, installed a pump and added several buildings to the town. A man was employed to look after the pump and keep the cistern full of water. His wages of seven shillings a week were recouped from the townspeople in the form of a quarterly levy ranging from one shilling for a householder to five shillings for a hotelkeeper. Today the war memorial occupies the site of the old town pump. The new buildings included a hotel called The Mercers' Arms which had good stabling and rooms for the company's agent, bailiff, magistrates etc.; also a dispensary, police barracks and market house with – surprisingly, since the cottage industry was in decline – an upper room for sealing linen webs. This had previously been done in a loft in Bridge Street.

Agents were strict and demanded a high standard from their tenants, who had to whitewash their houses regularly, both inside and out. A lease was sometimes granted for six months only, its renewal depending on the cleanliness and behaviour of the tenant, who was expected to uphold the law and act in a respectable manner at all times. A lease could be withdrawn if a

Courtesy of Ian McCullough

Selling local produce in Garvagh.

tenant was discovered to be a habitual drinker or to quarrel with his neighbour. The Mercers' Company prohibited dancing and forbade all nocturnal meetings, believing these would lower moral standards. They carried this to great lengths. At that time the people of the area were in the habit of meeting at a stream called the Clattering Ford, sitting down, washing their feet and discussing the state of the markets in Kilrea and Garvagh. Innocent enough you might think, but the Mercers' Company put a stop to it, seeing in it something that might lead to undesirable behaviour. They also put a stop to card playing, dice throwing and cock fighting. Well-behaved tenants might expect to have their rents reduced or their holdings enlarged. However changes were on the way. Towards the end of the nineteenth century Parliament passed several acts – unfavourable to landlords – thus enabling tenants to buy their land. By the outbreak of the First World War the changeover was almost complete. The London Companies, however, continued their good work albeit in an increasingly charitable role. The final severance took place in the 1960s when the Mercers' Company decided to break their links with the Irish Society. At the same time tenants in Kilrea were given the opportunity to buy out the leases on their premises. Most did so.

In the beginning Garvagh had a weekly market held every Friday and just four fairs which were established by George Canning, the first agent for the Ironmongers' Company. The number of fairs increased to twelve in the nineteenth century. They were notorious for their faction fights which continued to the late nineteenth century while stick fighting continued until the 1920s.

Several roads converged on Garvagh, which made it an important meeting and crossing place. It was on the direct road from Coleraine to Dungannon and was served on that route by the 'Wellington' coach, which was drawn by three horses and stopped regularly at the local inn.

It was on the (Newtown-) Limavady–Kilrea route by which pork, butter and other merchandise were conveyed to Belfast and it was on a road favoured by cattle jobbers taking their animals to Larne and other ports en route to England and Scotland. These started off with anything from fifty to eighty animals, buying or selling as circumstances dictated along the way. The town had the usual markets for dairy produce, grain and pork but the commodities sold were said to be very limited, mainly due to the fact that there was no market house or shelter for the storage of goods as no proprietor had up until then devoted his attention to improving the town. However in 1829 along came a certain Archibald Fisher who built a new pork and grain market, together with two dwelling houses intended for shops, some sheds and storehouses, and a black hole [lock-up] with an upper storey for holding petty sessions. The markets improved immediately, particularly for the sale of dairy produce, pork, yarn and flax; also churns, tubs, milk strainers, books, crockery, ropes, baskets and much, much more.

The nearby village of Swatragh had four fairs. The patent, originally granted to the Stewart family in the early seventeenth century, passed to the Mercers' Company in 1830 'under whose fostering care it was expected to improve.' No tolls were charged on the horses, cows, pigs, sheep, goats and yarn sold there. Of the thirty-one houses in the village, sixteen were occupied by weavers who also laboured, each having an acre of land and a cow's grass (enough ground to graze a cow). All these places changed to monthly fairs in the nineteenth century though Kilrea and Coleraine had a score or more with extra days set aside to include hiring and the sale of horses.

The cluster of villages lying between Swatragh and the Bann included Upperlands, Bovedy, Inishrush, Gulladuff and Tamlaght (or Tamlaght O'Crilly). Upperlands is synonymous with the Clark family whose mills have flourished there for over 300 years. Bovedy once had a pleasure fair held on Christmas Day. Gulladuff and Inishrush each had a small weekly corn market which lasted from October until the following May. Tamlaght had quarterly fairs which ceased about 1800 for the usual reason – drunkenness on Fair Day. However there were good fairs in Kilrea, Maghera and Portglenone, and farmers and weavers simply took their custom elsewhere. One of them was Andrew Smyth, farmer and linen manufacturer, from Tamlaght village itself. Trade was good in the early part of the century but times were changing and he would soon need to think of other ways of making a living. Whole families were emigrating, mostly to America. This was due partly to bad farming years at the beginning of the century and a near-famine in 1817 when many perished, but none compared with the Great Famine years of 1845 to 1848. The Smyth family had weathered those years of misery, but around that time they left Tamlaght and went to a farm at Falgortreavey, a short distance outside Maghera. However Andrew was not content to farm so he asked his old friend and former minister the Reverend James Smyth of Drumbolg for a reference, before setting off into the wide world to seek his fortune. He eventually arrived in Australia where he tried his hand at panning for gold. He must have had some success at this for the family still have some jewellery made from Australian gold.

Meanwhile yet another Smyth family was farming at Lakeview, not far from Tamlaght village. The last of that family inherited with the farm an old retainer called Hugh Whyte who had been with the family since 1893. Hugh's duties revolved round the yard work. He fed pigs, helped the servant girl with the milking, cleaned out the byre, brushed and tidied the yard. He is remembered as a small man who travelled everywhere on foot. He had his own quarters in the big house and lived in it for eight years on his own after Joseph Smyth married and moved

Letter of recommendation from Pastor James Smyth for Andrew Smyth.

to more modern premises nearby. He could lilt, dance and sing and was a popular figure at local gatherings. When his final call came he was laid to rest in the Smyth family plot at Drumbolg. He had served the family for seventy years.

After a few years Andrew came home from Australia to look after the old folk and with their passing married Eliza Little, who was one of seven sisters from the Little family of Orritor near Cookstown. He then moved to County Tyrone, living first at Cady and then at Drummond near the village of Rock. It was while living at Cady that Andrew unwittingly offended his landlord by letting the smoke from his chimney drift towards the manor at Tullylagan. The Tullylagan butler was despatched post-haste with orders to extinguish the fire immediately. No reason was given but perhaps Landlord Greer was afraid of soot falling on the linen on his bleach green. At this point in his life Andrew was appointed tithe and cess collector for the district of Dungannon and moved to the lovely old farmhouse at Drummond. Andrew and Eliza's last resting-place is in the shade of some tall trees in Sandholes Presbyterian Churchyard.

Andrew in his younger days often attended the fairs and markets in Maghera. The origins of that town go back into the mists of time. It was church property and existed as a village

Andrew Smyth.

The now over-grown farmyard where Hugh Whyte once lived and worked. Hugh's living quarters were on the left.

before the Plantation, in consequence of which the streets are narrow, unlike the newer towns and villages 'planned' by the London Companies. Its narrow streets and old church bear testimony to its venerable ecclesiastical history. Saint Lurach is said to have built his church there at the end of the fourth century. A patent for fairs was granted by Charles II in the late-seventeenth century, but it is likely that there were fairs in the vicinity of the old church from a much earlier date. It is known that the old market house at the eastern end of the town was built with stone and lime and thatched with heather. Another was built at the opposite end for marketing butter, beef, flax and mutton. The old one was then used for selling meal and grain. The new building is said to have been used to hang the staunch Presbyterian Walter Graham for standing by his principles as a United Irishman in 1798 while McKeever, his chief and companion, fled the country. Another school of thought believes that the hanging took place on a tree near the church and that the body was displayed on the market house afterwards as a warning to other would-be rebels.

Maghera came into its own as a Post and Market town. Around 1800 coaches travelling between Dungannon and Coleraine met regularly at Falls' Hotel at twelve noon. The Londonderry–Belfast coach also arrived at noon. Market Day was Tuesday; the last Tuesday in the month was Fair Day, and the day for selling corn was Friday. There were no tolls collected after 1832, when the townspeople purchased that right from Alexander Clark, then-proprietor of the town. Mr Clark remained, however, their main benefactor. He built the two market houses, established the butter market, provided the poor with turf, and set up a spinning fund for twelve poor housekeepers. He also encouraged the building of a Presbyterian meeting house and the making of new roads with the active support of the Drapers' and Mercers' Companies under the guidance of the Irish Society.

Courtesy of Ian McCullough

Maghera May Fair Day in 1909. The men on the left are carrying cabbage plants.

Maghera's fairs and markets were extensive, encompassing hiring and the sale of potatoes, sheep, pigs, horses and cattle of every description; also wearing apparel, hardware, tinware, delph, riddles, tubs, chairs and the hundred and one miscellaneous items needed in every home in the countryside. Its linen market ceased even before the slump in the linen trade because of a row which broke out between the weavers and merchants over the quality of a web of cloth. Vitriol was thrown over the merchants who thereafter took their custom to Magherafelt.

Two fairs were held each year a few miles away in the village of Curran – one in June and the other in November. Sometimes they were of so little consequence that hardly anyone turned up. On 23 November 1836 only twenty cows and one pig were exhibited for sale.

The nearby village of Castledawson supported markets and fairs until the 1800s but after that they declined there but began to flourish in Bellaghy. Castledawson, once called Dawson's Bridge, was a former linen village founded by the Dawson family from Westmorland. Its four fairs died out altogether in the 1830s due mainly to the nearness of the excellent fairs in Magherafelt. However the village was well supplied with meat, dairy products, poultry and eggs; also Bann eels from Toome, and Lough Neagh trout and pollan – all abundant and cheap in their season.

Bellaghy started off with two fairs which increased to twelve in 1805. Thereafter they were held regularly on the first Monday of every month until fairs ceased in the middle of the twentieth century. The usual farm animals were bought and sold (but no horses), also pedlars'

Harvesting Flax near Maghera

Top: Fordson tractor with flax puller near Maghera.
Bottom left: Tying beets (sheaves) of flax. Ties were usually made from rushes.
Bottom right: Boon of flax pullers. A boon could have any number up to thirty workers.

Courtesy of Peter McGuckin

Courtesy of Peter McGuckin

Courtesy of Peter McGuckin

Top: 'Drowning' the flax. Beets were placed heads down in the water (weighed down with stones) for seven to twelve days.
Bottom: Load of retted flax on its way to the mill after being gaited and retied.

Feeding the flax into the crimpers in the scutch mill.

Line of scutchers in bays (stalks) in scutch mill. Flax went to market laid lengthways in boxes. Each length was tied in three places and weighed one stone. Hence the scales with the weight hung on the end (left of the picture). It was sold in the market as a stone of flax.

goods and earthenware. There was a weekly market for flax and yarn. There were in addition two registered fairs on 12 May and 12 November which in all probability were hiring fairs. Bellaghy has a fine example of a Plantation bawn which was built in 1622 for the Vintners' Company, though the Vintners were seldom there. At the same time a church was built; also a corn mill and twelve wooden houses, all of which were either slated or tiled. Bellaghy Church was yet another destroyed by rebels in 1641. The Vintners' and Salters' Companies (who undertook to 'improve and plant' lands north and south of the Moyola River) did not make the progress on their estates they might have done, due to the fact that they let their land out to agents or middlemen whose aim was to make as much money out of it as possible. These agents could (and did) put rents up at will, whether the tenants could afford it or not. Tenants were known to sell every last item of food produced on their land and do without food themselves in order to meet the agents' demands.

Magherafelt was in the Salters' estate for which a grant was obtained in 1631. In that year a licence was granted to Ralph Whistler, agent of the company, to hold a market every Thursday and two annual fairs each lasting two days. The fairs were so successful that they increased to four sometime in the eighteenth century, twelve by the nineteenth and were actually being held twice monthly at the end of the nineteenth and into the twentieth century. They were held on the streets until 1840 when the lessees (the Bateson family) provided a Fair Hill for the purpose. They also built a market in Charity Street. At the time (1836) it was considered a great asset to the town, but within a short space of time the markets for grass seed, hay, straw, pork, young pigs, flax, etc. were back on the streets. The town had a market house, market yard, courthouse, grain market and corn store; also a linen hall situated beside the courthouse at the north end of Broad

Bellaghy Bawn - now restored and used as a visitor attraction.

Courtesy of Muriel Bell

The Diamond Magherafelt. This picture was probably taken on a market day about 1910. The spire on the left belongs to Our Lady of Assumption R.C. Church and that on the right is 1st Magherafelt Presbyterian Church.

Street. The linen hall had wooden stands on which the merchants stood when the market was in progress. Linen was sold twice monthly. Large quantities of grain and pork were at one time exported from the Magherafelt area to Belfast and Newry, both by road in carts and by lighter from Ballyronan.

Magherafelt is a good example of Planters' planning, the Salters having created a large Square (or Diamond) from which the main streets radiate. A castle was built in the centre of the town, though no one took possession of it until the reign of Charles I. A castle and a few wooden houses were also built at Salterstown on the shore of Lough Neagh but the proposed town was never built. A recent dig by archaeologists revealed the foundations of the original houses. In 1641 the castle in Magherafelt was wrecked, the rector of the parish church murdered, and the church itself (which had been dedicated to St Swithin, the patron saint of the Salters' Company) burnt to the ground. However the town flourished in spite of these setbacks, due in no small measure to its linen trade, its markets and its fairs. Thursday was the general market day, with special days set aside for set commodities. Sam Brown remembers the markets well. His memories span most of the twentieth century:

> The grass seed market was always on a Monday in Magherafelt. All the farmers roun' about had in loads of grass seed. It was all horses an' loads. It woulda' been from the market yard right up till the Diamond. There wud a' been a row of horses an' carts all stannin' along gettin' weighed an' gettin' delivered. The men come from Belfast an' wud a' punched the bag wi' a' scoop they had;

Sam Brown on hiring day.

had; throw the seed on a black sheet an' they wud a' bought it at such 'n a price an' that was every Monday during the summer (from August 'til the grass seed finished). About two months redd it up. The same men come to Cookstown on a Tuesday an' bought it there too.'

If he was free, Sam liked to attend the hiring fairs in Magherafelt, Maghera and Cookstown, whether or not he needed to hire. On one occasion he hired on condition that he was allowed to go to Magherafelt Fair on the day before he started work. The woman (a widow) had come to see Sam in the hope that he would hire with her. When he saw her he wasn't sure whether he wanted to hire with her or not. Sam was small. She was tall and well built and looked as though she could tackle any job on the farm herself. He'd heard the talk about Paddy Wilson having been hired with her, and Paddy was a great man with a scythe. As these thoughts were running through Sam's head she suddenly spoke:

'I've no mowing machine. I've about seventy acres of land. My husband died and I have to carry on. I've four daughters and a son. I pay good money. What are you looking?'

Says I, 'Ten poun'.'

'Big money,' says she.

'Well,' says I, 'if you can get anybody at less that's up to you. I'm a horse man an' any other way it comes.'

Says she, 'I've a young horse an' I'm feedin' him for 'The Moy' [Fair]. He's sixteen hands high an' nobody can ride him.'

'Then you couldn't sell him,' says I.

Sam liked the challenge of 'breaking in' the horse and decided to go, provided she allowed him to go to Magherafelt Fair the next day. He remembers that fair well, for someone in the throng tried to steal his pocket watch:

There was that big a crowd that you had to go through it sideways through the stalls. I felt a pluck and there my watch chain was cut in two. But she was that well in the breast pocket they didn't get 'er out. Then there was shootin' galleries an' there was everything to ketch [catch] the money. I didn't bother me head wi' them. There was Pretty Lizzie an' Hairy Mary. That was a hairy family. They were figures of wee men an' weemin wi' curly hair on them. Anyway they were all stannin' up in a row. 'A penny buys three more. Where are all the lucky lads? Three shots a penny.' You give a penny, an' you got three of these balls that you clodded [threw] at them. Then a man at the side pulled a cord an' they all stud up again. I didn't spend much. I might have bought a penknife; very little. You maybe got a cup o' tay an' you went through an' watched these boys.

Then away at the west corner – it used to be called Douglas's Corner; an' then the Constitution Corner – the like o' me if I was goin' to hire, I wud a' had a red tie roun' me neck tied, an' a bunnel [bundle] annunder [under] me arm. You wud a' went an' stud along that fut-pad maybe two or three row deep. Out the' come. This was the oul farmers. 'Are ye hired? Wud ye engage? Can ye lead a horse an' cart? Can ye plough?' An' the' wud say, 'I can plough an' mow corn. I can put on a sheet an' sow it wi' the han'.' That was in 1912.

I just went till it to see how things was goin' on. An' the whole fun of it was – there was an oul fella an' an oul hussy up at the Fair Hill – fernenst the Fair Hill School. The' called him Davy Berry. He had a corduroy kep [cap] an' corduroy coat an' corduroy trousers. An' the wife an' him fell out an' he was away a piece an' she had a stick – she was threat'nin' him. An' what she wud do! Then a wheen of us was comin' up walkin' home at night tired, an' there she was, busy liltin' a fancy tune an' he was dancin' on an oul tin lid. An' we stopped. If you'd a' heerd the dances o' that! Step-dancin'! A lid about three fut wide. He was step-dancin' an' she was liltin' a fancy tune. That finished it up an' we come on home. A lot of the boys woulda got drunk an' started fightin' an' you were better out of it. You could get into trouble.

Anyway I started wi' Mrs Sloss the next day. Then wan night that year I went to Coagh. There was a bit of a carry-on an' a band practice. I went into John R. Elliott's shop for a message. John R. Elliott's son (Rowley Elliott) was a member of the Stormont Parliament an' the word come that the *Titanic* had hit an iceberg an' was split in two. So that night Coagh was in an uproar. We were all late of comin' home. I come home to Sloss's where I was workin' at the time. Slosses was all in bed but they had left the back door open that I cud get in. I took off my shoes an' slipped up the stairs. Some of them slept in the room below. One of the girls spakes up, 'Sam, is there anything wrong in Coagh the night? You're late.'

'A terrible thing,' says I. 'The *Titanic*'s sunk.' Well the' all got up an' it was two o'clock in the mornin' before the' went to bed. It was powerful. Ever so many men had lost their lives.

It come on then till the twelfth of November an' Mrs Sloss says, 'Are ye stayin' on?'

'Naw,' says I, 'Am not stayin'.'

'An' what's wrong wi' your house?'

'Not a ha'p'oth,' says I. 'It's a tarrible good house.'

But her an' me had had our ups an' downs. Says I, 'You have a son an' he's fond of a horse. An',' says I, 'I'm fond of a horse. Him an' me wud be fightin' over these horses.'

'Ye'll get all the horse work ye want.'

'I'm the pickle nixt the wind,' says I. 'I'll go. Your son's entitled to the horses. The horses is yours an' they'll be his.' So I left. The house was a brave piece aff the road and they left me to the road. 'You'll be back,' they said. 'I might be back an' I might not be back.' I said; an' away I went.

It wasn't as easy to find a good place to hire as Sam thought and to be truthful he was embarrassed at the situation in which he found himself. It reminded him of an old poem called 'Magherafelt Hiring Fair' that he had heard many years before. It is thought to have been written about 1800.

1   *Would you hire with me, Tam Bo, Tam Bo?*   2   *£2 5s 0d, Tam Bo, Tam Bo,*
    Would you hire with me, my heart and my Jo?   *£2 5s 0d, my heart and my Jo,*
    Would you hire with me, say you and say I,   *£2 5s 0d, say you and say I,*
    And what an' a rantin' young widow am I.   *And what an' a rantin' young widow am I.*
       What wages mistress?   **Too little wages mistress.**

3   *Then two pounds ten, Tam Bo, Tam Bo,*   4   *Sowans and eels, Tam Bo, Tam Bo,*
    Two pounds ten my heart and my Jo,   *Sowans and eels, my heart and my Jo,*
    Two pounds ten say you and say I,   *Sowans and eels say you and say I,*
    And what an' a rantin' young widow am I.   *And what an' a rantin' young widow am I.*
       What diet mistress?   **Too slippy diet mistress.**

5   *Then potatoes and beef, Tam Bo, Tam Bo,*   6   *You'll lie in the laft, Tam Bo, Tam Bo,*
    Potatoes and beef, my heart and my Jo,   *You'll lie in the laft, my heart and my Jo,*
    Potatoes and beef, say you and say I,   *You'll lie in the laft, say you and say I,*
    And what an' a rantin' young widow am I.   *And what an' a rantin' young widow am I.*
       Where will I lie mistress?   **The rats might eat me mistress.**

7   *You'll lie wi' the weans, Tam Bo, Tam Bo,*   8   *Well then we'll get married, Tam Bo, Tam Bo,*
    You'll lie wi' the weans, my heart and my Jo,   *Well then we'll get married, my heart and my Jo,*
    You'll lie wi' the weans, say you and say I,   *Well then we'll get married, say you and say I,*
    And what an' a rantin' young widow am I.   *And what an' a rantin' young widow am I.*
The weans might kick me mistress.

The words in bold were spoken.

Meantime, unknown to Sam, his father had taken earls (two half-crowns) on Sam's behalf from a farmer called Willie Clarke of Lakeview near Ballyronan. Sam was furious at not being consulted by his father before he accepted the earls:

'Under no circumstances will I go to Willie Clarke. Will ye give me the earls?'
     An' we had it up an' down. Says I, 'Give me the earls.' An' m' father put 'is han' in 'is pocket an' give me the two half-crowns. Out I go an' I niver stopped till I landed in the fiel' to Willie Clarke an' a fella. Well the fella was fit till handle horses alright if you were in the fiel' wi' 'im. He was scourin' these potatoes wi' two horses an' Clarke was back an'

forrad wi' 'im.

'Are ye comin' home?'

'Naw,' says I. 'I'm comin' to give ye these earls ye give me father.'

'I'm not takin' them,' says he.

'Ye didn't give them to me. Ye'll hae them to take.'

'Under no circumstances,' says he. 'Catch that plough to you see the way she's runnin'.'

'O naw,' says I. 'I'll ketch no plough.' So I struck on up to the house. I was right an' smart on me fut at that time. An' Mrs Clarke says, 'Who are you?'

'I'm Sam Brown.'

'Are ye comin' home?'

'Naw,' says I. 'I'm comin' to give ye these earls.'

'I'll take no earls.'

She was stannin' in the door. An' I just threw them through the door into the kitchen between 'er feet. An' I luked roun' an here wasn't the oul boy comin' as hard as he cud footle. An' I made aff. He didn't speak to me for about two years after it.

Sam worked for a spell also with a namesake of his – George Brown of The Loup. He was fourteen and it was the first place that he hired. He continues:

George lived his lone, well – just him an' the father. The father was old and kinda dotin'.

Sam Brown in later years.

Courtesy of Sam Brown

So I left school to attend the oul man an' keep house. I hadn't been rared wi' the rest of the family so I didn't really mind. I lived wi' me father. He was the keeper of a farm at Ballybriest belonging to a vit [vet] in Magherafelt. He kep' short-horn cattle an' had a stud horse. A brother [of the vet's] went to the market wi' this stud horse on a market day. He [the horse] went along the road nickerin' [whinnying]. You'd 'a been afeard till a' met 'im. There was no such thing as lorries till transport them then. This man walked 'im. He walked 'im to Cookstown. He walked 'im to Magherafelt. That wud be away about nineteen hundred an' six or seven. M' father got a fiel' for grazin' a cow an' he had to see after these kettle [cattle] for this vit, an' me an' m' father lived in the house.

Anyway, I went to George Brown's an' I attended to the oul man. I done the cookin'. We had a small wee pot that wud a hel' maybe a stone o' potatoes; potatoes an' butter. Whiles we wud a' fried a wheen o' cuts of bacon an' broke an' egg on it. He lived a couple of years after I went there. The first year I just had three poun' for the six months. An' the next year a poun' more an' the next year a poun' more an' so on. I lived wi' George 'til 'e got married an' a year or two after 'e married. He got a tar'ble good woman. Every six months I got paid. Well, I'd 'a got a wheen o' shillin's or a pair o' shoes if I needed it or some clothes. George had a washing machine. It was wooden. You turned a han'le roun' an' roun' an' as you turned the han'le a spindle inside it wi' lugs on it went backwards an' forwards. There was a wringer on the top of it. That was the first place I hired.

The last place I hired was Jackson's. I was fifty years in Jackson's. She was a wee woman an' she had a son an' daughter an' they were lookin' someone to look after the horses. The son had a bad heart. I was goin' to leave it one time an' go to Scotland. I didn't like this wee woman tellin' me how to do things. She was no size. She was the real boss. The son couldn't walk about or do anything. He died in 1914. When the son died I said, 'If you were a pair o' wise weemin now, (they had a farm of about fifty acres) yez wud call an auction, sell all the stuff aff, set the lan' an' you could live 'private'. Where's the use in youens carryin' on farmin'?'

An' the oul woman got out the handkerchief an' she sat awhile an' she said, 'As long as you stay, I'll pay you whatever you charge for you're trustworthy, an' I'll farm. I wouldn't like to see the things that me an' my son have gathered up goin' away. D'ye see?'

So I stayed. She lived to she was ninety years of age. I still stayed on after she died an' the daughter carried on. I tuk the stuff out an' sold it in the market an' kep' an account. I used to take maybe a litter of pigs or two or three head of cattle. Then the daughter died an' the place was sold. I had a wee place of my own bought between Moneymore an' Coagh. Then war broke out an' anybody that had more than ten acres had to plough it; an' the lan' was better for grazin' than labourin'; so I sold it again on Moneymore Fair Day by auction an' bought another place at £400, all good lan' an' arable. That's this place. I'm eighty-seven now so I'll har'ly ever move again.

Girls hired in Magherafelt too. The trials and tribulations of one are recalled in the poem, 'Magherafelt May Fair' supplied by James Mulholland of Randalstown:

Manor House, Moneymore, home of the Agent of the Drapers' Company.

I am a bouncing fair young girl, my age is scarce sixteen
And when I'm dressed all in my best I look like any queen;
Young maidens fair from far and near that want till sell your ware,
On the twelfth of May I'll make my way to the Magherafelt May Fair.

My mother cautioned me going out, 'Do not stay late in town,
For if you do, your father and I, on you we both will frown.
Be sure to shun bad company and of all young men beware
They nice may be but don't make free in the Magherafelt May Fair.'

'Mother dear, oh do not fret, and set your mind at rest,
For I must leave this house some day as the white swan leaves the nest.'
I dressed myself in my blue gown and combed my bonny brown hair.
There'll be many a boy from Toome to Moy at the Magherafelt May Fair.

I bade them all Good Morning and hoisted then my sail,
Hoped providence would guide me with a sweet and pleasant gale
And though to my misfortune on my arrival there
There were females ten for each young man in the Magherafelt May Fair.

151

Like any sprite or air searchlight I wandered up and down.
I was puffed with pride and vanity – my feet scarce touched the ground,
And as I walked the young men talked and at me they did stare,
Though I was nice, none asked my price in the Magherafelt May Fair.

I stayed there till the evening still trying to make my sale,
I hoped for the best – believed the worst and my courage near did fail.
Then night came on, all hopes were gone. I may take my sale elsewhere,
At a dance or wake my chance I'll take and leave that hiring fair.

Moneymore and Draperstown were once celebrated for two things – their fairs and their cleanliness. It was not always so. When taken over by the Drapers' Company at the beginning of the seventeenth century, Moneymore was described as 'but a collection of wretched mud cabins and crooked streets'. Draperstown was little more than a few scattered mud-walled houses at a crossroads, giving it the title of The Cross at Ballinascreen. In Moneymore the Drapers' Company proceeded to build a castle overlooking the main street and lined the street on either side with six fine, two-storied thatched houses. Running water was installed (a very advanced amenity for those days). Pynnar described the castle as 'one of the finest and most perfect in Ireland.' However, like many others it was attacked in 1641 and disappeared altogether during the next century.

During these years the settlers were learning to live with and obey the rules of their new landlords – the Drapers' Company. Certain standards had to be met in their behaviour and in the tidiness of their houses. They were also bound by their leases not to cut or burn turf – this in an effort to make them cut down trees for fuel, so that the area might be rid of the forest that provided covering for the outlaws which still roamed the countryside. And outlaws were not the only ones lurking in the woods. Wolves abounded and there were some leases by which tenants were expected to kill a certain number annually.

It was during this time that Good-Will Conyngham (a Scots Presbyterian who came to Ireland in the late seventeenth century) arrived in Moneymore with his sixteen-year-old bride Ann, and decided to build 'a convenient dwelling house of lime and stone, two stories high, with necessary office houses, gardens and orchards.' This was to be known as 'Springhill', and the Conyngham family and their heirs were to live there until it was presented to The National Trust by Captain W.L. Lenox Conyngham in 1957. The same served on the committee which had assumed responsibility for the affairs of the Drapers' Company in 1904. Their main duties were to see to the continued upkeep of the Company's property and supervise the sale of land to the tenants.

To return to the early days: as it turned out the Drapers' estate was leased to agents throughout the seventeenth and eighteenth centuries. The Drapers did not take possession of it themselves until 1817. In 1818 the former Cross at Ballinascreen became known as Draperstown. From then on the aim of the Company was to educate and advance the district for the good of their tenants and the ultimate advancement of the estate. They built houses, dispensaries, market houses, corn stores, court houses, inns, schools, Presbyterian Meeting Houses, Episcopal Churches, and in Moneymore a stately Manor House. They contributed towards the improvement of other churches including the Roman Catholic Chapel. They made roads, built bridges, constructed mill races and planted trees. It was the Drapers who planted the trees around Lough Fea and in

Courtesy of Ian McCullough

Fair Day in Draperstown.

the intriguing and beautiful Reuben's Glen (recently swept away in the name of development). They provided residences for, and paid the salaries of the teachers – £50 for the master and £35 for the mistress, with turf for a fire in both cases. They contributed £10 towards the salaries of the priest and the ministers of religion. Clergy were also presented with either the rent of their farms or their tithe and bog. The dispensary surgeon got 100 guineas, a house with a good garden and forage [grass] for his horse. Roads were cut through districts hitherto almost unknown. These were used by coaches travelling regularly from such places as Dungannon and Cookstown to Coleraine and Belfast. At the same time the Drapers were managing the tenant farms which paid rent to the company. This was collected by their agent Rowley Miller Esq. who lived in the Manor House in Moneymore. Small wonder then that a report based on an inspection by the Irish Society in 1836 advised that anyone visiting the County of Londonderry should make an effort to visit Moneymore and Draperstown to see for themselves the amount of work carried out by the Company.

Both towns had excellent fairs and markets which contributed in no small measure to the economy and social life of the people. Wednesday was market day in Draperstown. The first Friday in every month was Fair Day. Today sales are held weekly. Sheep are still sold in the open street but nowadays they are sold by auction. The Market House is now a library.

The number of fairs in Moneymore increased to twelve early in the nineteenth century and from then on were held regularly on the twenty-first of every month. The markets were held at the front of the Market House, which was just one of a number of fine buildings built by the

Horse Fair in Moneymore. The horse was still very much part of the farming scene in the 1930s.

Courtesy of Ian McCullough

Drapers' Company on High Street. The ground floor was used as a corn market until the new Market Yard and corn stores were built across the street. The first floor doubled as both town hall and court for petty sessions. Linen merchants used it on fair days to pay for their cloth.

The new Market Yard had an impressive entrance off High Street and a second wider entrance on Market Street. These led to corn stores with cellars and overhanging balconies. Some grain went to local corn mills, one of which was conveniently situated by the creamery at the back of the Market House. Large quantities went to Gaussens, Huguenot immigrants who in 1788 built a pier and extensive stores in Ballyronan; also a brewery and distillery which manufactured grain into beer and whiskey. The surplus was exported via the lighters which plied regularly across Lough Neagh en route to Belfast and Newry. Local tradition has it that the last surviving Gaussen lost a fortune on the greyhound track. Although lighters had no regular passenger service, it is thought Ballyronan was the chosen point of departure for some Derry and Tyrone emigrants in the nineteenth century on the first stage of their journey to America.

Hundreds of cattle were sold in both towns. Many of these were purchased at fairs in Connaught, brought north to be fattened and then sold to dealers who exported them on the hoof to Scotland and England via such ports as Larne and Donaghadee. They were then sold on at fairs in Dumfries and Carlisle and even as far south as Norfolk and Hertfordshire. Many Irish harvesters followed this same route in their search for seasonal work. With the coming of the steamship, Glasgow, Birkenhead and Heysham became the main points of entry to the mainland.

Both Moneymore and Draperstown had good horse fairs. At a fair held in Moneymore on 21 July 1836, for instance, 343 horses were sold at prices varying from three to forty pounds, also 675 cows, 283 sheep, and 117 pigs. Other animals included 17 goats and 47 litters of sucking pigs, none of which cost more than ten shillings. Thirteen asses changed hands at from fifteen to thirty shillings. At the same time, the market was well supplied with linen, linen yarn, flannel, stockings, shoes, gates, crocks, rakes, noggins [wooden container used for storing buttermilk], churns and a hundred and one other things probably sold in both places by the same people travelling from fair to fair. Bedsteads sold at six shillings and sixpence, gates at half-a-crown, wooden pig troughs at eightpence. Itinerants played their part by trying to persuade people that they needed clothes pegs, handmade tin-ware, wire toasting forks and even paper flowers.

Tobermore and Desertmartin had fairs but no markets. Local tradition has it that the fairs held in Tobermore were originally held at the gort beside Kilcronaghan old church. A gort was a portion of land attached to a glebe, on which in ancient times clergy kept a bull, a ram and a boar for the convenience of the farmers in the parish. It contained about four acres and was enclosed by stakes and brambles. Farmers brought their animals there when in season. In later years when the practice of bringing animals to the gort died out, it was used for fairs and as a place of safety for horses while parishioners were at worship. Since fairs were never held on the Sabbath, it would have served the dual purpose admirably. Tradition has it that long ago hangings took place at Kilcronaghan too, possibly for the theft of linen or sheep. Interestingly, when the old church was being taken down, the timbers used in its roof were of such good quality that local weavers purchased them for making looms.

The neighbouring parish of Desertmartin also had a patent for fairs, but these died out in 1821 when just two of the original eight were held. While the main support of the people was linen manufacture and trading in cattle, a considerable number were engaged in the lime trade, either in quarrying it or burning it, and some were employed in the numerous small shops which sold such things as tea, sugar and tobacco to cottagers. If the cottager had not the money to pay for his purchases the shopkeeper was quite willing to accept goods in kind – usually butter, yarn or raw hides.

The Dungiven and Brackfield areas were Skinners' territory, while the Haberdashers under Sir Thomas Phillips held sway around Limavady. Both towns are beautifully situated on the banks of the River Roe. In the eighteenth century Dungiven had just two fairs, each of which was liable to last a week to the accompaniment of drinking, racing and cock-fighting. Limavady, or Newtown-Limavady as it was then known, had five. By the nineteenth century Dungiven's fairs were being held regularly on the second Tuesday of every month, though the two old patent fairs were still held in May and October. Market Day was Saturday; in Limavady it was Monday. By the nineteenth century extra fairs were being held in Limavady to accommodate people wanting to hire. For some reason these were known in Limavady as the Gallop. They continued well into the twentieth century. The poem 'Copper John' captures the atmosphere:

1   *I'm a civil fellow called Sandy Bond*   2
    Sure I'm hired with a man called Copper John
    For the second Gallop I was bound
    For to take my stand down at Magowans
    As I dandered [strolled] up through Market Street
    It's Copper John I chanced to meet
    With his brother Willie with him I seen
    Likewise Sam Dale of Drumadreen.

    Sammy Dale he says to me,
    'Will you hire wi' these two men this day?'
    Says I, 'I will if you give good pay:
    I'll engage with them till the twelfth of May.'
    'For what sort of money?' he says to me
    Says I, 'Nine poun' and I think it's fair
    And for nothin' less will I go there.'

3   *Copper John bein' standin' near*   4
    'You're a fine big fella but you're far too dear
    And since I've come into this town
    I tell you what we'll do – we'll divide a pound.'
    'Oh,' says I, 'I'm sure you will,
    But I had far more at the foot o' the hill.'
    'And now,' he says, 'Mr. Bond,
    Are you for the grass wi' the Cruiskeen Lawn?'

    Then we all went up to Martha Graham's
    And he says to me, 'What is your name?'
    Says I, 'My name is Mr. Bond,
    And from what I hear, you're Copper John.'
    We went out and we did start
    Sure John came home wi' an iron cart
    And he says to me goin' up the street,
    'I suppose you'll come to us this week.'

5   *We have a maid and of her I'll sing*   6
    This maid's name is Liza King
    And I'll flit in till the twelfth of May,
    If she'll l'ave down the bread and tay.
    Sure Copper John's a civil man
    When he's out in the market he likes a dram,
    And a jolly boy when he gets that
    Sure he looks a swell wi' his wee hard hat.

    And to conclude and end my song
    I hope I have said nothing wrong,
    I'll bid farewell, and I'll be gone
    To spend six months wi' Copper John.

    (Last line spoken)

A *Northern Whig* of November 1922 states that a feature of the fair in Limavady that month was 'the increased supply of labour, both male and female, for agricultural work, but there was still unwillingness to accept a lowered wage. The low prices prevailing for all farm products made the farmers reluctant to pay high wages. A large number were not fitted up during the day.'

Lizzie Scott was one of several I met who hired herself out in Limavady. She spoke about her experiences with an enthusiasm that belied her ninety-three years:

Yes. I was hired at the Gallop. I was twelve. My mother brought me. My father was hired. My brothers and sisters, they all hired too. There was always a big crowd at the Gallop for the working class was all redd at that time. They had two or three days holiday in May and November – the two days they galloped. Yes. You spent the day goin' roun' the town just lookin at the stalls an' wan thing an' another. That was a great evening – the

156

Courtesy of Stanley Burns

Lizzie Scott, Limavady.

Gallop – for there was mostly a Dance on somewhere that night; up in the Orange Hall here; and they all went up there that was hired. Aw, it was always a good night's dancin' 'til the mornin'. The music; it was just an ordinary fiddle and a drum, an' sometimes you had a melodeon; and we danced till the mornin'.

I was hired to John Loughrey. I stayed there at night. My room was just the kitchen loft. I went upstairs and my room went right in at the head of the stairs. I had to get up at six. It wasn't high feedin' in a man's house then. You got plenty of porridge an' plenty of spuds an' plenty of buttermilk. When you got a wheen o' good spuds an' a drop of salt an' a mug o' buttermilk you were rightly done for.

My work was feedin' pigs an' milkin' cows an' feedin' calves. One of the other women helped me to milk twelve cows: six apiece. An' then we fed twelve calves. That was our first route. An' we didnae get much 'til we had that done, an' then the old lady that kep' the house had the breakfast ready. After that I had to boil a boiler o' spuds. You had to boil that before you fed the pigs. You couldnae a' fed them without boilin' that boiler o' stuff. I wheeled the potatoes from beside Balteagh Church till Loughrey's over at Cloughan. That would be about a mile; a barrowful; I dug them myself an' gathered them and wheeled them in a barrow.

Many a time I churned. The skim milk went to the calves. There was plenty of hard work wi' them oul farmers an' you couldnae a' wrought to them. There was that much work milkin' cows an' feedin' pigs an' calves.

Then I got married when I was twenty-four. We got a cottar house wi' people my husband wrought till – just a room an' a kitchen.

Lizzie reared a large family and in later years was to be regarded as handywoman of the district. Very few could afford to call out a doctor in those days, so every neighbourhood selected its own midwife. Lizzie was the first to be called when a birth was imminent, and was the layer-out of the dead when their days on earth came to an end.

Not far away at Carrick East William Purcell also hired help. Robert Allen was a good worker but frequently appeared in the morning with a black eye or cuts and bruises, depending how he had fared the night before when he boxed at the crossroads. John Simpson first hired there when he was barely fifteen. William felt so sorry for John that he bought him a coat and pair of trousers in Paddy Burke's second-hand shop in Limavady before he left the fair. They cost him one shilling and sixpence.

Then there was Ruby Meighan the servant girl. Ruby enjoyed her time at Purcell's, though she didn't always toe the line as regards the rules:

Courtesy of Ian McCullough

Fair Day, Dungiven.

When I worked at Purcell's you had to be in at ten o'clock. 'Deed many a time you were watchin' fellas at the crossroads shootin' marbles or throwin' horse-shoes at a peg, an' you had to ring that peg; an' you forgot all about the time. But anyway this night I was late an' the back door was locked an' I says, 'What am I goin' to do?' I'll have to knock somebody up.' And the pantry was on the left. And for some reason or other the window hadn't been snibbed [closed]. And there was a barrel of flour always kept wi' a lid on it. An' of course I opens the window nicely an' I steps in the window an' stepped into the barrel

Courtesy of Stanley Burns

Home of the Purcell family, Limavady.

of flour. The lid was on the barrel but it toppled over when I stepped in. And you talk about a mess! And I had to clean that up an' keep quiet an' not waken anybody. And it wasn't easy because the boss and mistress slept in the room exactly above that. I tell you I was the sorry girl that I'd stayed them wheen o' minutes late. It wasn't worth it. I tell you I was never late from that 'til the day I left. John Simpson worked at Purcell's too. The boss used to go across the landing at half five in the morning and shout, 'Come on boys, we've slep' in.' They had to work wile hard then. There was a lot of heavy work carryin' water to cattle. Sure you'd'a pumped for about two hours. Many's a time you'd a give them a kick wi' your fut to see if they'd stop drinkin'. It was all hard work them days.

As in most other places, fairs were established in Dungiven and Limavady in the seventeenth century. At that time Dungiven had just twelve houses and Limavady eighteen, set around a crossroads with a stone cross at the intersection. The cross would indicate that fairs may have been held there at an earlier date (as in Dromore in County Down). Cattle were bought mainly by jobbers who made a living by dealing and by exporting them live through the various seaports. Drovers or dealers boarded the boat with the animals and stayed with them until they were either sold or handed over to a drover on the other side. The nearest port was Derry but they were just as often taken to Larne or Donaghadee for the short sea crossing to Portpatrick. Butter, eggs and poultry were also exported, mainly to Glasgow. Butter was put up in firkins. A firkin was reckoned to be a quarter of a barrel or 56lb weight. Eggs were sold by weight too.

Public buildings in the form of a market house, hotel, parish church and schoolhouse were built in Dungiven by the Skinners' agent, Robert Ogilby, Esq. around 1830. The old fortified bawn erected by them in 1618 had by this time long since gone. Gone too were the hundreds of humble homesteads that once furnished the valleys and lower slopes of the mountains, and the sod houses built by the young folk in the hills when they went booleying with their cattle in the summer months. Emigration and the ravages of time had taken their toll. By now farm houses, though fewer and further between, were much improved. Most were thatched and white-washed, with a fireplace and chimney to carry away the smoke (no more blackened faces or sore eyes due to the smoky atmosphere indoors). The poorer classes still lived in 'abodes of want and misery' – not surprising when a girl's wages seldom exceeded £2 10s and a man's £5 for six months.

The erection of the market house and the introduction of a public crane in Dungiven saw a big improvement in the grain and butter markets. At the same time the Haberdashers saw to it that churches, meeting houses, schools, hotels, lodging houses and a library were built in Limavady. All the usual commodities were on sale in both towns. Both also sold sea shells which were gathered on nearby beaches, crushed and used by farmers for improving the texture of the soil. Dungiven specialised in the sale of locally grown scollops [sally rods] which sold at sixpence for ten dozen. These were used for pegging the straw in thatching and in making baskets and stable loft hurls. Misshapen and waste ones, along with briars and pieces of thorn bushes, were useful for making bases for haystacks. The criss-cross of sticks kept the sheaves off the damp ground, though they provided a hiding place for vermin in winter. There was great excitement when the day came that the last row of sheaves was being fed into the thresher, for it was then that rats and mice tried to make their escape. It was not unknown for a mouse to run up the inside of a man's trouser leg. The trousers weren't long in coming off if the mouse threatened to make the distance.

Of the two, Limavady had the better linen and yarn market. It was to Limavady that yarn dealer John O'Neill was riding on an August day in 1831 when he was murdered and robbed in the Glenshane Pass. His attacker pulled him from his horse, hit him on the head with a hammer and stole the £100 he had for purchasing yarn in the Monday market in that town. It was all too common an occurrence in those days. Murders also took place on the other side of town on the

Courtesy of Ian McCullough

Old Cattle Market in Limavady.

aptly named Murderhole Road, where highwayman Cushy Glenn attacked travellers in a similar way.

Limavady will be remembered by musicians the world over as being the birth place of Jane Ross, who in 1851 saved the 'Londonderry Air' from almost certain oblivion. Jane is believed to have been so enchanted with the tune that she noted down the music when she heard it played in the street by Jimmy McCurry, a blind fiddler. Jimmy arrived into the town on market day and took up a position between the shafts of an upturned cart outside Jane's home at 51 Main Street. He played his music and collected alms, until overtaken by ill health and advancing years when he was admitted to Limavady workhouse. He died in 1910 and was mourned by all who knew him. He lies buried in the graveyard at Tamlaghtfinlagan. Jane's last resting place is at Christchurch in Limavady.

Between Limavady and the Faughan Valley lay the territory of the Fishmongers' and Grocers' Companies, who early in the seventeenth century built fortified bawns at Ballykelly and Muff (later called Eglinton). Like their sister companies, these built many fine buildings some of which are known only to local people, like Ervey old school-house built by the wealthy Grocers Company in 1831. Until recently this retained the distinctive symbol of the company in the form of a camel embedded in the wall. The chapel and burial ground of the Fishmongers and

160

Walworth Wood, planted in memory of Sir William Walworth, governor of the company at that time, were situated near the bawn at Ballykelly.

The slump in the linen industry in the early nineteenth century put many out of work, causing large numbers to emigrate. Those that were left found work in the mills and tan-yards prettily situated on the banks of the streams which drained towards the Foyle. The Fishmongers arrived in person around this time, constructed new roads and improved the old ones and erected several useful public buildings. They built a canal from Ballykelly to the Foyle but although this was used to transport building materials from Londonderry, it never fulfilled its original promise.

Two fairs were held in Ballykelly until 1807, when they succumbed to the success of those in Limavady. The grain market went the same way in 1830. An *Old Moore's Almanac* of 1895 mentions a fair at Muff on 11 December but it was probably a fair in name only, or it may even refer to the Muff across the Foyle in Donegal. There is no mention of the bustling fur and meat market once held at Benone every Friday. The fur and meat were obtained from rabbits which inhabited the sand dunes on nearby Magilligan Strand. Buyers came mainly from Belfast.

The stretch of coast from Magilligan to Killowen was the territory of the London Guild of Clothworkers, though it was dominated from the middle of the eighteenth century by the wealthy and flamboyant Earl of Bristol, Bishop of Derry. It was he who built the church at Ballykelly and numerous other smaller churches throughout his diocese, not to mention his contributions to Catholic Chapels and Dissenting Meeting Houses. He also started negotiations for building the first bridge over the Foyle, thus connecting the city with the rest of the county. His benevolence towards the poor was legendary. He put forward ambitious schemes for improvements to agriculture and planted thousands upon thousands of trees in the glens near his residence at Downhill. This once fine building is now quietly disintegrating in the winter gales that sweep across the open Atlantic. However the elegant temple named after his cousin Mrs Mussenden still survives, thanks to the care bestowed on it by the National Trust. His official residence was, of course, the Bishop's Palace in Derry, a modest building by his standards.

The portion of land lying east of the Foyle and stretching to the border with Tyrone fell to the lot of the Goldsmiths' Company. It included Clondermot, the Waterside and part of Faughanvale – about forty-five townlands in all. They chose New Buildings as the centre of their territory and it was there that they built their bawn, only to see it destroyed during the Revolution of 1688. According to a rent roll of Sir Thomas Phillips, their lands were let out at an annual rent of £331 in 1628.

Camel Plaque, Ervey school-house.

Courtesy of William Stevenson

Between New Buildings and Dungiven lie the villages of Feeny, Claudy and Park, all once famed for their fairs. Friday was the usual Fair Day in Park, Tuesday in Claudy, while it varied from month to month in Feeny, the only certain date being 17 March. Like most other towns all three were strongly influenced by their respective London Companies. Although there was no market as such, hawkers of all descriptions attended the fairs of both Park and Feeny, and bought and sold their wares without having to pay any custom. The fairs in Feeny were much favoured by both cattle jobbers and butchers.

However, the nearest and surest market for the district was to be found in Londonderry. The town, clustered round a hill overlooking the Foyle, was once small enough to be contained within its famous walls. Its history has been well documented from its beginning, when it was known as Derry Calgagh (Calgagh's Oakwood) and Derry Columbkille, when it was granted to Saint Columba for a religious settlement. It was plundered by the Norsemen time and time again, and was a completely ruined town when taken over by the Irish Society 'for the promotion of religion, order and industry'. The Society gave them a town to be proud of, a fact embodied in words on the porch wall of St Columb's Cathedral.

IF STONES COULD SPEAKE
THEN LONDON'S PRAYSE
SHOULD SOUNDE WHO
BUILT THIS CHURCH AND
CITTIE FROM THE GROUNDE

The city walls were assailed several times during that century, the most notable being in 1641, again in 1649 and during the historic siege of 1689. It was during this century also that cannons were presented by the various London Companies, the best known being *Roaring Meg* which was presented by the Fishmongers in 1642.

From the Diamond, four main streets at right angles to each other lead to the four original gates. Three more were added later. This was (and still is) the heart of the city. Fairs and markets were established and held there from the seventeenth century. The number of fairs rose to fourteen in the nineteenth century, and increased to sixteen by the twentieth century. Most included the sale of horses. The Derry horse was said to be a very good animal, never more than fourteen hands high and indefatigable. He was called a clib or clibbock in reference to his long unkempt coat. Highland ponies were also highly esteemed, especially in the Magilligan district where they did not need a heavy horse which might do damage to the soil. In the best areas the farms were good enough and prosperous enough to afford good horses and this was evidenced at the fairs in the city. A market house was built in 1622, destroyed in 1689 and rebuilt in 1692. It served also as a Town Hall, guard room, weigh-house and meal market and held the Mayor's Office. Law Courts were held on the floor above until the nineteenth century when the building was demolished. Markets were held twice weekly. The main one was held on Wednesday, with a smaller one for provisions on Saturday.

On Market day carts rumbled towards the city along the Letterkenny, Buncrana, Springtown, Culmore, Prehen and Dungiven Roads, for the economy of Donegal as well as that of Londonderry was intimately linked with the port and markets of the city. The carts were loaded with coarse linen, linen yarn, drugget, grain, flax, knitted stockings, cheap crockery, brushes, tinware, butter, buttermilk and eggs. The city was famous for its pre-Christmas goose fair, to which farmers sometimes walked their geese from places as far away as Dunfanaghy, Co. Donegal. Generally geese fed on grass and the value of the grazing of twenty geese was reckoned to be equal to one 'summ' (or 'sum'); in other words the amount of grass that a cow would graze over a season. Eggs and feathers were also sold. Londonderry had by far the best linen market in the area, though its sales never reached those of places like Lisburn, Lurgan or Dungannon. The great linen areas were proud of their success. The name 'Coleraine' for instance, stamped on a piece of linen was a mark of very high quality as were Gilford, Dungannon and Dromore (County Down). In some linen markets only gold and silver coins were accepted in payment by the sellers. This caused difficulties for the buyers, who were sometimes forced to exchange bank-notes at unfavourable rates. Apparently this was particularly true in Londonderry and Monaghan.

When the linen trade failed in the 1820s, shirt making started to take the place of weaving. It began as a cottage industry but changed when William Tillie introduced the sewing machine to the city in 1856. Factories were built, and shirt making became the main industry in the city for well over a century, employing thousands of women. Men, especially in the Bogside, Rosemount and Lecky Road areas, reared pigs and sold them to the ham- and bacon-curing factories in Foyle Street and Bishop Street. These in turn supplied the shops with such delicacies as spare ribs and pigs' feet.

Dealers came from far and near to sell their wares, including Johnny McIlroy, the same Johnny who appeared in Omagh, Strabane and other places. Johnny was short and stout with a robust voice and matching sense of humour. On one occasion the crowd remained silent while he expounded to them the merits of a batch of press-button umbrellas. At the end of his demonstration pointing out their usefulness and the necessity for everyone present to own one, the crowd remained silent, hands in pockets. He asked for an opening bid of £2 without response, progressively dropping the price till he reached 12s 6d. Not one in the assembled crowd made a move. At this stage he flung the umbrella down in simulated anger and roared, 'I hope the bladder of the heavens busts and drownds the lot o' yiz before yiz gets home.' The response to that was a roar of laughter and the umbrellas were sold in minutes.

In Donegal going to hire was referred to as going to the 'Laggan'. This was understood to be that part of the country along the Foyle, the Finn and the Mourne which specialised in agriculture. Most Donegal hirelings hired in either Strabane or Londonderry, where the hiring fair was held a few days after that of Strabane and was known as the 'Rabble'. The scene is described vividly by an unknown author in the poem 'Derry Hiring Fair':

1
Ah say there young Willie,
D'ye think ye'll stay on?
Of course I will, sorr
Till the first Rabble morn.
It's then I'll show you
A clean pair of heels,
For I'm sick to the teeth
Of your stony oul' fields.

2
They came in their hundreds
From all arts and parts
Some running, some walking,
Some riding in carts,
Like pilgrims to Mecca,
All banter and babble
But the road was to Derry,
Today was the Rabble.

3
Six months have they laboured
In cornfield and bog,
They've worked like a slave
And lived like a dog.
For a couple of hours,
They intend to be free,
There's a fair in the Diamond
They're set for the spree.

4
With red rosy faces
And navy-blue suits,
Flat caps of all sizes
And great hob-nailed boots
With eyes full of wonder
and mouths full of sweets,
Ignoring the footpaths
They walked on the streets.

5

The tradesmen are early,
Displaying their wares,
'Twas 'Yes sor, no sor,'
'Was it one or two pairs?'
Warm coats for the winter,
Stout boots for the feet,
There were bargains in plenty
Up Waterloo Street.

6

Oul farmers are looking
For labour to hire,
A man that can plough
Or a girl for the byre;
A healthy young lad
That can do what he's told,
For twelve hours a day
In the heat or the cold.

7

An oul' man looks round him,
He's been here before,
'Tis years since he left
His beloved Gweedore;
He's spent his life holding
Another man's plough,
And there's acres of furrows
All over his brow.

8

A young lad all eager
And raring to go,
Far away out of range
Of his father's big toe;
Away from a mother
Who went without dinner,
That he might grow stronger,
While she would grow thinner.

9

The day passes quickly
For some far too fast
For once they are hired
The die is then cast;
A shake of the hand
And a trip to the pub
Where the bargain is sealed
In brown porter suds.

10

At the end of the day
They go off for their tea,
There's still the bright lights
And the pictures to see;
If they haven't been hired
They've still got their pay
And there's still two weeks left
Till the last 'runaway'.

11

A mother stands weeping,
Her son waves good-bye.
He's only a lad
And there's a tear in his eye;
His worldly belongings
Are tied up with string
And he won't see his home
Till the following spring.

12

If those were the 'Good Days'
Thank God they are gone,
When the people were pledged
Like a coat in the Pawn;
They've left us forever,
They're now history,
Good-bye dear old Rabble,
Good-bye memories.

Hiring normally took place in the Diamond, though often the crowd spilled over into the surrounding streets. When Jeannie O'Neill of Carrickatane wanted a servant girl in 1912 for instance, she headed straight for Butcher Street. On that particular occasion she took her eleven-year-old son Andy with her for company on the journey.

Andy O'Neill.

Jeannie O'Neill.

Girls were in good demand in Derry at that time, as more remunerative work was to be found in the shirt factories. Andy's mother knew that if she didn't succeed the first time out there was always the second Rabble the following week and as a last resort the Runaway fair a week after that (so-called because if you were unhappy in the place where you had hired, you could run away and rehire with someone else on the third day). The minute she set eyes on Bridget McFadden Jeannie liked her, but she did not understand Bridget's reluctance to commit herself, until someone told her that she was anxious to hire in the same general area as her two sisters so that the three could get together now and then. In the event Bridget came to O'Neills and stayed until she married three years later.

Andy loved the day of the fair for he knew he was sure of a treat or two – like a wafer of ice-cream or a bottle of lemonade or tenpence worth of peas and chips from the Italian cafe on Carlisle Road. It was also exciting to go into Woolworths. On Rabble day Woolworths placed mirrors here and there to discourage thieves and Andy saw a boy being challenged for helping himself to grapes from a bran barrel. The boy seemed surprised and pointed to a nearby mirror saying, 'Sure that other boy's taking some!'

Eating houses did a roaring trade on hiring day. Most of them were situated in the streets surrounding the Diamond – Foyle Street, Waterloo Street, William Street. The fare on offer was plain but substantial. Boiled beef or bacon was usually served with cabbage or turnip, together with the inevitable boiled potatoes. This was followed by a bowl of rice with either raisins or a spoonful of jam. A cup of tea, strong and sweet, rounded off the meal.

Alex and Agnes Buchanan.

Andy's abiding memories of that day were of the many fiddlers and ballad singers, the blind man on the footwalk collecting pennies in a cap, and the tables with people throwing dice and placing thimbles over something. These things fascinated Andy as he was never allowed to stop and have a good look. He was puzzled by the number of people going through Butcher Gate. Some, no doubt, were interested in the hiring but others were likely going through to the pawn shops, Andy's mother thought. In the second-hand clothes shops boys and girls no bigger than himself were being kitted out for the next six months. A blouse or a skirt could be bought for sixpence, a pair of trousers for tenpence. One boy, his face wet with tears, was pleading with his mother, 'Mammy, please don't make me go.' Little did he know that she was just as heart-broken as he was.

To the townsfolk, the people for hire were inferior beings; an amusing diversion. These townies did not know the despair that had driven many of them from their homes. Some had lost their mothers. Others had been living in such abject poverty that they were forced out to fend for themselves. Their appearance too would often give rise to amusement.

> *The cloth cap with the button undone, thus raising the crown, the flannel shirt, sometimes collarless, or the white shirt with the narrow stiff collar, jacket and narrow lapels, drain-pipe trousers – or perhaps breeches and leggings, ending in huge boots, these together with the person's ruddy complexion, and great callused hands epitomised to us sophisticates the country dweller, or 'culchie' as we referred to them. [...] Here they were now, in their hundreds, slow of speech, shrewd of decision, solid of outlook – neither overawed, nor impressed by the glossy facade of city life, as though being close to the soil imbued them with a natural appreciation of the fundamentals of living.*

Agnes McKeague was typical of the many who were forced to leave home at an early age. She was not to have a place to call home again until she met and married a young servant-boy called

Alex Buchanan. Here is Agnes's story:

> My mother died and we had to squanner [spread] out. There were five of us – four girls
> and a boy. The boy was just a baby and was reared with a step-mother. My sisters went to
> farmers. An old lady took me. I was twelve and a half at the time. She was very frail and it
> was my job to look after her. I even had to sleep with her. She died when I was seventeen.
> I then helped her daughter for a while, but she couldn't afford the £5 a year to keep me
> so I ended up at Derry hiring fair. I hired at several other places and then I got married.
> At that time Alex was working for a farmer called Johnny Gilfillan. Johnny gave us the
> use of a cottage, free fuel, a couple of drills of potatoes and all the buttermilk, sweet milk
> and skim milk we wanted. I used the skim to make rice. We got butter when we needed
> it too. It created a roughness of food and we were glad of it.

Alex Buchanan tried several jobs before settling down to farm work. While he was still at school
he did grouse-beater at shoots on the Clark estate at Clady. Later he worked with a dealer who
bought and sold horses for shipping across the water. There he gained valuable experience, not
only in working with and breaking horses, but also in understanding and respecting them. He
could never understand the saying, 'To plough the lone furrow'. 'It was never lonely with the
horses,' he maintained. 'You talked to them and you knew by the way their ears fell back that they
were listening to every word you said.'

At a busy time on the farm Agnes helped Alex in the fields. These in the main were
family occasions with the older children minding the baby while the younger ones played on
the head-rig. They did all kinds of farm work – pulling flax, setting potatoes, thinning and
snedding turnips [slicing off the roots and tops with a knife]. Alex always pulled the flax while
Agnes made the ties, twisted them round the sheaves and tucked the ends neatly out of sight. For
this and thinning turnips they were always paid by the acre. When the children were older they
helped with the thinning and weeding. They also helped with gathering nettles, which were not
only used for feeding the turkeys but also for making delicious stew, broth and champ for the
family. Blackberries were gathered and sold at five shillings a stone. These were busy days for the
Buchanans but they didn't complain.

Not all hired people however were so lucky. Alex knew of one farmer whose hired men
slept in a barn loft. At five o'clock on a summer morning the farmer would come out and look
at the barn windows and then look at the crows flying overhead and say, 'Yous is not sleepin' in
– all the way frae Convoy an' my men not even up yet!' Another discovered his hired man lying
on the broad of his back when he should have been working. 'It just takes me the half of my time
watchin' you Jimmy,' he said.

'You're lucky,' replied Jimmy. 'It takes me *all* my time watchin' *you*!'

But on the whole Alex enjoyed his work and looked forward to each new day. In his own
words, 'In days gone by people went whistlin' an' singin' to their work. Now they go cursin' an'
scowldin'.'

COUNTY TYRONE

And the first money ever he got, he got thirty-one shillings for four pigs in Fintona fair and he told me he was shaking hands with himself. And he got a pound a month out of the creamery. If he got 22s 6d you'd think he'd got a tall hat.

— John Martin of Augher, talking about his father

County Tyrone, like most of Ulster, was linen country in the eighteenth and early nineteenth centuries. Weaving occupied at least half of the male population, some full-time and the rest during slack times in the farming year, for most farmhouses had a loom which was constantly in use during the winter months. The farm (which seldom exceeded twenty acres) provided the food, and the loom provided the money for the landlord's rent and hopefully a few small luxuries for the family. Markets and fairs were held in almost every town and village in the county. Some, like Fintona, started off with four in the early days and other places like Gortin, Fivemiletown and Sixmilecross had just one. By 1800 one of Fintona's old fairs had ceased to exist but twelve more were granted by George III at that time making fifteen in all.

According to Pynnar's 1619 survey, 2000 acres called Fentonagh were allotted to John Leigh Esq. who lived in 'a good large stone house within a bawn of lyme and stone.' Near the bawn there was a village of eight houses which grew into the town of Fintona. The markets were noted for the quantity of oatmeal sold at them and the fortnightly brown linen markets which attracted buyers from the bleach greens of Counties Londonderry and Antrim. Other goods were on offer too. Customs ranging from one penny to fourpence were due to the lord of the manor on every item sold. Fairs held on Saints' Days were said to bring out the idle and dissipated and to offer temptation to the idler. The number of fair days in Fintona, it was said 'could advantageously be curtailed as tending only to riot and disturbance and being profitable only to the spirit dealer and distiller.'

In nearby Dromore it was a similar story. According to records the quantity of whiskey drunk in Dromore in the eighteenth and nineteenth centuries was quite disproportionate to the number of inhabitants. The town had no hotel, nor was it patronised by any post conveyance but out of forty-four tradesmen's houses nineteen were spirit shops. However farmers in the area were said to live comfortably having plenty of beef and bacon and an abundance of tame and wild fowl besides a great variety of vegetables. The labouring class on the other hand could barely afford potatoes, and ate mainly oaten bread, flummery and stirabout. Cooking was done over an open fire. Fuel was plentiful in Tyrone. The mountains and bogs provided plenty of hard black turf which in some cases was supplied free of charge. Others paid half a crown to five shillings for a day's cutting.

In Tyrone the settlers were brought over by families such as the Abercorns and the Hamiltons who proceeded to build towns like Strabane, Newtownstewart and Omagh. The settlers formed the nucleus of each new town. Fairs and markets were established soon after. In those days these towns had just two, four and six small fairs respectively in the year. By the nineteenth century all three towns had twelve fairs. The weekly markets were well supplied not only with linen but with many other articles of provision. Everything had its allotted space in each town. In Omagh, for example, corn and potatoes were sold in Brooke Street, sheep at the front of the Infirmary and at the corner of Church Street, cattle between the church and the Presbyterian meeting house and pigs in the open space near the courthouse. You could have bought a good horse at the Dublin end of the town at that time for under £20. The goods manufactured in Omagh included hats and shoes and there were two tanneries. There was a gaol as well as the courthouse mentioned above. In the four years after 1829 no executions took place but thirty-four people were transported for life, five for fourteen years and ninety-four for seven years. There is no record of how many returned.

Hiring took place in all these towns. Labourers' wages in the nineteenth century were small at tenpence a day in winter – a shilling in summer. By the outbreak of the First World War, hired men were earning £10 and women £6 a half-year together with their food and lodging. Many came from Donegal. Some were accompanied by their parents. Others were cold, dejected and alone and bore all the signs of homesickness. Amongst them was the young Rose Welch who hired in Strabane but was to settle in the countryside near Drumquin, though she obviously had no idea of the geographical position in which she found herself. This is Rose's story:

> Times was hard and we used to walk from Dungloe to Fintown to get the eight o'clock train to Strabane. There were about thirty of us all heading for Tyrone and we had a great time walking to Fintown in our bare feet. We put on our boots when we got on the train. All the mothers and fathers came with us. We were to get no money to the six months was up an' we were to get every other Sunday to Chapel. When the farmer hired you, you be to hand over your wee bundle of clothes. I never seen my sister after – she was

Fair Day, Newtownstewart.

Courtesy of Ian McCullogh

Leap Bridge and Mills, Omagh - just one of the hundreds of water-powered mills once scattered throughout the country.

hired somewhere an' I was hired somewhere – 'til May come, an' then we met up again in Strabane.'

Someone else was eagerly waiting on that day too. Rose's mother was not only looking forward to seeing her daughters. She also desperately needed the money they had earned to pay the rent and feed and clothe her ten younger children. When the girls had re-hired she took them to McGarrigle's second-hand shop and bought them whatever they needed in clothes. Rose got fitted in a skirt and blouse for a shilling. They got sixpence each for themselves and their mother tucked the rest of their earnings into her bosom for safekeeping until she got home. Rose hired that day with a man who had a farm and a butcher's shop. She wasn't sure whether she wanted to go home with him or not:

I mind runnin' after that oul man for about four mile. He was on horseback. I'd heard him tellin' my mother he was a butcher and I thought, 'Jesus, he'll kill me!'

An' when I got up the next mornin' an' went to milk; I milked three cows an' took a bucketful off every cow. I thought that was enough. I threw it into the creamery can when I had the bucket full. So the oul boy came after me an' he says, 'There's not much milk in the creamery can. How many cows have you milked?' And I says, 'I have three cows milked.' He says, 'You couldn't have three cows milked an' only that wee drap o' milk in the can!' So he took the stool off me an' he sat down and he got another bucketful. Then

170

we went in for our breakfast. When I saw it I could have cried. He said, 'What's wrong with you, Rose?' Says I, 'I don't want spuds. I want my breakfast.' Says he, 'You ate them before *they* ate you! If you're hungry you'll ate them,' he says. And so I did.

Then when I'd be boilin' the spuds for the pigs in the big boiler I used to – if I got an egg handy I'd put the egg into the boiler and boil it. And when I'd be emptying the boiler I'd break up the shell and ate the egg. But you had to hide the shell or they'd find you out – that you'd ate the egg.

Then he'd go to the creamery and I'd start an' feed the hens an' feed the ducks, make drink for the calves, feed the pigs, sweep out the pig-house 'til it would be near dinner time. Then the spuds was boiled and a big rough bag was put on the table an' a hoop on it. An' the spuds was heeled up in this hoop to keep them from scatterin' over the floor. And there was a wee lock of salt put on every corner of the bag – no plates or nothin'. And we'd to peel them an' ate them. Then I was told to go down to the pantry an' bring up the buttermilk. Well – the buttermilk – I don't know when it was churned. There was blue hair on the churn and it would have cut your throat. Every time they came back from the creamery there was a pan of stuff threw into this churn. That was the buttermilk.

I used to have to make the porridge for the supper after dinnertime. She used to make me put on a pot of water and throw in a bowlful of oatmeal and a big bowlful of Indian meal and mix the two together. That was boiled for six o'clock for the men stoppin'. The two meals was mixed together and boiled. That was it then. You got no tea or nothin' 'til the next mornin'.

We never went out of the house them six months only to Mass. We were too young you see at fifteen. We didn't know where the town was even. You didn't know where you were just. I begun to think long an' I began to cry one day. I went outside and there was all these bushes and this big hill. I sat up against the bushes and I thought, 'If I went over the top of that hill I would see home.' I think it was Bessy Bell [mountain] maybe I seen. But I didn't get. I'd to stick out my six months.

Rose had hired in Strabane which was easily the biggest and best hiring fair in the county. Its fairs served not only the immediate area but a wider hinterland stretching from Tory Island to Cavan and Monaghan. As in most towns the main fairs, each lasting two days, were held in May and November but the quarterly fairs held on the first days of February and August drew large crowds too. Boys and girls converged on the town for days before, some walking bare-foot with their boots slung round their shoulders, others getting lifts in traps and carts, but many travelling on the wee Donegal train from such places as Glenties, Stranorlar and Letterkenny. Some came from the offshore islands such as Aran and Gola. Jimmy Quigley, a native of Strabane, was familiar with the town's hiring fair and wrote the poem, 'The Hiring Fair:'

> Sad did I stray one twelfth of May, far from my native home,
> To earn an honest living in the valleys of Tyrone.
> I left the hills of Donegal and looked back with a sigh –
> I mind it yet, I'll ne'er forget until the day I die.

Courtesy of David Fleming

Fair Day, Strabane in the early 1900s.

I'm on my way this hiring day to the hiring in Strabane:
And not alone on the banks of Mourne where Red Hugh took his stand.
Sure I will take my stand to-day outside the oul Town Hall,
And down thon street 'tis there we'll meet the lads from Donegal.

It's up the Back and down the Main and round the town we'll go;
We're ready now to take our place where Mourne waters flow,
Ach, there's a farmer now in sight outside McGiffer's pawn,
An' we know the first thing he will ask – 'An' lads are ye stayin' on ?'

Says this big farmer with a smile, 'Can you plough barren land,
And milk the cows and feed the sows just ten mile from Strabane?
We rise at six an' break the sticks to light a fire grand.
Of course I am a bachelor and not a married man.'

This farmer made me shiver as he took me by the hand,
Like a lamb being sold I was feeling cold till I reached the coffee stand.
Says he, 'Drink up your coffee boy, for our bus is on the Square,'
And homeward bound to Newtown town, we leave the hiring fair.

The Rosses, Donegal. Thousands of boys and girls left here to hire in Tyrone.

With speed of dash and still no cash, this farmer fooled me on,
And night and day I worked my way till all my strength was gone.
He made me do the work of two; this was his careful plan,
Till I got wise and cut my ties and headed for Strabane.

Strabane became almost a boomtown in the days before the fair. Eating houses were established overnight and food supplies were in great demand according to Mary Ann Elliott of Lower Main Street:

My mother would have been cookin' for two days before it – bakin' bread – this lovely treacle bread – big, big scones baked in the pot oven hung over the open fire and the red coals heaped on the top of it. She would have baked maybe twenty scones from a bag of flour – treacle bread and soda bread wi' big raisins in it. As well as that she left in dozens of loaves and Paris buns. The loaves all had to be sliced and we would have had welts on our hands cuttin' bread. You always sliced it thick for they were brave and sore on the butter and jam – young fellows and girls wi' big appetites and them half-starved in some of the places. If we run out of bread I was sent to Tom McElhinney's for more. You could have carried a dozen loaves in my mother's big basket. They were joined together in fours. Every four was (called) a 'ticket'. The people that came the night before got a bit o' supper – porridge it was them days.

Most of the ones that we had came from around Gweedore. My mother came from Gweedore and she knew all the generations of them. We had eight beds here. She would have said to the older ones, 'There's two double beds in there and two in the front room and four in the return at the back. Youse is all frien's. Sort yourselves out whatever way you like.' Some of them didn't like to lie down – you know – the oul weemin talkin'. Sometimes they had a singsong if somebody had a mouth organ or jew's-harp.

Next morning they would have been up from six getting themselves ready, tying their bundles together. That front room was redd out to make room for tables and forms for teas. When they had hired, some of them arranged for the farmer to lift them here later in the day. I have seen them cryin' in the street there – didn't want to go when the farmer came for them at evening time and the trap or cart waiting outside. If they got it hard they walked back to my mother in the night. Sometimes in a day or two a farmer would come and ask, 'Have you a girl you could recommend?' And somebody would get another chance.

In the area surrounding the main street there was hardly an inch that wasn't put to use. A cattle market was held in the Abercorn Square, Castle Street and Castle Place; also from Buchanan's garage on the Railway Road to the courthouse on the Derry Road. Horses and horse-dealers congregated in Irish Street and Newtown Street. Since a deal was usually completed in a pub, dealers became more drunk and quarrelsome as the day wore on. One man is reputed to have looked at the clock and exclaimed, 'Dammit! Four o'clock on hiring day and not a blow struck yet,' and promptly hit the man beside him with an ash plant!

In the Main Street there were swing-boats, hobby horses, fiddlers, singers, three-card-trick men, trick-of-the-loop men, Crown-and-anchor men, rickety wheelers, thimble ringers, fortune tellers, shooting galleries, roulette wheels and much, much more. There was an Italian organ grinder from Londonderry who got a squeak of music by turning a handle on the side of a box. He had a monkey which was trained to collect pennies in a cap. Sometimes it snatched the cap from a passing schoolboy's head causing merriment. An organ, or 'hurdy-gurdy' as it was called, was the centrepiece of Mary and Paddy Corrigan's act too. Their organ was surmounted by a birdcage containing two budgies and the whole outfit was trundled about on a handcart. Their patch stretched along the Main Street from the Provincial Bank to the Commodore Cinema. Paddy provided the music – usually old Irish airs – while Mary brought the birds out on a stick and asked them to pick your fortune out of a hat – blue paper for a boy, pink for a girl.

Not far away a man was selling kitchen utensils, tin-ware, crockery, cutlery and knick-knacks of all descriptions. Every so often he would hold up half-a-dozen teaspoons – every one guaranteed to sweeten your tea without sugar, or so he claimed. He also sold fine combs (for de-lousing heads) which he said would kill ninety-nine out of the hundred! Next to him very special Initial brooches were being sold at half-a-crown. It was big money, but worth it for the pretty girl you had fallen in love with earlier in the day.

Further along Peter Harte from Stranorlar had set out his stand. If you gave Peter a penny you were allowed three kicks at a football which you aimed at a doll sitting on the edge of a tea chest. If you managed to knock the doll backwards you got a free kick. The ball was attached to a rope spiked to the ground. For a penny also you could peep at a picture show. You could choose between Irish scenes and cartoons and you were allowed to see just six. Then there was big Hughie Gibbons who took his stand at the Post Office and offered the people a silver watch for ten shillings. He always wrapped it up with the instruction that you were not to open it until you got home. In the end you were charged just one shilling but when you got home the silver watch had gone and in its place you would find an old brooch or medal. Hughie could provide a minor attraction by touching his chin with his nose. Lilter Meehan was another regular visitor to the fair. He invited people to throw coppers into a bowl from a certain distance. They either missed the bowl altogether or the penny bounced out again so there weren't many prizes. Once in exasperation somebody threw a stone and broke the bowl. This started a row, much to everyone's delight.

Mick 'the Whang' and his wife Betty sold leather laces, Willie Puzzle sold wire puzzles and rat traps and Bounce Gallagher sold purses filled with half-sovereigns which turned out to be new half-pennies. Another character called 'Tie-the-boy' visited all the fairs. He was heavily tattooed and claimed to have sailed the seven seas. He was strong enough to bend iron bars and could wrestle himself free no matter how well he was tied up. When the ropes were being tied he would whisper, 'Hi boy, give us a chance.' Sometimes he would lie down on the ground and invite strong men to swing a sledgehammer and smash a stone on his chest. Pat McAllister, an ex-boxer with a cauliflower ear and a nose to match sold bottles and rubs for pains. His patter didn't vary. 'D'ye see this bottle. It's made from a secret recipe that I got from Jack Johnson, the heavyweight champion of the world, the night I knocked him out wi' wan big punch in Madison Square Gardens in New York – and as he lay there in the ring dyin' he whispered the secret to me, *black an' all as he was* (these last words were muttered under his breath), 'Take it back to dear old Ireland and put the people on their feet.' 'And here it is specially for you in Strabane at half-a-crown a bottle.'

In the midst of all this there were street singers and music-makers galore – Mickey Harron with his violin, the man they called Ghandi who had no legs and went about in a specially made small cart playing an accordion. Mick Corrigan sold penny broad-sheets there and his voice could be heard above the general din singing 'Lovely Martha (The Flower of Sweet Strabane)':

> *If I were king of Erin's Isle*
> *And all things at my will,*
> *I'd roam through recreation*
> *New comforts to find still.*
> *But the comfort I would seek the most*
> *As you may understand,*
> *Is that lovely maid called Martha*
> *The Flower of sweet Strabane.*

Old Malachy Kelly usually stationed himself under what was known as the iron staircase. He played the fiddle and sang 'Killeter Fair'. Some even said he composed it. Other favourites of Malachy were 'The Day Bella Brooks was Drowned' and 'The Killygordon Train'. These he certainly composed. Yet another fiddler played jigs and reels and danced to the rhythm of his own music. Every now and then Beezer Cassidy was seen to close his shop and depart for a 'pint'. Here and there, boys were distributing handbills notifying the crowd of where Dances were being held that night. The biggest one was at the Town Hall but there were others at Barry's Hotel, the Forester's Hall, The Corkscrew and one known as 'The Little Heaven' in Railway Road.

But the biggest attraction of all was Johnny McIlroy who stood aloft on his four-wheeled horse-drawn lorry selling horse-collars, harness, bridles, ropes, nails, whips, straps, buckles, kidney covers, and second-hand clothes. Johnny could always be relied upon to raise a laugh, usually at the expense of some unsuspecting by-stander. A young Donegal lad could suddenly find himself the centre of attention as Johnny pointed and shouted, 'Here young fella, catch a hoult o' that rope and see if it would stretch as far as that! Man there's enough rope there to hang the wife or anything you want – and all for three shillin's. (Haven't yiz all heard of Milton the famous poet? When he got married he wrote *Paradise Lost*. Then when the wife died he wrote *Paradise Regained*). Occasionally Johnny got a bit blue and while the by-standers roared with laughter, the police would sidle up – just to keep him under observation. Johnny would watch them out of the corner of his eye not once breaking his line of patter until they were close enough to hear and then he would address them. 'What did you think of the trousers I sold you at the last fair Inspector? Did they wear well?' Then he would look hard at his victim and shout with feigned delight, 'Be damn but that's them you've on. Sure they're as good as new yit. Would you like another pair?' And the crowd would roar louder than ever.

In the midst of the mêlée, usually somewhere near the Town Hall, stood the boys and girls waiting to hire and the farmers waiting to hire them, amongst them Ellen McFadden and Sheila Gallagher who like Rose Welch had left the west coast of Donegal to seek their fortune in Tyrone. Ellen was fortunate in that she hired at a place where she was to remain happily to the end of her days while Sheila, like Rose, married and settled in the area in which she hired. Other servant girls weren't so lucky. WF Marshall sums up the attitude of one of them towards a previous employer in his poem Sarah Ann:

> 'Sure ye min' the girl for hirin' that went shoutin' thro' the fair,
> "I wuntered in wee Robert's, I can summer anywhere".'

Ellen was fifteen when she first left home in 1922. She had intended hiring in Letterkenny, but had mistaken the date and found herself travelling a further twenty miles to the Strabane fair which was being held the following Monday. She knew that an Evelyn Logue who had a lodging house somewhere in the main street always welcomed boys and girls from her native Gweedore and it was to her that she made her way on arrival. Here in Ellen's own words is her story:

'I was with some other girls. We had left home anonst and we were anxious that we would hire for we didn't want to have to go back home. I hid my clothes in the hen house the night before, all ready for leavin' in the mornin'. My father was dead from we were weans [children] and I wanted to earn some money for my mother. We would all have liked to hire in the one place, but no, it was one here and one there. I had this notion that I would like to hire with a woman, and here didn't this widow-woman come up to me and says, 'Are you for hirin'? I'm lookin' for a good girl to help me on the farm. I need somebody that can milk.'

She was a Mrs Kelly – Margaret Kelly. She had a farm near Clady and a pub in the town. Her daughters looked after the pub and her son managed the farm. She was very good to me – even better than my own mother. This was her farm. It's mine now. When her son died he said in his will that he was leavin' the farm to his housekeeper that had been so good to him and his mother. This was his house. It was thatched up 'til last year. When I came here first that floor was flagged and that was an open fire. There's the big black kettle yet. My room was through that door beside you there. I nursed old Mrs. Kelly

Sheila Gallagher.

for the last three years 'til she died. It used to be that if I was going to chapel or going to town, my first stop was at her grave but I'm not fit now.'

Sheila Gallagher travelled the same road at the same tender age. Her parents had prepared her by sending her out to work locally at the age of eight. She attended school in winter but come the month of May off she went to earn a few shillings herding cattle. Oddly enough she remembers those days with affection, especially the time spent with the O'Donnells who had no family and treated her like she was their own.

However all this was merely a preparation for the big hiring in Strabane. Like Ellen, Sheila arrived the day before the fair and took lodgings for the night. She was out early the next morning at the eye of the market house along with hundreds of others – just like a herd of cows. Those for hire always stood under the market house clock. It was the biggest clock Sheila had ever seen. Before long a man tapped her on the shoulder. 'Are you for hirin'?' he asked, staring hard at her. 'I need a girl to milk the cows, wash spuds, clean the house, help wi' the washin'.' Could Sheila do these things he wanted to know. Sheila replied that she had learnt to do all these things. He offered her three pounds and she was hired. For a while she kept up the pattern of working away from home in summer and going home in winter but eventually hired full-time, returning to Strabane to re-hire each May and November.

Farmer William Mehaffy hired his servant girls in Strabane. William farmed around 90 acres in the townland of Carricklee about a mile and a half outside the town. He hired both men and girls as did his father before him and probably his grandfather before that. Mostly hired men and women worked hard, were happy in their work and lived as one of the family. William remembers those years:

We mostly managed to get servant men that we knew. My mother came from Donegal and there were people up there beside where she came from, the name of McKnight. We had three of them at different times. One of them came and spent two or three years with us and went to Canada and then down to the States. The next brother spent five or six years with us, joined the Specials while he was with us and he went to Canada too. He came back then during the last war and he had joined the Canadian Army. He was on his leave and when he came to us we gave him a suit of clothes and a bicycle for he couldn't go back to see his people in Convoy in his uniform. The third one worked with us for a few years and then went home.

I had different other people. There was that fellow in the photograph – Bob Montgomery. He was from Carnone. Then he went away and joined the army. Mostly

I knew who I was getting but I did have to hire girls in the hiring fair – had to make a bargain with them. I hired one girl one time and nearly got two but she got away just in time. She used to let the servant man in through her bedroom window when he came home late at night and you can guess the rest. She married a neighbour man after that and had thirteen children. Sometimes you had to clean the fleas off them but mostly they were clean and honest. The girls used to work with farmers for a year or two, then get married and get a job in Herdman's mill. That entitled them to get a mill house. They came from all over Donegal, mainly the Rosses, Bloody Foreland and the off-shore islands. This part of the country is full of their decendents – thousands of them! Girls worked both inside and outside the house. You see long ago the water had to be carried from a well across the road. Then there were pigs and calves to feed, cows to milk by hand, hens to feed. The girls would have helped with those things. In those days we lived in a thatched house. Then in 1923 we built a new house and had all the facilities we needed after that.

The servant girl lived in. She maybe slept in a room with my sisters. When I was wee I slept with the hired help too. My brother and I slept in one bed and the hired man slept in another. The people we got were treated like ourselves – ate the same food at the same table. If they lived near, they got home on a Sunday and took their washing with them. There was no contracts; just word of mouth. We kept a wee book, a wages book, and they gradually lifted so much to keep them smoking. Sometimes at the end of six months a man would have nothing to get. One fellow we had was overdrawn and cleared off. He had done the same with the previous farmer only we didn't know that at the time. But most of them were honest.

My father would sometimes have hired men for a quarter – August till November to help with the harvest and potato digging. That was over and above the ploughman. He did all the ploughing and horsework. There was no such thing as 'hours'. The ploughman got up about six, fed the horses, cleaned the stable and maybe fed the cattle before he got his breakfast. Sometimes he harnessed the horses before he got his breakfast too. On a wet day he would have cleaned the harness. We used to have two horses. Then when we got a binder we had to borrow a horse till such times as we could buy one, for it took three to pull the binder. Before that we used a reaper and somebody had to tie the sheaves behind it. We would have got extra help for that at harvest time and paid them half a crown a day. I think the last hiring in Strabane was about 1949.

Two of Donegal's most famous sons have described the hardships of a servant boy – Patrick MacGill in his books *Children of The Dead End* and *The Collected Poetry of Patrick*

Courtesy of William Mehaffy

Bob Montgomery (hired) from Carnone, Willie Haire (shaving pig), William Mehaffy (farmer).

MacGill and Patrick Gallagher in his autobiography *Paddy The Cope*. Patrick MacGill's poem 'The Farmer's Boy' could only have been written by someone who had seen the tears of his mother and felt the loneliness of leaving home at the age of twelve:

> *When I went o'er the mountains a farmer's boy to be,*
> *My mother wept all morning when taking leave of me;*
> *My heart was heavy in me, but I thrept that I was gay;*
> *A man of twelve should never weep when going far away.*
>
> *In the country o'er the mountains the rough roads straggle down,*
> *There's many a long and weary mile 'twixt there and Glenties town;*
> *I went to be a farmer's boy, to work the season through,*
> *From Whitsuntide to Hallowe'en, which time the rent came due.*
>
> *When Virgin pure, the dawn's white arm stole o'er my mother's door,*
> *From Glenties town I took the road I never trod before;*
> *Come Lammastide I would not see the trout in Greenan's burn,*
> *And Hallowe'en might come and go, but I would not return.*
>
> *My mother's love for me is warm; her house is cold and bare:*
> *A man who wants to see the world has little comfort there;*
> *And there 'tis hard to pay the rent, for all you dig and delve,*
> *But there's hope beyond the mountains for a little man of twelve.*
>
> *When I went o'er the mountains I worked for days on end,*
> *Without a soul to cheer me through or one to call me friend;*
> *With older mates I toiled and toiled, in rain and heat and wind,*
> *And kept my place. A Glenties man is never left behind.*
>
> *The farmer's wench looked down on me, for she was spruce and clean,*
> *But men of twelve don't care for girls like lads of seventeen;*
> *And sorrow take the farmer's wench. Her pride could never hold*
> *With mine when hoeing turnip fields with fellows twice as old.*
>
> *And so from May to Hallowe'en I wrought and felt content,*
> *And sent my wages through the post to pay my mother's rent;*
> *For I kept up the Glenties name, and blest when all was done,*
> *The pride that gave a man of twelve the strength of twenty-one.*

Tears fell in Patrick Gallagher's home too on the day that he left for his first hiring in Strabane:

'*The big people warned us we would not have such a rush in our feet when we had the thirty-seven miles' tramp to Ballybofey past us, but we only laughed at them.*
   I'll always mind the morning I first left home to go to the Laggan; that was what we called the

countryside beyond the mountains where boys went on hire. I think I see my mother as she handed me four shillings for the journey. She was crying. She kissed me again and again. I can't say whether I was crying or not, though it's likely I was, for to this day it's easy to make me cry. It was in Irish she spoke and this is the sense of what she said: 'Paddy, son, here is four shillings. Two shillings will take you to the fair. If you hire, keep the other two shillings 'til you come home; if you don't hire, it will take you back to me.'

Patrick and his friends reached Ballybofey that night as planned, paying threepence for the privilege of sleeping in a barn. They were up early the next day to catch the train to Strabane where they made their way to the main street feeling both small and vulnerable. He continues:

> *'When we reached Strabane we all cuddled together, and were scared at first, but the big fellows told us to scatter out so as the farmers would see us. They made us walk up and down to see how we were set up and judge what mettle was in us. Anybody who looked tired or faulty in any way was passed over, and I was getting scared I would be left. In the end two men came to me.*
>
> *'Well,' said one of them. 'Wee fellow, what wages do you want for six months?' I said: 'Three pounds ten.' He said: 'Get out, you would be dear at your meat. Walk up there to the market clock until I see what you are like.' I walked up, he followed me and made me walk back to where I started from. I heard him whispering to the other fellow: 'He is wee, but the neck is good,' and he then offered me two pounds ten.'*

Patrick goes on to describe how after a bit of haggling he hired for three pounds. After the fair, the farmer trotted the horse out the Donemana road with Patrick running after, slowing down occasionally when he thought the *horse* was tired. When they reached the farm, they had covered a distance of fourteen miles. In spite of all this Patrick worked hard and counted himself lucky that he never went hungry. At the end of the six months his trousers were threadbare and his master bought him a pair of corduroys so that he would look respectable at the next fair. The sum of four shillings and sixpence was withheld from his wages in lieu. However even this did not spoil the excitement he felt at the prospect of seeing his friends again. He takes up the story once more:

> *'When I arrived in Strabane most of the Cleendra boys and girls were there. (…) They made fun of me about my trousers. Some called them 'Fiddler's trousers.' I did not mind what they said, I was so glad to be going home.'*

Before leaving the town Patrick went to a stall and bought a halfpenny clay pipe for his father, rosary beads for his mother, and threepence worth of sweets for his sisters. He then set off for home with a group of others from his own townland. They reached the first house at two in the morning and to their surprise all their mothers and fathers were waiting for them. Patrick's mother hugged him so tight he thought she would never let him go.

He was to hire at a number of places before he had the idea of forming a Co-operative for the benefit of farmers. The seeds of the idea were sown when he and his neighbours decided to get together to buy a large quantity of artificial manure so that they could get it at a cheaper rate.

The plan worked and Patrick later formed the Templecrone Co-operative Society in the Rosses area of Donegal. It was an enormous success and he became its first chairman.

Other Tyrone fairs going back to the seventeenth century include those at Trillick, Killeter and Drumquin; also at two smaller places i.e. Killen and Magheracreggan. The latter had ceased to exist by the end of the nineteenth century; Killen still had one held in October and the rest, together with Dromore and Castlederg, all had monthly fairs and almost certainly hiring fairs as well. Castlederg benefited from having good landlords in the eighteenth and nineteenth centuries. Sir Robert Ferguson built a good inn in the town around 1830. It was a handsome building and served as a halt for the Londonderry to Enniskillen stagecoach. He also gave a piece of land free of toll for a cattle and pig market and saw to it that the town had a reservoir and a piped water supply. This was installed in 1829 at a cost of £170.

    Hiring certainly took place at Trillick with the usual entertainments and sideshows. A report in the *Tyrone Constitution* of 1883 states that the attendance of public and supply of stock was very large in Trillick in May of that year. The report further states that a large number of male and female servants attended and that numerous contracts were entered into at wages satisfactory to the employed. At one of the last fairs in Trillick a party of tinkers (both men and women) livened up the proceedings by having a family fight in the open street.

    By the nineteenth century tolls had been abolished in Killeter Fair, which encouraged sellers, and premiums to the value of £2 were awarded to the highest purchasers of cattle, yarn and pigs, which encouraged buyers. Henry Smith Esq., landlord, contributed £10 a year towards this and the rest was made up by the inhabitants of the town. Killeter Fair is immortalised in the song of the same name:

> *Oh attention pay you country folk, and listen to me plaise,*
> *I'll sing to you a verse or two to content you at me aise;*
> *It's all about a fair maid, her equal wasn't there,*
> *And the first time that I met the girl 'twas in Killeter Fair.*

> *For her eyes they shine like diamonds and her cheeks are like the rose,*
> *She is my first and only love no matter where she goes,*
> *She stole my heart completely, boys, the truth I do declare,*
> *And the first place that I met her it was in Killeter Fair.*

> *I invited her into Edmund Hughes's, all for to have a 'trate'*
> *We both went in together and sat down to have a sate;*
> *She said that she'd have lemonade, I said I'd have a share,*
> *For I never like to take strong drink when in Killeter Fair.*

> *She invited me to see her home in Aghaloney Glen,*
> *Where many a pleasant afternoon with her I since did spend;*
> *Her father bid me welcome, and said he didn't care*
> *If I'd like to wed his daughter I met in Killeter Fair.*

From left: Bridget Rodgers, Minnie Corr and Gracie McBride. All travelled from Donegal to Tyrone to hire. Bridget's fine clothes were probably cast-offs from her mistress. I don't know the name of the shy little girl with Minnie but Gracie's charges are Katie Dunn and John Laird.

Och, now that we are married we are happy as you know,
We always feel right pleasant, let the weather freeze or snow.
She says, as she sits by the fire, and laughs right hearty there,
'John, the first place that you met me, it was in Killeter Fair.'

Drumquin is described by the Ordnance Surveyor of 1834 as a 'poor-looking place, the houses mean and out of repair.' However it had a weekly market on Thursdays and quarterly cattle fairs which were attended by English dealers.

The countryside in which these towns were situated was renowned in those days for the excellent whiskey made in the stills hidden away in the hills and mountains. In 1820 there were upwards of sixty private stills in the Killeter area alone. Ten years later the number was said to be 'greatly diminished' owing to the exertions of Lieutenant Hunt, a sergeant, and eleven privates of the Revenue Police. Three-quarters of the inhabitants were said to be Catholics, the remainder Episcopalians and there were a few Presbyterians. The former were said to be 'civil and obliging', the latter 'uncouth'. The former were however also said to be often 'dishonest and insincere' and the latter mostly 'upright men'. (*O.S. Memoirs* Vol.5 p.129)

The South Tyrone area included the three Clogher Valley towns – Augher, Clogher and Fivemiletown, together with Caledon, Aughnacloy and Ballygawley. All had at least one fair by 1700. Aughnacloy had five. All (with the exception of Augher) had a small linen or yarn market. By the end of the nineteenth century all (again with the exception of Augher) were market towns and had monthly fairs. Most had hiring fairs.

By then too the Clogher valley tram had arrived and could be seen crawling by the roadside, cutting across fields or clearing a way through village streets as it made its way from Maguiresbridge to Tynan. In 1894 four cattle wagons were added to its existing stock of thirteen carriages. On Fair Days the cattle wagons were crammed with livestock of all descriptions.

(Hundreds of cattle in those days made their way to sidings all over the country to catch the shipping train on the GNR (Great Northern Railway) for Belfast Quay and the cross-channel steamers). Tommy Caruth looked after the tram for many years, perhaps too many, and old age and tiredness often caught up with him especially in the heat of summer. Tommy (known as Tam or Tammy) is remembered in the poem, 'The Clogher Valley Railway'.

It's Clogher Fair and we're running late
And Tammy the Guard's in a terrible state,
'For it's bad enough,' he's heard to say
'To miss the mail on an ordinary day.'
'For people,' says he, 'if they're left behin'
Can look after themselves – barrin' they're blin'!
'But bastes,' says he as he peers ahead,
'If they're left behin', they've got to be fed.
And the Manager'll curse to bate the band
At fattenin' bastes for a dalin' man!'
The carriages dance in the summer heat
And Tammy sits down in the corner seat;
His ticket punch slides to the floor
And Tammy the Guard begins to snore.
For 'tis hard enough at the best of times
To manage a train at seventy-nine.

The carriages on the tram were cleaned out, whitewashed and pressed into service on the day of the Clogher Valley Show – also on the Twelfth of July to transport local Orangemen to their big day on the Caledon estate. With the extra load the train used to stick going up Tullyvar hill. Legend has it that when this happened the second-class passengers were asked to get out and walk and the third-class to get out and push. The tram made its final journey on the last day of December 1941.

The town of Clogher is dominated by its cathedral which dates back many centuries – back indeed to Saint Patrick who founded it in the year 443. Over the years it was destroyed and rebuilt many times, one of them being in 1041 when it was renamed Saint Macartin's. In the early nineteenth century a post horse could be obtained at a place called Shepherd's near the church. Since there was no good hotel in the town, Shepherd's must have been one of the several 'miserable' inns that served as staging posts at that time.

Clogher had two old fairs held on 6 May and 26 July which were, like those of Carnteel, formerly Bishop's fairs. The July fair was said to be very big and was known variously as the Gooseberry Fair and Spolian or Spolien Fair. The former referred to the sale of gooseberries as it occurred at the time of year when gooseberries were ripe, and the latter to the tents and bothies set up to provide food for the crowds. The sale of second-hand clothes was also a feature. The people were said to amuse themselves on the day by stuffing themselves with mutton and mutton broth. As the day wore on many found their way to McAleer's Pub and the inevitable fighting broke out before the day was over. As in other places sheep, cattle, cows and pigs were sold – especially sheep. The roads approaching the town were filled with them on the morning of the fair. Long ago selling took place in the main street but nowadays animals are sold at a modern mart near the old tramway station. The markets in Clogher were always well supplied with eggs, poultry, potatoes and oatmeal. The last three before Christmas in Augher and Clogher were each called *An Margadh Mór* (Great Market). They specialised in the sale of ducks, geese, turkeys and heavy hens.

Markets were held in Augher on Mondays for the sale of corn, potatoes and meal. There were four fairs in the year, held at hiring times. Hiring took place near the church, the boys and girls standing in separate groups 'with their heels in the water trinket [gutter] be it wet or dry'. Willie Martin (Sunday School teacher and blacksmith in the townland of Screeby) hired his men in Augher. When his son John reached the age of thirteen he was taken from school and brought home to serve his time in the forge. John takes up the story:

> My father had land forby [as well as] the forge. When I left school at thirteen he sent the man that had been helping him in the forge out to do farm work and brought me into the forge whether I liked it or not. I didn't like the black-smithing no more I had to stay at it. It wasn't like now. You had to do what you were told.
>
> It was a very heavy job. Everything had to be done wi' fire and heat. There was no electric d'ye see, not like now. They can pull the electric down now an' stick two bits together. We had to do it all wi' the fire an' the hammer. Sure I was nearly 'murdered' at it. The whole country come till us. Hooping [cart] wheels too. Sure that was a tarra [terror] on a hot day. You put the fire right roun' them hoops and you got that hoop on when it was red hot. It contracted then as it cooled. The sweat would be runnin' down your face – an' maybe a dozen wheels lyin' there. You'd be near burned alive keepin' the fire up to the hoops. Still an' all it wasn't so bad in a certain way for there was plenty of help an' the crack was good. You couldn't get out of it 'til eleven o'clock at night, me father an' me.
>
> In the Springtime it was a tarra. They used to come. There was no chill ploughs that time. It was all swing ploughs. The men would pull in their horses at six o'clock and they would land into the forge wi' a couter [coulter] and sock; throw them down there. And on a wet day they would gather in too. But he hired his men in Augher.

Hiring died out in Augher shortly after World War I. The village was said in the nineteenth century to have a 'wretched appearance' – in marked contrast to the beautiful little lake and demesne of the castle which was known locally as Spur Royal. Dean Swift is said to have married Stella under a tree in the castle grounds.

Two fairs were held during the 1830s at Newtownsaville, a hamlet a few miles north of Augher. Fivemiletown, so called because it was five Irish miles from Clogher, was the most commercial of the Clogher Valley towns. On hiring day there were the traditional stalls selling such things as delph, toys, watches, razors, and boots – in fact anything that people from the country might ever need. The fair also had its quota of fortune tellers, hobby-horses, swing-boats and the same variety of catch-penny artists that frequented other fairs. Five of its monthly fairs were originally patent fairs. For a time animals were sold just outside the town at a place called The Commons but eventually they returned to the streets. John continues:

© Belfast Telegraph Newspaper Ltd

Blacksmith's Forge. Hooping cart wheels, shoeing horses, making and repairing gates, repairing plough parts: These were all jobs for the local blacksmith.

Cattle, sheep, pigs, goats, ponies, horses; all were sold there. And the old women dressed like men wi' oul felt hats on them and big overcoats. They would have come in with an ass and cart with their butter and eggs; fowl too, maybe even vegetables. There was a woman one day brought heather – heather from the mountain. She sold it in wee bunches – lovely heather it was. The smell would have done you good. Sometimes they'd bring turf too. Anything to make a few pence.

Caledon had two fairs, also great markets selling the usual produce (including linen) on the second Monday of every month. In 1770 its markets were attended by one hundred weavers. Later it had a general market on Saturday and a grain market every Tuesday. The Earls of Caledon were good landlords who not only distributed clothes and money to the poor but did all they could to benefit the village. By the nineteenth century it had two corn mills and a flour mill which ranked among the most extensive in the kingdom and was said to supply the country from Belfast to Lough Erne. The refuse of the grain was used as fuel – it was found that a ton of refuse equalled four hundredweight of coal.

The nearby town of Aughnacloy was also of considerable importance, though said by the Ordnance Surveyor in 1834 to be small and dirty with not more than four good houses. Linen to the value of £41,600 was sold there in 1803 but by 1820 the takings were down to £4,618 an indication of how the demand for linen slumped at that time. It also had a weekly market held on Wednesdays, a grain and a fruit market when in season, monthly fairs and twice-yearly hiring fairs.

Hiring Fairs and Market Places

The latter died out about 1930 but left their legacy in a poem entitled 'My Father's Servant Boy':

Ye lovers all, both great and small, attend unto my theme,
There's none on earth can pity me but those that feel the pain;
I live between Dungannon and the town of Aughnacloy,
But now I'm in America with my father's servant boy.

Where is the man that will or can a farmer's son despise,
His bread to win he does begin before the sun does rise;
My love and I are Adam's seed, I never will deny,
There in none on earth I love as well as my father's servant boy.

My parents they wished to have me wed unto a gentleman,
And in the church we were to meet and join in wedlock's bands;
The night before I stole from them unto a village nigh,
Where there I met my own true love, my father's servant boy.

I took my love along with me, I could do nothing more;
I bid adieu to all my friends and to the Shamrock Shore;
To Belfast town we both went down where the Ackythere did lie,
And in that ship I sailed away with my father's servant boy.

When we reached the other side, our money was all gone;
Some time we were supported by a friendly Irishman;
Till gentlemen from Ireland did give us both employ;
Two pounds a week I do receive with my father's servant boy.

I left my parents lonesome: in sorrow they did weep;
Day and night condoling without a wink of sleep;
Until I sent a letter to the town of Aughnacloy,
Saying, 'I am in America with my father's servant boy.'

They sent an answer straight to me in Philadelphia town,
Saying if I would come home again I would get five hundred pound.
But I was joined in wedlock, which crowned my life with joy,
And until I die I'll ne'er deceive my father's servant boy.

This is the news that I did send from Philadelphia town,
That where they were worth a shilling I was worth a pound;
With pleasure and contentment I never will deny,
I am living in America with my father's servant boy.

– Author unknown

Courtesy of Ian McCullough

Main Street, Aughnacloy.

Courtesy of Ian McCullough

Fair Day, Ballygawley.

The usual tradesmen carried on business in the town including nailers, saddlers, leather workers, shoemakers, tailors, reedmakers, bakers, milliners and smiths. Almost every house was licensed to sell ale and spirits. No doubt these did a good trade on fair days when police were expected to remain on duty until all public houses closed and the people had dispersed. It was their duty also to patrol the roads leading to the fair. After the 1939-45 war boys and girls used to come across the border from Eire to Aughnacloy (quite illegally) to look for work on local farms. They congregated at the top of a side street leading down to the old railway station, sitting on the kerb until someone came to offer them a day's work.

Carnteel was one of several places to have bishop's fairs. Others were Armagh, Clogher, Dromore (Down) and Tynan. These date back to the thirteenth century and were literally owned and ruled by the bishop in whose diocese they were held. The Bishop of Armagh was granted two in Carnteel, each lasting two days, one on 15 August and the day after and the other on 8 September (the Nativity of the Blessed Virgin Mary) and the day after. The town was granted to Sir Thomas Ridgeway in 1611. Ridgeway erected a bawn and established more fairs at that time making seven in all.

Ballygawley was said to have a good fair which on hiring day was an excellent place to find a servant girl. They stood in a line, bundles at their feet, along the south-east side of the street and side-walk. Most came from the surrounding countryside but many came from Monaghan, Cavan and Donegal. Ballygawley was famous far and wide for its horse fair.

In the east of the county was the village of Moy – also famous for its horse fair, the action taking place in the town's eighteenth-century tree-lined square. Horses were needed by the thousand in both town and country not to mention those needed by the cavalry and artillery regiments of the British army up to and during the Great War. Buyers came also from Holland, Belgium and Switzerland. The horses offered for sale in Moy were said to be of high quality and to have great stamina. If the buyer (usually an agent) liked the look of a horse he asked the seller to first walk him and then trot him for a short distance along the street so that he could watch his action first from behind and then again as he cantered back towards him. If this was satisfactory he proceeded with a closer examination. He looked at his teeth to ascertain his age. The army liked three-year-olds so he looked for four big teeth. He then checked that he was sound in wind and limb. A strong cough indicated strong lungs; a soft cough the opposite. Finally he ran his hand along each leg to check for side-bone growths which were a sign that the horse might later go lame. A farmer from Aughamullen near Lough Neagh reminisces:

> I went there with cattle. I always walked it. There were always horses in the Moy. Buyers came from all over the country. The English ones came over on a Wednesday and bought all the best horses for the army. They would be jockeyin' horses and ridin' horses. Then there was second-class horses bought for ploughing. There was a row of vits [veterinary surgeons] an' when you bought a horse you could have him examined to see if he was soun' for five shillin's. There was nowhere better than the Moy, even for cattle. The butchers came there to buy first-class beef.

Moy in days-gone-by had the advantage of 'cheap and ready transit to Belfast and Newry from the Quay, 150 yards distant from the market place by Blackwater River, Lough Neagh, Belfast Canal, Bann River and Newry Canal'. Towards the end of the nineteenth century competition

Courtesy of Ian McCullough

Moy Cattle Fair.

Courtesy of Ian McCullough

Moy Horse Fair.

came in the form of rail transport with 'Cheap Inland and Through Rates for all descriptions of produce sold in Moy Market and transported direct from Trew and Moy station.' The horses have gone and the cattle have gone but the memories linger on in this old poem entitled 'The Moy Fair'. The author's name is unknown.

1
Man, about the ould horse fair
Some a thousand yarns could spin.
Soon 'twill be an ould man's tale.
Hokey sailor, dang it skin!

2
Horses once did line the street.
Ach! it is a mortal sin,
Now a horse you'd hardly see.
Hokey sailor, dang it skin!

3
Motor cars now hould the Square,
Deeving people with their din.
'Roar away for all I care!'
Hokey sailor, dang it skin!

4
Boys, them horses were a sight!
All decked out the eye to win,
Mane and tail straw-plaited tight.
Hokey sailor, dang it skin!

5
Dalers flocked from far and near,
Dalers fat and dalers thin,
Dalers from across the say.
Hokey sailor, dang it skin!

6
May Fair Day they swarmed like bees:
No hotel could take them in,
So they slept around the trees!
Hokey sailor, dang it skin!

7
Gipsies, tramps and quacks were there,
Begged and stole and peddled ware,
Varmints steeped in ivery sin,
Hokey sailor, dang it skin!

8
With the Moy none could compare,
But I'm feared its day has bin.
Goodbye, Ireland's best horse fair!
Hokey sailor, dang it skin!

In mid- and north Tyrone there was scarcely a village (small though some of them were) that didn't have its monthly fair by the end of the nineteenth century. They included Carrickmore, Mountfield, Donemana (or Dunnamannagh), Plumbridge, Rock, Gortin, Beragh, Sixmilecross and Pomeroy. Most had hiring fairs. Sixmilecross was particularly good for hiring according to John Ewing, a native of those parts. John left school at the age of eight unable to either read or write and hired with three old bachelor brothers who lived a few miles away. He remembers:

Their name was Myles. They farmed - mostly raisin' spuds an' sellin' them. I slep' in a wee bed on a sort of shelf above the kitchen. There wasn't much room, just room for a bed. They used to boil a big pot of spuds over the fire. When it was boiled they pulled the crane out, lifted the pot off and carried it to the door and teemed the water off them. Anyway you got pirties (potatoes) and salt for your breakfast − in a basket in the middle of the table. You never got a knife and fork to peel them or anything. You peeled them wi' your thumb nail and you ate them wi' your fingers. You got that for your breakfast an' your dinner an' your tea. It was always the same. I looked after the cattle; took them to

Courtesy of Ian McCullough

Gortin Cattle Fair.

the mountains. You would have got peewits' nests in the heather. I used to look for nests. It passed the time.

A number of places had just one fair in the year e.g. Seskinore, Ardstraw and Altmore. In the eighteenth century Gortin had one fair. At the beginning of the nineteenth century it had two, one held on the Monday after old Midsummer day and the other on the Wednesday after old Hallow day. By the end of the century it had twelve. Gortin was the place to go if you wanted a good ass or goat or if you had a pet lamb or pig to sell. At the beginning of the nineteenth century a fair was held on the first Monday of every month at a place called Charlestown in the townland of Tullynacross for the sale of mountain stock. It did not have a single fair in 1895.

Pomeroy's fairs were held on the second Tuesday of every month for the sale of provisions, yarn, mountain stock, pigs and horses. Stock was sometimes bought by jobbers at the farm and resold at one of the fairs. The horses were said to be of poor quality, the breeds of cattle and pigs also poor. Up to the early part of the nineteenth century there was a steady demand for yarn as nearly every cottager was engaged in weaving the narrow webs of coarse linen which fetched 7d. or 8d. a yard in Dungannon and Cookstown markets. Apart from weaving and labouring, the only other work in the area was to be found in the cornmills. Some illicit distilling went on in the mountains. It fetched six shillings a gallon in quiet places.

Around a century later Michael Martin selected Pomeroy for his first hiring. Michael was born in 1914 and reared at Upper Kildress outside Cookstown. Although he was christened

Bella and Mickey Martin.

Michael he could not remember ever being called anything but Mickey. One evening in the Spring of 1922 a stranger arrived to see his father. Eight-year-old Mickey was sent outside while the two talked and when the visitor was about to leave he was summoned. His father told him that the man's name was O'Connor and that he came from a mountain farm a couple of miles away in the townland of Teebane. He told him also that he was soon to leave home for he had just hired him to this man for six months, at the end of which time he would have earned £1. Mickey was to rise early each morning and take the cows out to graze before he went to school. The cows would stay indoors during school-time and when Mickey came home he would take them out again.

The O'Connors were kind to Mickey. They fed him well, bought him clothes when he needed them and sent him regularly to school. If he felt lonely, he went off home for an hour or two until he got over it. Never at any time however did he see his wages which were paid directly to his father. After a couple of years Mickey was hired with a different farmer at the increased wage of £2, the arrangements again being made (and the wages collected) by his father.

At fifteen Mickey decided to strike out on his own and went off to the November fair in Pomeroy. He noticed a number of people for hire strung out along the street outside O'Neill's pub. Mickey couldn't make up his mind whether to join them or not. Mickey wandered about aimlessly for a while, unaware that he was being watched by an interested farmer. Suddenly the two came face to face and the farmer, seizing his chance, said, 'Are ye for hirin' boy? What's your name?'

'Mickey Martin.'

'You wouldn't be a son of Barney Martin's that works up at Cappagh?'

Mickey said that he was, and this seemed to satisfy the farmer for he hired him immediately, gave him a shilling and made arrangements for him to come the next day. His name, he said, was McGeogh and he lived just outside the town in the townland of Cornamaddy. Mickey was to start at seven o'clock the next morning and he was to make shores, clean sheughs, cut hedges. For this McGeogh would give him £5.

With the serious business of the day behind him, Mickey began to take stock of the fair itself. One man was selling all kinds of harness – reins, winkers, breechin', collars, straddles. Another was dealing in wheelbarrows and wooden gates. A woman was resting her basket of wares on the street. As far as Mickey could see it contained four hens for there were two heads over one side of the basket and two over the other. He was fascinated at the way their heads darted from side to side while their bodies remained absolutely still. A dealer from Dungannon was trying to buy them as cheaply as possible. Other women were selling butter and eggs.

Mickey then turned his attention to the stalls. He would have liked to buy a penknife but sixpence was a lot of money so he decided against it and bought a cup of tea and a bun instead. Thus fortified he watched the shooting galleries for a while; then proceeded to the wheel of

Courtesy of Ian McCullough

Hay Market, Cookstown.

fortune. Nobody was winning much at either so he moved on to the next attraction which was a contraption with wooden men on it. All you had to do was knock one of them down to win a prize. It was so easy he couldn't believe it. He had a go and lost his money in seconds. Fortunately his attention was taken almost immediately by the sound of an accordion and someone singing. It was none other than Bob Magee, the popular ballad singer from Cookstown. Bob attended all the fairs and wherever he went a crowd gathered to listen to and enjoy the rich tenor of his voice which had that authentic lilt which only comes to the natural untrained singer. He was singing a favourite song of Mickey's – 'The Spinning Wheel'. Before going home Mickey went back and bought the penknife. He was a man now and he would make his own decisions. Tomorrow he started at McGeogh's. He would have to work hard but he didn't mind that. The spring would soon come and with it the warmer days and the putting in of the crop. In fact he stayed with McGeogh for a second term until the crops were harvested as evidenced in the following words:

> One of my duties was to take the corn to the mill to be ground and then to take it to be dried at the kiln head. There was a mill out there – Loughran's they called it. Then there was one in Dunnamore or Dungate. There was mills all over the country that time. And you brought it home and you boiled it and you supped it and fed calves with it and fed everything with it – but yourself in particular. You'd make porridge with it and oat bread. And you took the hulls home and you steeped them in a crock to make sowans. It sat there for a couple of days and then you drained the water off it. Then you put it in a pot or an oven and boiled it and it was lovely stuff.

In the years that followed Mickey hired at a number of places, his wages varying from £5 to £11 10s, and the time he stayed varying from six months to eight years. He worked hard and was rewarded by being treated well wherever he went.

The main towns in the east of the county were Dungannon, Cookstown, Stewartstown and Coalisland. When Chichester was awarded lands in 1608, he not only acquired 144 townlands (including Belfast); he also gained 'the manor of Dungannon with the fort, castle, town and lands, water mills and water courses, alias Drumcoo, Kenemele, Gortmerron, Moycashell, Mullaghmore, Mullaghedun and twenty-five additional townlands.' His patent authorised him to continue Hugh O'Neill's Thursday market (established in 1591) and to hold two fairs, 'one on the feast of the apostles Philip and Jacob and the day after, and the other on the Monday after the feast of St Michael the archangel with a court of piepowder.'

Dungannon soon became 'one of the most prosperous in the North of Ireland in the linen trade'. By the end of the eighteenth century there were dozens of bleach greens centred round the town and in places like Tullylagan, Desertcreat, Derryvale, Newmills, Coalisland and Moy. In its heyday (around 1800) about twelve hundred weavers and one hundred and twenty buyers attended each market. Its cloth market was far superior to the dozen or so others in the county, well over £200,000 worth being sold annually – not surprising since almost the entire population were weavers and spinners. It is not by chance that in the well-known ballad '*In the County Tyrone near the town of Dungannon, Bob Williamson lived, a* weaver *to trade.*' But by

Market Square, Dungannon.

1839 the number of weavers had dropped dramatically and the number of buyers was down to ten. However when the linen trade declined the markets and fairs generally began to improve. Doubtless its cornmarket found a ready customer in the local distillery. Thursday (then as now) was market day and once a month also fair day. Four registered fairs had died out much to the regret of the inhabitants of the town as they were said to be 'much superior to the present monthly fairs'. By then the landlord was Lord Ranfurly who collected tolls ranging from one penny to four shillings on every item sold. The Ranfurlys sold the market rights to the local council in 1911.

The people of the area were said to be 'industrious' and those wanting work (generally called 'corner' men) used to assemble at the corner of Market Square where Scotch Street meets Irish Street until someone came to offer them work. This remained a favourite place for hiring until hiring ceased in the 1930s. People for hire also stood at other places in the Square and a few went to faraway Ann Street. There was always a big turn-out on hiring day particularly if that day happened to coincide with Ascension Thursday or Corpus Christi. Wages were often drawn by the father of the person hired (as with Mickey Martin), this system only changing when the hired man either got married or reneged at having to give up the wages he had worked so hard to earn. Fathers were quite happy to collect their sons' earnings as long as the sons were willing to put up with it. Hiring was already dying out in Dungannon in the mid 1930s as evidenced in *The Tyrone Courier* of 16 May 1935:

Courtesy of Ian McCullough

Ann Street, Dungannon.

Fleming family, Lamey. Jack is on the far right. His father Sam is seated in front.

'Thursday last was the May Hiring Fair in Dungannon and judging by the number of farm servants on the streets in search of labour, this method of hiring is dying out. Wages being offered £12 to £13 plus board for half year. Extra police were on duty but things were quiet.'

Aran Victory and Kerr's Pink potatoes could also be bought on that day for 2s 6d per cwt. Hen eggs had dropped to 5d. per lb. while duck eggs remained at 6s 8d for ten dozen.

It was to Dungannon that the newly married Jack Fleming went to look for a man in 1928. Jack was one of a family of eleven (even Presbyterians had big families in those days) but there was always plenty of work on the seventy-five acre farm at Lamey and a hired man was usually kept. Since Jack had done the hiring this time the hired man stayed with him at 'Hutchinson's' – the name given to an outfarm belonging to his father. Being teetotal and a regular church-goer Jack did not take his man into a pub when the bargain was made but he did give him the half-crown earls. Jack's father kept a dairy herd and Jack regularly took his turn at taking their own and their neighbours' milk to Mullnagore creamery. His spring-cart easily held the cans of five of their neighbours along with their own. It was not necessary to go as often in winter when the cows gave less milk and the creamery opened on just three days a week.

Jack's father took pride in the way he looked after the horses; also the pony which was said to be the fastest trotting pony in the countryside. As well as the usual farm work, the horses were used for threshing which took place in a barn at the top end of office housing (byre, stable, meal house etc.) stretching from the entrance gate to well beyond the dwelling house. The horse walk was on open ground beyond the barn. The hay-shed was close by. Jack hired his

Courtesy of Peter McGuckin

The girl is driving the horses which supply the power to drive a barn thresher.

Courtesy of Peter McGuckin

The same team of horses as above seen from inside the barn. One of the horses is wearing ear muffs to deaden the noise of the thresher.

197

Barn thresher. It took two men to loosen the sheaves and feed the thresher and another to fork away the straw.

Barn threshers were superseded in the 1920s and 1930s by huge machines made by manufacturers such as Ransome, Marshall, Boyd and others. This Ransome thresher was powered by steam.

man in Dungannon but his father preferred to do business in Cookstown. He also considered Cookstown a better town for hiring. It was a great fair in which to look for a clean respectable girl. Farmers' wives were particular about cleanliness as often the girl lived as one of the family, even to the point of sharing beds with the younger children.

Hiring took place at what they used to call Hirin' Lane Corner (now the corner of Coagh Street) and anywhere along the main street from the Fair Hill or Loy Street to the Oldtown. Hugh Pat Hampsey was one of many who hired there:

> I hired with a man the name of Tommy Harkness – 'Tiressan' the' called the place. Tommy picked me out at Hirin' Lane Corner an' then my father an' him went for a drink. He gave me two shillings earls. There was older ones too an' ploughmen. The farmers all went roun' talkin'. It was just like buyin' a baste.
>
> I was second in a family of nine. My mother was rearin' the rest of the family an' I never got any money only tuppence on a Sunday for a packet of cigarettes. If my mother needed a poun' to get something she went to that man an' got it on the strength of my wages.

As Hugh Pat said, many farmers viewed and judged those for hire in much the same way as they vetted a horse or cow and as the slapping of palms rang out it was hard to tell whether a young lad had been hired or a good donkey sold. They arrived in the town from an early hour, unharnessed their horses, watered them at the nearest watering trough and quickly stabled them at the rear of a pub or hotel. On fair day the action took place at the Fair Hill. The most indispensable person there was Dick Crane who acted as go-between thus helping buyer and seller come to an agreement. Dick could also be found at social functions, auctions, funerals and even serving the occasional summons on a law-breaker.

Cookstown's fairs date back to 1628 when Charles I granted Dr. Allan Cook (a Dublin lawyer) a weekly market and twice-yearly fairs. Cook had earlier leased his lands from the See of Armagh as they were termon [or church] lands. At that time the place was a mere hamlet of a dozen or so mud and daub houses and remained so until Cook sold his lease on the land to the Stewart family of Killymoon in 1666. It was William Stewart who in 1726 hatched the bold plan of the present town with its mile-long main street earning it the name of Long Hungry Cookstown. The Saturday market transferred from the Oldtown common to the main street in 1752 and has been held there ever since. All the usual commodities were on offer. The sale of turf was a speciality. The most anticipated market in the year was the one before Christmas called *An Margadh Mor* (pronounced Margymore), as in Augher and Clogher. On that day the atmosphere changed to one of expectation and excitement as the town thronged with people wanting to buy ducks, geese, hens, turkeys and whatever other bits and pieces they could afford. Shopkeepers made a special effort to be festive by placing sprigs of holly amongst the assortment of match boxes, candles, clay pipes, jew's-harps, bottles of castor oil, ginger ale, shoe laces, liquorice, tins of sweets and the hundred and one other things that were likely to adorn their shop windows for the occasion. Fairs were held on the twentieth of the month throughout the nineteenth century but changed later to the first Saturday in the month.

Outlying villages and hamlets had their own fairs though they declined as those in Cookstown became more successful. In the eighteenth century Dunaghy and Orritor had

Egg Market, Cookstown.

© Green Collection, Ulster Folk and Transport Museum

quarterly fairs. By the nineteenth they had just two and by the twentieth they had died out altogether. Several bleaching establishments had also ceased to exist though those at Tullylagan and Desertcreat lasted longer than most.

It was near Cookstown also that Hugh and Samuel Faulkner started their beetling business in the eighteenth century. Beetling is the final process in finishing linen – after retting, hackling, scutching, spinning, weaving and bleaching. Faulkner's mill at Wellbrook was one of many at that time. Surprisingly it functioned until 1965, was given to the National Trust in 1968 and can still be seen working on certain days each year when its doors are open to the public. The thunder of the beetling hammers as they crash down one after the other on the linen is an unforgettable experience.

Coagh in those days had regular fairs held on the second Friday of each month when 'an extensive assortment of cattle, sheep, goats and hogs' were offered for sale. These included cows, calves and heifers but never beef cattle which were always taken to neighbouring larger towns. There was no pork market in Coagh either though there was a good supply of live pigs. You could have purchased a milking goat for around seven shillings or a young kid for a shilling. The town had no market as such but the commodities needed by farmers were usually on sale i.e. harrows, ploughs, barrows and some yarn for the benefit of local weavers. Most of the implements could be purchased for fifteen shillings or under. A box barrow cost seven and sixpence, a hand barrow or a turf barrow about half a crown. The shopkeepers and tradespeople provided the rest, basing their prices on those reached in Cookstown

Courtesy of Ian McCullough

Flax Market, Union Street, Cookstown.

market the previous Saturday. They also had a good supply of turf spades, scythes, teethed hooks, iron hoops, deal planks and boards and fresh pollan and eels daily from Lough Neagh. Though cheap coal could be obtained locally at the pit-head in Coalisland, farmers preferred to burn turf which could be bought by the gauge (a cubic yard, or enough to fill a donkey cart) for one shilling and sixpence half-penny. By 1900 almost all of this had gone. In 1895 Coagh had just one fair held in the month of May. Tullyhogue held one in December that year. Successful monthly fairs were once held in Castlecaulfield, Rock, Donaghmore and Stewartstown. Hiring probably took place at all of them. Fairs were still operating in all but Donaghmore in 1895.

Coalisland never claimed to be a successful market town though it had both fairs and markets at the beginning of the nineteenth century. The corn market flourished, due no doubt to the convenience of the canal which was used to transport grain and other commodities to Newry and Belfast. But Coalisland was not dependent on its markets for success. It was the discovery of coal in the area in the seventeenth century that provided the impetus for building the canal in the first place. The enterprise proved uneconomic however due to the fact that the seams of coal were short, and mixed with layers of sand and gravel or sometimes heavy clay. Ironically coal was to be the main commodity carried upstream in the opposite direction. There was always plenty of work to be had on the farms in the Coalisland area, not to mention the spade mills, quarries (both limestone and freestone), bleach greens, flour mill, potteries, tile manufactories and of course the cottages themselves where linen was woven extensively.

Courtesy of Ian McCullough

Fair Day, Stewartstown.

Stewartstown's markets and fairs were much like those of Dungannon but on a smaller scale. The market was held on Wednesday and was said to be amply supplied with 'all agricultural produce, provisions, cloth and yarn'. Maggie O'Neill remembers it well:

> Graips and shovels and buckets were set out on the street outside the shops. An' somebody singin' a song an' goin' roun' with a hat for you to throw in a penny or a ha'penny. An' a row of carts turned up an' some o' them wi' eggs an' butter an' things an' they just kep' all in the cart – sold it out of the cart; fowl too. There were plenty of second-hand clothes stalls an' other stuff. I might as well tell you the truth. I was reared off them. They called it the 'cant' (or kant). That was the name of the market where they were shouting and selling things. They would talk about the cant in the Square in Stewartstown.

Those for hire stood on the footpath along the main thoroughfare. Maggie used to feel sorry for them and showed them friendship by inviting them to her house:

> I was born in Ballywhilloan outside the town. I hardly ever went to school. There were nine of us. I was the oldest so I reared some of them, for my mother had to go out to work. She had it to do. I'm sure her heart was sore many a time not knowing what was going on when she was away. They were hard times.
> I run about with a girl that was hired. She was from Moneymore. She met up with a

boy here in this part of the country. Then they got married and I was bridesmaid at the wedding. We walked to Stewartstown Chapel, just the four of us. And the Charlemont Arms Hotel; we went there for our breakfast and that was it – and back home. She was hired. I suppose she went back till her work the same day.

Then when I come thirteen or fourteen I got a job across the road from where I was living for three days in the week and three days some place else. Then the next place was Whitetown near Newmills. He was a farmer. She was a schoolteacher. I lived 'in' then. I run the house; done the cookin', washin', ironin'; done the churnin', made the butter. I baked every day – soda bread and wheaten bread. There were no dainties. I'd to work in the fields as well. If you had an hour to spare you'd to go out an' take your turn. I never pulled flax. I spread it. I lifted it, but I never pulled it. I did everything else. I built rucks of hay. I built stacks of corn, milked cows an' fed them, fed horses, calves, reared turkeys an' chicks an' all them things. I did a man's work. When I went to Sinclairs I got two pounds and ten shillings a month. That was good wages, because I had the run of the house an' responsibility. But my stamp [National Insurance] had to be taken out of that.'

In the early 1700s Stewartstown had three fairs and the fairs were held regularly on the second Wednesday of every month. Sometimes there were two fairs in the month e.g. in 1895 there were two in each of January, February and October.

The only other fair in the County Tyrone of long ago was that held at Washing Bay on the south-west shore of Lough Neagh. It was held purely for pleasure occurring on the Sunday before and the Sunday after Mid-summer day. Since the lough was invested with a magical origin it is not surprising that healing powers were attributed to its waters. Invalids, especially those with skin sores, bathed and became whole. Even cripples declared themselves restored to health and strength. It seems likely that 'washing' in its waters gave rise to its name and the fairs were a later addition. On fair days stalls were erected for the sale of sweetmeats and other dainties. In one respect, however, it was no different from other fairs of the time. The main occupations were said to be 'dancing, drinking and broken heads'!

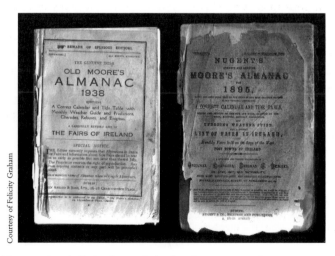

Courtesy of Felicity Graham

Old Moore's Almanac *listed all the fairs in Ireland and continues to do so.*

EPILOGUE

Research for this book began around twenty years ago and many of the people whose memories fill its pages have long since gone to their reward. I am glad to have encountered them – ordinary country people who gathered potatoes, milked cows, threshed corn, and churned to put butter on the table. I am glad to be able to remember these things from my own childhood.

I particularly remember the harvest. It took a team of men to cut, tie and stook the corn and the same again to stack and thresh it, not to mention the time and effort required to see the task through. Today the same job is done in a few hours by a combine harvester and baler. Grain leaves the field in trailers, and straw in huge bales wrapped in plastic netting. These winds of change have swept through every aspect of farm life whether it be haymaking, the growing and harvesting of potatoes or even the role of the farmer's wife in the kitchen. The toil and drudgery have gone. Gone too the camaraderie that existed between farmers, neighbours and hired men who joined forces to help each other in time of need.

And gone are the hiring fairs. These died a lingering death before and during the Second World War but did not end officially until 14 July 1948 with the implementation of the National Insurance Act. This culminated in the Beveridge Report which promised better working conditions and social benefits for all.

The selling of farm animals changed too when the Department of Agriculture introduced Tuberculosis (T.B.) Testing of cattle. From then on cattle had to be taken to approved saleyards, and marts sprang up all over the country. This put an end to any remaining fairs. Open-air sheep fairs linger (no T.B. restrictions for sheep) and are still held in one or two places – Draperstown and Cargan for instance, though nowadays, the animals are sold by auctioneers. Even bigger changes have taken place in our towns and cities. Supermarkets, car parks and houses have replaced the fair greens and market places.

The Waterfront Hall and Hilton Hotel stand proudly where growers once sold their produce from the back of a cart in May's Market. Motor cars have taken over roads along which farmers once drove their sheep and cattle to the fair.

I hope this book gives a glimpse into the lives lived by our farming forefathers – people like ourselves who in their time faced and overcame problems as great as those we face today.

Courtesy of Kathleen Acheson

Horse-operated churn. It took one horse to pull the 'lying' shaft of the crown wheel that drove a churn, but two horses were needed for a thresher and three to pull a binder.

BIBLIOGRAPHY

Adamson, Ian. *The Cruthin: The Ancient Kindred* (Pretani Press, Belfast 1991)

Barry, John. *Hillsborough: A Parish in the Ulster Plantation* (Mullan, Belfast 1982)

Bartlett, R., Parkhill, S., White, S. *The Hiring Fairs* (Queen's University Belfast Teacher's Centre, Belfast, 1983)

Bassett, George Henry. *County Antrim 100 years ago: a guide and directory, 1888* (Friar's Bush Press, Belfast 1989)

Bassett, George Henry. *County Armagh 100 years ago: a guide and directory* (Friar's Bush Press, Belfast 1988)

Bassett, George Henry. *County Down 100 years ago: a guide and directory* (Friar's Bush Press, Belfast 1988)

Belcoo & District Historical Society & Belcoo & District Development Group. *If Only* (unknown)

Bell, Jonathan (Ulster Folk & Transport Museum). *People and the Land: Farming Life in the nineteenth century* (Friar's Bush Press, Belfast 1992)

Bell, Muriel. *A Hospital At Magherafelt: The Workhouse and Famine Times in South Derry*

Clarke, Edith M. *City Set on a Hill* (Outlook Press, Rathfriland 1979)

Corcoran, Doreen; W A Green. *A Tour of East Antrim: historic photographs from the W.A. Green Collection at the Ulster Folk and Transport Museum* (Friar's Bush Press, Belfast 1990)

Corporation of London, Public Record Office. *The Livery Companies of the City of London* (Corporation of London, London 2001)

Crawford, W.H. 'Fairs and Markets in Ulster' (Federation for Ulster Local Studies, Winter 1987, Vol.10, No.1, Omagh, 1987)

Crawford, W.H. *Domestic industry in Ireland; the experience of the linen industry* (Gill and Macmillan, Dublin 1972)

Croker, Thomas Crofton. *Popular Songs of Ireland* (Early nineteenth century)

Curl, James Stevens. *The Honourable the Irish Society and the Plantation of Ulster, 1608-2000 : the City of London and the colonisation of County Londonderry in the Province of Ulster in Ireland: a history and critique* (Phillimore, Chichester, West Sussex 2000)

Evans, E Estyn. *Irish Folk Ways* (Routledge & Paul, London 1957)

Foster, Jeanne Cooper. *Ulster Folklore* (H.R. Carter Publications, Belfast 1951)

Fraser, Colin. *Harry Ferguson, Inventor and Pioneer* (J. Murray, London 1972)

Gailey, Alan (edited by). *Gold Under the Furze: Studies in folk tradition presented to Caoimhín Ó Danachair* (Glendale Press, Dublin 1982)

Gallagher, Charles. *Acorns and Oakleaves*

Gallagher, Patrick. *Paddy the Cope: My Story* (Dungloe Templecrone Co-operative Society Ltd., Dungloe, 1948)

Gilmour, John A. 'Fairs and Markets in Ulster' Vol.10 No.1 Winter 1987 (Federation for Ulster Local Studies, Omagh 1987)

Gwynn, Stephen. *Highways and Byways in Donegal and Antrim* (London, New York, Macmillan and Co. 1899)

Hagan, Felix. *Around Dungannon* (Gill & Macmillan, Dublin 1998

Hayward, Richard. *In Praise Of Ulster* (W. Mullan, Belfast 1946)

Her Majesty's Stationery Office. *Ancient Monuments of Northern Ireland Vol. 1* (1975)

Hill, Myrtle & Pollock, Vivienne. *Image and experience: photographs of Irishwomen, c. 1880-1920* (Blackstaff Press, Belfast 1993)

Hunter, Jim. *Jane Ross and The Londonderry Air* (Cranagh Press, Coleraine 2000)

Hutchinson, W R. *Tyrone precinct; a history of the plantation settlement of Dungannon and Mountjoy to modern times* (W Erskine Mayne, Belfast 1951)

Hutchinson, W R. *A Short History of Ireland to 1955 (W Erskine Mayne, 1955)*

Institute of Irish Studies (The Queens University of Belfast). *Ordnance Survey Memoirs of Ireland 1830 – 40 Vols.1 - 38*

Irvine, Alexander. *My Lady of the Chimney Corner* and *The Chimney Corner Revisted* (Appletree Press, Belfast)

Kee, Frederick. *Lisburn Miscellany* (Lisburn Historical Society, Lisburn 1976)

Kennedy, Michael G. *By the Banks of Mourne: A History of Strabane* (Strabane Historical Society, Strabane 1996)

Logan, Patrick. *Fair Day: the story of Irish fairs and markets* (Appletree Press, Belfast 1986)

Lutton, William; Bigger, F. J.; Armagh Guardian *Montiaghisms: Ulster Dialect Words & Phrases* (Linen Hall Library, Belfast 1976)

Lynn, Adam. *Random Rhymes from Cullybackey* (Belfast, 1911)

McCusker, Breege & Morris, Frances. *Fermanagh, Land of Lake and Legend* (Cottage Publications, Donaghadee 1999)

McDonnell, Pat. *They Wrought Among The Tow: Flax and Linen in County Tyrone, 1750-1900* (Ulster Historical Foundation, Belfast 1990)

McKinney, Jack. *They Came in Cars and Carts: A History of the Markets and Fairs in Ballyclare* (Area Resource Centre, Antrim 1989)

McKinney, Jack. *Where The Sixmilewater Flows: Historic Photographs of the Ballyclare area, Co. Antrim* (Friar's Bush Press, Belfast 1991)

Mackey, Brian. *Lisburn, The Town and Its People, 1873-1973* (Blackstaff Press, Belfast 2000)

MacGill, Patrick. *Children of The Dead End* (Birlinn, Edinburgh 1999)

MacGill, Patrick. *The Rat-Pit* (Birlinn, Edinburgh 1999)

MacGill, Patrick. *The Navvy Poet, the Collected Poetry of Patrick MacGill* (Caliban, London 1984)

Magee, John. *A Journey Through Lecale: Historic Photographs of Co. Down from the W.A. Green Collection in the Ulster Folk and Transport Museum* (Friar's Bush, Belfast 1991)

Maguire, W A. *Hey Days, Fair Days and Not-So-Good Old Days: A Fermanagh Estate and Village in the Photographs of the Langham family, 1890-1918* (Friar's Bush Press 1986)

Maguire, W A and Hogg, Alex R. *Caught in Time: The Photographs of Alexander Hogg of Belfast 1870 –1939* (Friar's Bush, Belfast 1991)

Marshall, W.F. *Tyrone Ballads* (The Quota Press, Belfast, 1949)

Mitchell, Brian. *The Making of Derry: An economic history* (Genealogy Centre, Derry 1992)

Mullin, J E. *The Causeway Coast* (Rev. T. H. Mullin, Coleraine 1974)

Murphy, Michael J. *Ulster Folk of Field and Fireside* (Dundalgan Press, Dundalk 1983)

Murphy, Michael J. *Tyrone Folk Quest* (Blackstaff Press, Belfast 1973)

Moore, W 'Speedy'. *Beyond the Big Brae: A Novel on Rural Ulster of Yesteryear* (Cuilrathan Pub. Coleraine 1994)

National Trust (The). *Mid-Ulster Houses (Ardress House, The Argory, Springhill, Wellbrook Beetling Mill)*

O'Byrne, Cathal. *As I Roved Out: A Book of the North: being a series of Historical Sketches of Ulster and old Belfast* (Blackstaff Press, Belfast 1982)

O'Donnell, Peadar. *The Knife* (Irish Humanities Centre, Dublin 1980)

O'Hanlon, Michael. *Hiring Fairs & Farm Workers in North-West Ireland* (Guildhall Press, Derry 1992)

Old Moore's Almanac (1895 and 1838)

Richardson Rev. Alfred. *A Guide to Portrush, Ballycastle and Neighbourhood* (Ballymoney 1913)

Rogers, Mary. *Prospect of Erne: a study of the islands and shores of Lough Erne, Co. Fermanagh, Ulster's first national park* (Fermanagh Field Club, Belfast 1967)

Rocks, S. *The Hiring Fairs – Cookstown No Exception* (Derrychin Primary School, Coagh, Cookstown, unknown)

Rotary Club of Portadown. *Portadown* (Export & Freight Publications, Portadown 1986)

Saintfield Heritage Society. *Saintfield Heritage No.2* (1982)

Sandford, Ernest. *Discover Northern Ireland* (Northern Ireland Tourist Board, Belfast 1976)

Shearman, Hugh. *Modern Ireland* (Harrap, London 1952)

Smyth, Patrick. *Osier Culture and Basket-Making : a Study of the Basket-Making Craft in South West County Antrim* (P Smyth, Lurgan 1991)

Smyth, Patrick. *Whipping The Cat: Tales from Lough Neagh's Banks* (P Smyth, Lurgan 1991)

Stewartstown & District History Society. *The Bell: Journal of Stewartstown and District local History Society: No.1 1985-86*

Strabane History Society. *Strabane Hiring Fair: Memories, Views and Attitudes* (Strabane Historical Society, 1996)

Thompson, Samuel, *New Poems* (Belfast 1799)

Walker, Brian Mercer. *Shadows on Glass: a portfolio of early Ulster photography* (Appletree Press, Belfast 1976)

Walker, Brian Mercer. *Sentry Hill: An Ulster Farm and Family* (Blackstaff Press, Belfast 2003)

Walker, Brian Mercer. *Faces of the Past: a photographic and literary record of Ulster life 1880-1915* (Appletree Press, Belfast 1974)

Watson, Charles. *The story of the united parishes of Glenavy, Camlin and Tullyrusk : together with short accounts of the history of the different denominations in the Union* (McCaw, Stevenson & Orr, Belfast 1892)

Watson, John (Bookseller). *The Gentleman and Citizen's Almanack for the Year of our Lord, 1746* (John Watson, Dublin, 1746)

Weatherup Roger. *Armagh: Historic Photographs of the Primatial City* (Friar's Bush Press, Belfast 1990)

GLOSSARY OF TERMS

anonst	without anyone knowing, e.g. 'to do something anonst'
arable	land which is suitable for growing crops
bart (of flax)	large two-storied stook of flax with thatched, hipped roof
bawn	fortification around a house or enclosure
beet	bundle of green flax as it is bound up in the field
bellows	instrument for producing a current of air to light a fire
bing	long heap (of potatoes etc.)
booley	wander about in search of grass for animals e.g. cattle
boom	bar with nozzles through which liquid pours as spray for crops
boon	group of labourers gathered at a busy time e.g. for flax-pulling
boxtey (boxty)	bread made from grated raw potatoes and flour
brave	indicates a greater degree than that expressed by the adjective which follows it e.g. 'brave and big –wet –high etc.
cant (kant)	that part of the market where sellers advertise their wares by shouting
ceilidhe	spending time at a neighbour's house: also an evening of music and song
chill (plough)	horse-drawn plough with two wheels at the front, the adjustment of which controls the depth of the furrow
cock (of hay)	a small pile (sometimes called a 'rick' or 'ruck')
common(s)	piece of ground common to everyone, usually on the outskirts of a village or town
coutre, couter, coulter	iron cutter in front of a plough-share
cowp	overturn
crane	that part of fire furniture on which a crook is hung
crock	earthenware vessel in which cream is kept
crook	that part of fire furniture on which pots are hung
dale/ daler	someone who buys and sells livestock aiming to make a profit
deal	haggle down price or reach an agreement
dress (flax)	straighten, set in order
drugget	woven and felted coarse woollen fabric
dung-hill	heap of dung or animal manure
dyke	trench (or the earth dug out and thrown up)
earnest (earls)	coin given by a farmer to someone who has been hired at a fair
farina	a mealy powder; ground corn
farrow	give birth (to piglets etc.)
fief	land held in fee or on condition of military service
flannel	soft woollen cloth of loose texture
flummery	an acid jelly made from the rusks of oats, sowens
fodder	hay; to give hay to animals
footer (foother)	do something in an unskilful manner

fother	see 'fodder'
fur	furrow
gauge	cubic metre (enough to fill a donkey cart)
gauger	Exciseman
graip	three- or four-pronged fork for lifting manure or digging potatoes
Great Market	larger than usual market, usually held at a special time e.g. Christmas
gruel	thin food made by boiling meal or oats in water
haggle	dispute price; to be difficult in bargaining
happoth	half-penny worth; meaning nothing e.g. not a happoth
hoke	scoop out; root – like a pig
kant	market where people shout out to draw attention to their wares
Lammas	first of August
lap	small quantity of hay rolled over the arm and set down so that the wind blows through it
luck-penny	small return made to the purchaser
madrig	saddle packed with straw
manger	upright trough (usually constructed against a wall) in which fodder is laid for horses or cattle
march (ditch)	boundary between the fields of neighbours
mercat	market (Scottish)
mercat cross	old cross around which a market was held
meskin	large oblong piece of butter usually around 3lb in weight
midden	dung-heap
near	mean, close, stingy
noggin	wooden container usually used for buttermilk
Ordnance	a department concerned with supply and maintenance of artillery
Pattern	festival associated with a patron saint
piepowder	wayfarer or itinerant
Piepowder Court	ancient court held in fairs and markets to administer justice in a rough and ready way to all-comers
pillory	wooden frame supported by an upright pillar or post with holes through which the head and hands were put in punishment (abolished 1837)
pound (animal)	enclosure in which stray animals are confined
pot-walloper	person allowed to vote (he qualified because he had a hearth where he could boil a pot of yarn)
pot-walloping borough	status granted by patent by Charles II, entitling a borough to send two members to the Irish Parliament
redd (up)	put in order
rick (ruck)	small stack, heap (of hay etc.)
rickle	small pile of turf
rundale	system of holding land in single holdings made up of detached pieces
scollop	rod used to fasten thatch
scour (potatoes)	cultivate and remould into drills to keep ground clear of weeds
shaft	handle of shovel or other implement
shamble	butcher's market stall
shambles	flesh-market, slaughter house
sheltie (shelty / shilty)	Shetland pony
sheuch (sheugh, shugh)	trench or ditch
shill	separate husks or pods from grain etc.
sloop	one-masted, cutter rigged vessel with fixed bow-sprit; light boat
sned	cut away superfluous parts e.g. 'to sned turnips'
sned (snead)	curved handle or shaft of a scythe
sock	ploughshare: iron point that lifts the earth to the board
sowens	dish made from the farina remaining among the husks of oats
sowl	sold
steer	a two- to four years old castrated ox
still	apparatus for making alcoholic liquor
stirabout	thick gruel, porridge
stirk	year-old bullock or heifer
store (cattle)	cattle kept for fattening, usually 18- to 24 months old
swing plough	plough without a fore-wheel under the beam (so-called because it could only be turned at the end of a drill by being swung round manually)
tarra	terrible (as in 'That's a tarra')
tenant at will	someone who holds land only as long as the owner pleases
tether	rope for leading or restraining an animal
toll	tax for the liberty of using a bridge or road, selling goods at market etc.
toll	portion of grain kept by a miller in payment for grinding
thewr	similar to pillory, but used to punish women
trencher	wooden platter
tumbrell	an old instrument of punishment; cart in which prisoners were moved though the streets of a town
wheen	a few
will (tenant at will)	one who holds land only so long as the owner pleases

ACKNOWLEDGEMENTS

Decades of friendly help from many people have contributed to this book which only in a relative sense is all my own work. Thanks are due to the people who not only shared their memories but allowed me to commit them to print. I must thank also the people who supplied the pictures which support and enhance their stories. Many of these came from private family albums and have never before been in the public domain. Thanks are due to Kathleen Acheson, Cecil Allen, Dorothy Arthur, Muriel Bell, Rowan Black, Edward Blair, Sam Brown, Stanley Burns, Bob Colhoun, Myrtle Colhoun, Hazel Dickson, Sheila Duffy, Jack Dunn, Terry Eakin, David Fleming, Norman Foote, Robin Greer, Rita Gribben, Annette Henry, Stuart Johnston, Matt Kelly, Patrick Kelly, Oliver McCaffrey, Ian McCullough, Sam McCoubrey, Jim McDowell, Peter McGuckin, George McKibbin, Colm McIldowney, William Mehaffy, Robert Murphy, Speedy Moore, Andy O'Neill, Arthur Ovens, Alison Patterson, Lily Scott, Molly Smyth, William Stevenson and Joe Warnock.

Every picture had a part to play in the overall scene but I would like to say a special thank you to Peter McGuckin whose father took the superb pictures of farm life in the 1920s, particularly those of barn threshing and harvesting flax. They convey more eloquently than words the intense effort that went into everyday life on a farm in the early decades of the twentieth century. For the beautiful cover on the book and many of the pictures of fairs within it, I am indebted to postcard enthusiast Ian McCullough. These two people have between them supplied almost half of the pictures used.

Quotes from the Ordnance Survey Memoirs have been used throughout the book. Acknowledgement must be made to Col. Thomas Colby and the army officers who wrote them in the 1830s and also the team who transcribed them in the 1990s in the Institute of Irish Studies at The Queens University of Belfast.

I am also indebted to the staffs of *The Belfast Telegraph*, Armagh Museum, The Ulster Museum, the Irish Linen Centre and Lisburn Museum, Roslea Heritage Centre and the Ulster Folk and Transport Museum for their courtesy and attention when researching for additional photographs. Thanks are also due to the latter for the award in 1984 of an Ulster Television Research Bursary which gave the green light for this work to begin.

I must also thank Raymond Clifford for his permission to use his father's poems.

It would be impossible for me to name the many others who encouraged me, people like Felicity Graham who handed me a small bundle of papers - yellow with age - which turned out to be almanacs listing fairs held in 1887, 1894, 1895 and 1938 and Sandy Heasley who produced one dated 1746. Little did these people realise how often these would be consulted in the ensuing years.

Last but by no means least I must pay tribute to my husband Edward who was always there when I needed enlightenment on some of the finer points of farming in the past.

I hope the end product is a record worthy of them all.

Yours in research

May Blair